Thro' My Eyes
A Memoir

Iain Matthews
with Ian Clayton

route

Published by Route
PO Box 167, Pontefract, WF8 4WW
info@route-online.com
www.route-online.com

ISBN : 978-1901927-85-6

Orginally published in hardback in 2018
This edition 2021

Iain Matthews asserts his moral
right to be identified as the author of this book

Photographs from the Iain Matthews archive

Front Cover Photo:
Gijsbert Hanekroot

Back Cover Photo:
Monique Nuijten

Cover Design:
John Sellards

Printed & bound in Great Britain by TJ Books

All rights reserved
No reproduction of this text without written permission

*This memoir sits on your shelf because of the unwavering
and unconditional love and encouragement from Marly.
My second-to-none, my Limburg girl, my rock of understanding.
My red and my green light, my inspiration and my soulmate.*

This book is for you babe.

Preface: Ian Clayton   9

Introduction   13

PART ONE: THIS TRAIN IS RUNNING
1. The Iron Fist   19
2. Searchin'   31
3. Let the Music Begin   49

PART TWO: THE SUMMER OF LAST YEAR
4. Learning the Game   65
5. Sudden Discomfort   83
6. A Child is Born   99
7. Along Came Plainsong   113

PART THREE: CHASING RAINBOWS
8. Valley Highs and Lows   131
9. Go North Young Man   147
10. Hi-Fi and Be Damned   165
11. Joy Mining. The A&R Years   187
12. The Big Idea   203

PART FOUR: WALKING A CHANGING LINE
13. Repair and Restoration   215
14. Practise Makes Perfect   227
15. The Road Goes on Forever   237
16. Making Watermelon Whine   249
17. Thoughts of Leaving   261

PART FIVE: GOT TO GET BACK HOME

18. Amsterdam	281
19. In the Dutch Mountains	293
20. Jazz is an Accident Waiting to Happen	307
21. All That Is	321

Acknowledgements	335
Index of Songs	337
Discography	339

THRO' MY EYES

Lord above us hear my song
Tell me if I'm doing wrong
I'm just a man and not like you
If you saw thro' my eyes
what would you do?

A simple life, that's what I feel
To want to sing, it's not unreal
So Lord in heaven let me know
If you saw thro' my eyes
where would you go?

I take the blame for where I've been
On all the ones I've had to lean
And now I've shared it all with you
If you saw thro' my eyes
what would you do?

PREFACE

This is wonderful 247 metres on the medium wave. Music! Too much! It's thirteen minutes past the hour of eight in the am and climbing up the wonderful fun thirty, this is the beautiful sound of a band called Matthews Southern Comfort with their brand-new single 'Woodstock'...

The chiming guitar of Mark Griffiths and the pedal steel of Gordon Huntley start one of the most memorable of musical introductions.

...And don't forget our amazing offer to win a brand-new, three-band transistor radio, just pop your name on a postcard and write to me Tony Blackburn at Broadcasting House right here in London, that's Tony Blackburn, Broadcasting House, London, W1A 1AA. I'll say that again pop fans, that's London, W1A 1AA. What do you think Arnold? Woof! Woof!

Blackburn's waffle and jingles stop just in time for us to hear the tender, tenor vocal of Ian Matthews. 'I came upon a child of God, he was walking along the road, when I asked him where are you going this he told me...'

Matthews Southern Comfort's take on the Joni Mitchell song about the Woodstock Festival is an ethereal, eyes closed, head-nodding gem. It's been part of my consciousness for going on fifty years now. On the way to George Street School I sing 'We are stardust, we are golden and we've got to get ourselves back to the garden'. I'm still humming it when I run a stick that I've picked up along the chain-link fence that encloses a patch of grass in front of our classroom.

In the spring of 2010, I open an email sent to me from the Netherlands. The email is from Iain Matthews. He says that he has just finished reading a music-based memoir that I have written called *Bringing it all Back Home*. He tells me that he has enjoyed it a lot. He asks me if I know his music. I am too embarrassed to tell him that I had run my stick along a fence whilst humming

'Woodstock' so I say I like his latest CD *Joy Mining* and that we have a mutual friend in his record label owner, David Suff.

'Oh! You know my latest music and you know David! I like these connections.'

I tell Iain that his duet with Sandy Denny on 'Thro' My Eyes' has given me a lot of comfort over the years. Iain and I become email pals for a few months and later that same year, when he is touring Britain, he asks if he might come to our house to see me.

He is touring with the Dutch guitarist BJ Baartmans and they have a gig about an hour from me and a day off after that. Iain and BJ come over to my house and we sit drinking tea at my kitchen table. We talk about music, books and people who we know in common. Iain tells me that he is thinking about writing a memoir and wonders if I might like to help him with it. I tell him that I'd be very happy to help, but I thought he ought to write some stories down himself first.

For the past six years or so, Iain and I have become good friends. I have helped to organise one or two gigs for him when he tours England and he did me a great favour by playing alongside his musical collaborator Egbert Derix at a charity concert I organise. We batted Iain's idea to write a memoir back and forth during that time. Last autumn we got down to business. I went over to his home in the Netherlands and this time we sat at his kitchen table and drank tea. We talked about how to distil a life of seventy-two years, more than fifty of them pursuing a career as a travelling musician. I said, 'Just tell some stories Iain, I'll write them down and then hand them back to you, you go through them and take out or add whatever you want and if it works, we'll end up with a book.' So that's what we did. This book is the result.

It has been an honour and a privilege for me to work alongside one of the great singers in popular music. At first Iain said, 'The sixties is a long time ago, I'm not sure I can remember.' He did remember though. And not only that, he remembered in sparkling clarity. Here then is a story of a young man who left home to seek the bright lights of London in the middle of a decade when anything seemed possible. A young man whose journey has taken him around the world pursuing a career doing something he loves. 'I asked him where are you going and this he told me' indeed!

Ian Clayton
Featherstone
March 2018

INTRODUCTION

I have a deep admiration for the writer James Salter. I think I've read most of his books, if not all of them. He wrote in his final novel *All That Is*, 'There comes a time when you realise that everything is a dream, and only those things preserved in writing have any possibility of being real.' If what he says is true, if all that exists in the end is what has been written down, then I need to write down my story. I've followed a dream and lived what many might consider to be the enviable life of a musician, but until now that life has been written in songs. This is my attempt to put it into a book.

The life of the professional musician can be unstable. Many of us throw in the towel early and choose the relative security of a job with a monthly income. I've tried to focus on the music rather than the financial gain. I'm fully aware that the living to be made from this business works on several different levels. It begins at one end with the old blues men and women playing what they called their 'starvation box' – a guitar. At the other end of the scale you can also discover unimaginable wealth, created by writing a mega hit. If you invest the proceeds from this stroke of good fortune properly, it can sustain you, your children and your children's children for the rest of their lives. I've experienced neither of those things, unless we count a month-long period in the summer of '67 when I survived by the skin of my teeth, suitcase in hand, relying on the generosity of others, or a brief spell three years later when I had a number one hit in the European pop charts.

In terms of success, I've been up and down a lot. At the somewhat tender age of twenty-one, I joined a band called Fairport Convention and by now I have trodden the middle ground too many times not to have complete respect and understanding for my fellow songwriters. Like me, they still do it year after year, simply for the music. I often encounter them on the road, all with the relentless urge to write and perform. It feels more like a virus than a career choice. My career continues to be a series of peaks and troughs and I'm now approaching my sixth decade of making music. A heady realisation.

Yet still my fascination with music and song continues. I feel as though I'm on a quest, embracing the inconsistencies of what a day might bring, as I still reach for some improbable, impossible perfection, keeping in mind those who went before me, calling the tune and paving the way like musical pied pipers.

In my darkest moments songs have always pulled me back to the light. This book is about that light and what it's meant to be saturated in song. It's about waking up every morning with the realisation that music is my life and my life is music.

Iain Matthews
Horst, Netherlands
April 2018

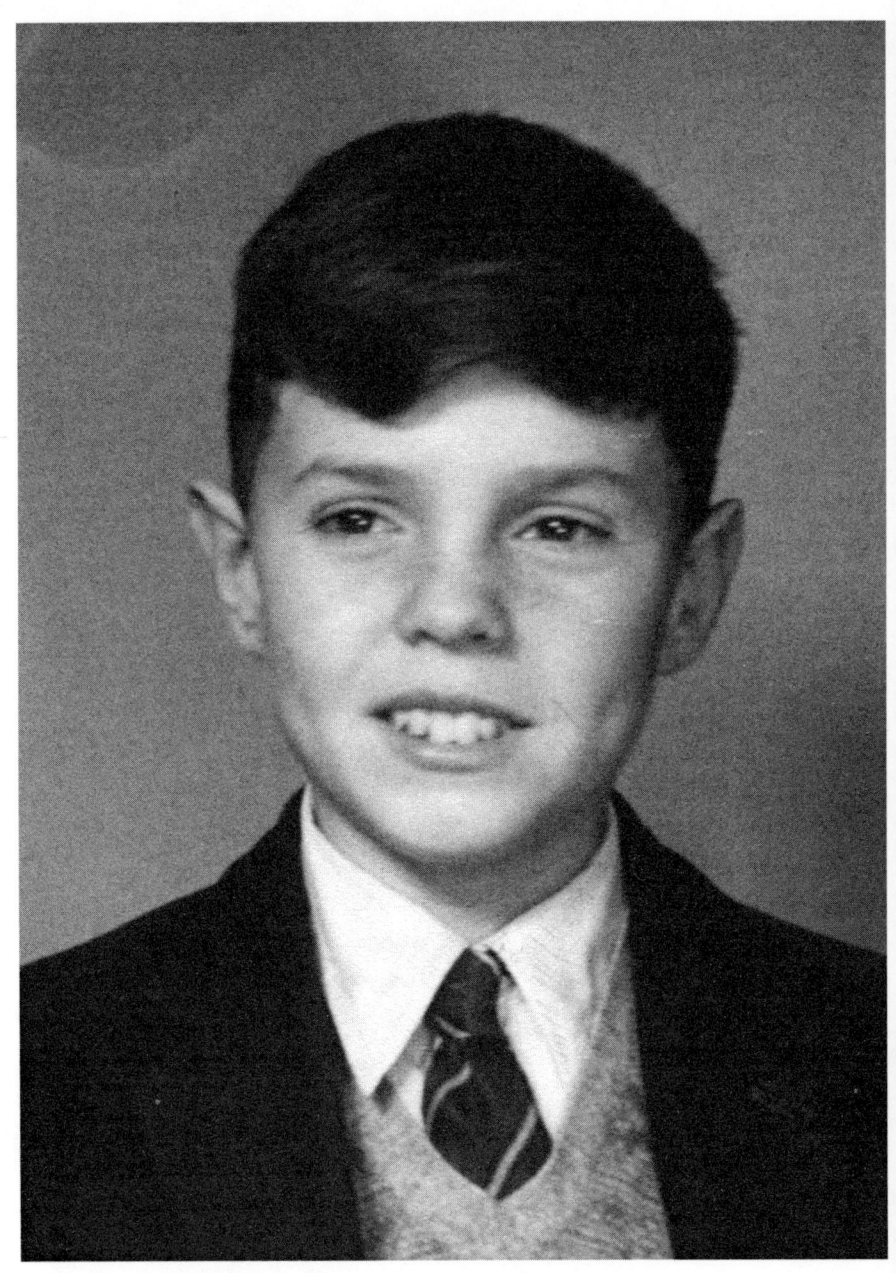

PART ONE
THIS TRAIN IS RUNNING

WHEN I WAS A BOY

Big steam engine whistle sings
Never mind the thistle stings
Before The Beatles did their thing
And skiffle took it on the chin
We were building carts from wood we found
From old pram wheels that won't go round
Matches at the Old Showground
Back when I was a boy

Bouncing marbles down the street
It was chips and cod's roe once a week
And tuppence bought a bag of sweets
After rationing was obsolete

We had holes in every pair of socks
Beano through the letterbox
Our front door was never ever locked

Days stretched on for ever then
Just dogs and dirt and oxygen
Bolton won the cup again
Just as Macmillan's crew were moving
Dad said work was tough and times were lean
As we lost a King and gained a Queen
And we gathered round that TV screen
Back when I was a boy

I know there's no returning to
Those days that seemed so free
But these are only childhood memories

The Russians put a man in space
Now the Yanks are stepping up the race
Mom says Grandma's gone to a far, far better place
Now Johnnie Ray's at number one
And Frankel's a phenomenon
While school went on and on and on
Back when I was a boy

Now it's PS3s and Wiis
And stay-at-home technologies
You and I had none of these
Back when I was a boy

These days kids grow up so fast
And nothing's really built to last
Their world's not quite as meaningful and innocent
As when I was a boy
Big steam engine whistle sings
Never mind the thistle stings
Before The Beatles did their thing
What's happening to Marilyn?

They built a wall from north to south
To keep the East Berliners out
Dad says Castro better watch his mouth
While Brian Poole says twist and shout
Now they're rioting in Budapest
While Tommy Dorsey's laid to rest
And Brigitte Bardot bared her breasts
Back when I was a boy

I know there's no returning to
Those days that seemed so free
But these are only childhood memories

1. THE IRON FIST

I look at photos from my childhood in Barton-upon-Humber and I'm usually scowling or solemn. Of course there were carefree days too, many of them, but in general I was a troubled child, stubborn and often self-defeating. I remember some of those moments.

I loved football, yet one year on cup final day I desperately wanted to watch the game and had invites from both my grandad and cousin Tim to watch it on their TVs, but instead I chose to lie motionless on my back on our front lawn, depriving myself, unable to get up until I knew the final whistle had blown, refusing to give myself permission to feel good and go watch it. On occasion I would invite my best friend Michael Fitzsimmons over to play. It was quite a long walk for him and when he arrived, for no apparent reason, I'd lock myself in the outdoor toilet. Despite his pleading, I would refuse to come out or even speak to him. He would eventually give up and go home. These types of actions blighted me for many years, well into adulthood.

The man I called Dad, Allan Beaton MacDonald, was a dour Scottish protestant, a salt on the porridge sort of person. He was a short man, slightly less than five foot seven, with an even shorter temper. He inflicted his frustrations on my mother and put the fear of God into my brothers and me with a thick, brown leather belt, something he'd learned from his own father. My friends were reticent about coming to the house, afraid that he might answer the door.

Mom called him Mac. He had a long, arched Roman beak, a real whopper. In a rare lighter mood, he once joked about it saying that when God was handing out noses, Mac thought he'd said 'roses' and asked for a big red one. He could be occasionally funny, rarely tender, but more often than not he was lightning-quick to anger and for no apparent reason.

I knew what I saw but never truly understood Mac. He was, by his own say-so, a smart man. He had been born in Dollar, just outside Bridge of Allan near Stirling in Scotland. His father worked as a gardener at Stirling Castle. Before the war he had studied at Stirling Academy and was an enthusiastic mathematician. After the war, when academic jobs were difficult to come by, he and my mom settled in Barton-upon-Humber. In order to create an income for his new family he signed on as a labourer at the Appleby-Frodingham ironworks on the outskirts of Scunthorpe. He would ride the daily 30-mile round trip on the works bus.

Mac worked rotating shifts. The day shift was six am until two pm. Afternoons were two until ten pm and nights would be from ten pm until six am. My least favourite of these was the night shift. He hated the night shift and would be getting up just as I got home from school. He'd be irritable and looking for trouble. If I had homework he would stand behind me while I did it. The one I disliked most of all was the math homework. I wasn't very good at math and he was excellent. He would stand there watching, terrorising me into making mistakes. I did it with the sense that there was a tiger behind me waiting to pounce. With a series of short quick flicks and sometimes slaps to the back of the head, he would tell me how easy it was and how stupid I was to not get it. I grew to dislike the man. I would try to avoid him, but it was impossible.

Mac's primary job was to reline blast furnaces – giant brick-lined kilns where the iron ore is melted down before the impurities are discarded and the remainder made into steel. At the end of the process, once the iron had been removed, my dad and his workmates would ride on small dump trucks into the kiln wearing face masks. In thirty-second stints, they would pull out the old lining. Meanwhile, the furnaces were still red-hot as it was considered inefficient to let the kilns cool down between blastings. The blast chamber is constantly full of poisonous fumes, which Dad and his companions couldn't help but inhale as they toiled. These fumes are ultimately what killed him in his bed one night, shortly before he reached retirement age. And this was the man who would slap my head and tell me I was stupid.

I grew up with a feeling that I was the black sheep of the family, at least until I hit my late teens. By then his mistreatment of me had escalated and become more brazen and, finally, unforgivable. The slaps and flicks turned into kicks and punches. He just wanted to fight me all the time. He would say, 'Don't you dare look at me like that!' If I showed a flicker of defiance he'd say, 'Don't you think about raising a hand to me or I'll knock you into the middle of next week.' By the time I'd turned sixteen things became unmanageable for me. I knew I could fight back, but by then I simply couldn't be bothered. He meant nothing to me. I had accepted this man as my protective parent and he'd betrayed me. I started telling my closest friends he wasn't my father.

My mother, Dorothy May Matthews, was born and raised in Barton-upon-Humber. My gran Carrie, her husband Tom and most of their kids lived within hailing distance of each other. It was an insular family support group. After I was born, I was brought to a small house tucked away next to The White Lion pub in the old market square. It was a narrow, white, two-storey building which we rented from a Mr Doughty, the landlord at the pub. Mr Doughty had a huge albino Alsatian that would roam free around the property, slobbering all over us should we let him within licking range. The house was barely big enough for one family yet I have a vague memory of us sharing it with Aunt Carrie and her infant son, my cousin Tim, who was the same age as me. Both of our dads were away in the military and the sisters had decided to hang together until their return. We didn't stay in that house too long. When Mac came home from the army we moved to No. 50 Bowmandale, a brand-new house on the newly-built council estate.

I carry an abiding image of one Saturday morning when I was five years old. Mac and I walked into town, down Bowmandale and across the green where the pensioners lived, through the alley past the Elswick Hopper bicycle works, then a quick right and into the market place to the butcher's shop. Hanging on steel hooks in the window were huge, lolloping cows' tongues. I was both mesmerised and disgusted by how long and hairy they were.

He bought two and we carried them home wrapped in white greaseproof paper. Once we got home he cut and peeled off the skin and hair before boiling the tongues. When they were done he pressed and steam-sealed them into jars, all bound together in some kind of jelly. He made me watch. I found the entire process sickening. The tongues remained in the jars at the back of the pantry for a month or so. One day he opened a jar, forked the meat out and sliced it up to put in his sandwiches. Each day, he took sandwiches to work with either tongue or cheese in them. He was a man of strict repetition.

Ever since that sickening day, I've been a vegetarian. Many was the night I sat staring down a plate of meat while the rest of the family were sprawled out in the front room watching television. On the wages my dad made, meat was a luxury in our house and my parents were determined that I would eat it. I was equally determined that I would not. Usually, one of my brothers would drift through the dining room to get a drink and eat it for me, or else the same piece of meat would appear on my plate the next night. The process would be repeated over and over until meat finally stopped appearing on my plate. My parents never fully reconciled themselves to it and years later, when I came back from London to visit them, they still gave me meat with my dinner.

Meal times at home were stressful events. We weren't allowed to talk. Dad had a rule that the dinner table was for eating and we could talk later. Most families I knew would share the day's events, but not us. Our dinners were silent affairs, the only sounds being those of jaws exercising. We ate that way under threat of 'the belt', our penance for breaking his precious code.

But kids can be cruel too. My younger brother Neil, the middle child and Mac's firm favourite, was a timid soul. My youngest brother Andy and I would tag team and try, undetected, to make Neil laugh, just to get him into trouble. He would try to ignore us and became so terrified of laughing at the table that he would make himself cry instead, sometimes peeing his pants in the process. Mac eventually realised what we were doing and those moments of light entertainment came to a halt when the belt came out.

Neil and Andy were closer in years and worked mostly as a team against me. On weekend mornings they liked to play by themselves in the room they shared. If I tried to muscle in they would scream bloody murder. 'Dad, Ian's in our room,' or they'd yell 'Get out, get out' until Mom or Dad intervened. Mac got sick of these early morning disturbances, particularly if he was on nights, so he and Mom decided to keep us apart by attaching a light chain to the outside of my bedroom door, where only they could get at it and only they were allowed to undo it. This meant I was imprisoned in my room from bedtime to breakfast. I would sneak slices of bread from the pantry and store them in a drawer, just in case my parents one day chained my door and forgot about me. Many nights I peed from my bedroom window in desperation rather than disturb anyone.

I suppose these days this behaviour would be considered child abuse, but back then I didn't really care about the chain. In some strange way I quite enjoyed the solitary confinement. It made me feel special. I had a small radio that my favourite cousin Judith had bought me for my birthday. That and a stash of good books. I became an avid reader. My favourite books were a series about an Amazon explorer with the unlikely name of Ross Salmon. I loved to lie in my bed and go into the jungle with him. That was until in one of his later tales he told of a giant anaconda snake that one day fell through the roof of a native's hut, squeezing him to death as he slept. I fitfully imagined one of these twenty-foot monsters lurking in the crawl space above my room, waiting patiently for me to fall asleep before dropping down to silently crush me in my bed. My imaginings became so vivid and frightening that I had to put away Ross Salmon and turn to lighter bedtime reading.

One morning I awoke to the smell of something burning. My mom rushed to unlatch the chain. My brothers had decided to play at being Red Indians and had pulled a sheet over their heads to form a tepee. Apparently oblivious to the consequences, they sat cross-legged opposite each other and lit a small fire to toast bread on. We discovered it in the nick of time. There was hell to pay for that little stunt.

Neil and Andy loved fires. Our local family grocer Mr Appleyard had a small corner shop stuffed to the gills with household items. Mr Appleyard wasn't a pleasant man at the best of times and he'd apparently said something mean to Andy and Neil. They decided to get their own back and set fire to his little wooden storage shed, burning it to the ground, destroying all of his overstock in the process. They didn't get away lightly with that one and for as long as I can recall their weekly pocket money went into a fund to rebuild and restock Mr Appleyard's shed.

I was a chubby child and some of my pals at school teased me by calling me 'Plum' after a popular comic strip called Little Plum in *The Beano*. Plum was a Native American – in those less enlightened times they called him 'Little Plum Your Redskin Chum' – who was also a bit on the chubby side and was always trying to prove himself as a valuable member of the tribe. I was also teased because I never got picked for the school choir. In my mind I was a far better singer than any of them, so I couldn't understand why I wasn't chosen. There were try-outs twice a year. Miss Riley our choir mistress had a selection system. The applicants, about fifty of us, would assemble in the main hall to be placed in lines of ten, leaving enough space between the lines for her to amble down. She would cup her right hand behind her ear, listen intently to our sweet young voices and, if she liked what she heard, the chosen one would be the recipient of a light tap on the shoulder. We always sang the same song, 'Masters in This Hall', an ancient carol. I still remember the lyrics now.

> Hear ye news today
> Brought from over sea,
> And ever I you pray:
> Nowell! Nowell! Nowell!
> Nowell, sing we loud!
> God today hath poor folk raised
> And cast a-down the proud.

I never did make any sense of why Miss Riley chose that song, but it didn't matter, I just wanted in. I craved the Riley tap, but never got it. At my third audition she waltzed right by me as if I didn't exist. She didn't even slow down to listen to my wonderful timbre. My friends knew I was aching to be part of the choir and let me know about it. After the try-out, Michael Mason said, 'Oi, Plum, did she choose you this time? No! Oh what a shame.' I hated Miss Riley and her stupid choir try-outs.

Mom told me that I didn't have to try so hard to get in to grammar school because I wouldn't like it. She thought the other school would be fine for me. She had been a borderline eleven-plus passer herself and to hear her speak about it she had a miserable time at grammar school. Her advice was, 'Stay small, keep out of the way and then get yourself a nice little job.' I felt trapped between the devil and the deep blue sea. Damned if I did and damned if I didn't. The 'stay small' riff my mother repeated still echoes around my brain more than sixty years later.

Because of Mac's intimidation, Mom did little to protect or reassure myself or my brothers. The truth was she dare not. Years later she told me that after an argument he could hold out for more than a week without ever speaking to her. One Sunday, we were just finishing our tea when a car pulled up outside and the horn blew. It was Mom's sister, my Aunt Olive, and her family from Hull. We kids were really excited when we lifted the curtain and saw them coming up the path to the front door. But not Mac, he just said, 'Bloody hell! I can't even have peace on a Sunday.' That's how he was.

Having children of my own, I now see what it takes to be a parent. It's not easy and at times I've been a lousy one too. But I've been dedicated and compassionate. I didn't realise the sacrifices that Mom had made on my behalf. I thought she had it easy staying at home all day, testing out jobs here and there, trying to find a meaning in her life. But being a housewife in that marriage must have proven stressful for her; she had to maintain her own peace of mind and keep Mac as even-keeled and contented as possible. He was the sole provider and we were never allowed to forget it. Mac was unhappy with what life had dealt him and someone had to pay, which usually meant Mom and, as I grew up, me too. When I think about it now, things can't have been too easy for him either; he'd taken a poisonous job that was beneath him and worked rotten hours in order to provide for us. In a working-class environment of the nineteen fifties and sixties north of England, it's what was expected. Meanwhile, Mom was supposed to assume the role of the dutiful housewife – barefoot, pregnant and chained to the kitchen sink. She did her best and created her own little buffers to soften the blows. She always seemed to be starting or ending a diet but never quite seemed to achieve the body shape she envisioned in her mind.

She insisted that Sundays would be her day of rest, a time when she could put her feet up. Every Sunday she packed my brothers and me off to the Salvation Army and for three hours we would be subjected to singing hymns and reciting scriptures. Twice every Sunday, once in the morning and a second session in the afternoon. A donation of three pence per child finally became too much of a financial burden and we were allowed to drop the morning session. Even then I recognised and pushed against the religious dogma we were forced to endure, and to this day refuse to embrace it, regardless of faith. Yet something in me liked going. My saving grace was the brass band and a small choir they called the Salvation Army Singers. Whenever possible, I would sit as close as I could get to the great sounds that little musical ensemble made.

Melvyn Thurlby was around the same age as me. He played the cornet and, more impressively, he sang in the choir. Whenever Melvyn sang, it was curiously different to everyone else. The words were the same, but somehow the tune was altered, yet it still fitted in with what everyone else was doing. It was both puzzling and uplifting for me. One Sunday I plucked up the courage to ask him what it was he was doing. He told me, 'It's called harmony.' He said his mom had taught it him. She was also in the band and had showed him how to play the cornet too. I liked the harmony very much. I could tell that he was singing an independent melody that was slightly above everyone else. If I focused very hard and followed his melody, ignoring what the others were singing, I could do it too, but as soon as my attention wavered and I listened to what the others were doing I fell back down to the main melody. At Mel's prompting, every Sunday

I sat right behind him and began to copy what he was doing. Occasionally he would turn to me with a grin and a quick nod of the head to let me know that what I was doing was correct. It was difficult, but lots of fun, and after a while I began to enjoy Sunday afternoons and the prospect of singing with Mel. With his guidance I became quite adept.

I discovered that Mel and I attended the same school. He was a year behind me. We became loosely-tied friends and would stand next to each other in school assemblies, letting loose weird notes and chuckling with glee when they worked. I realised for the first time that music was cool, fun even, and despite what the big people might say, there were no rules. What I had first perceived as unfair punishment from Mom had become a true blessing in disguise. At least for me it did. My unmusical brothers detested Sunday school and the Salvation Army to the bitter end.

I was never very close to my brothers as a boy. We were different in so many ways. I took after my mom, while they favoured their dad's Highland attitude. I was shy, they were forward and demanding. I was besotted with football and music, they ran the cross-country and swam. I cared about my brothers deeply and would defend them at the drop of a hat, but I wasn't interested in spending much time with them. They were younger than me. They had their group of friends and I had mine. In school they were more studious than me and went on to the grammar school while I attended secondary modern. I was scholastically disinterested at best and only came to life on a Thursday afternoon when we had the double sports period. During those couple of hours we'd play football and I would mimic my Manchester United idol, Duncan Edwards.

I came home from school one February afternoon in 1958 and Mom had just got in with her shopping. 'Have you heard about the crash?' she asked. I hadn't. 'Sit down,' she said and then told me that there had been a plane crash in the ice and snow at Munich airport and Manchester United was involved. I turned on our tiny black and white television with the magnifier on the front. The news came screaming at me. The Busby Babes, my Babes; David Pegg, Roger Byrne, Mark Jones, Billy Whelan, Tommy Taylor and Frank Swift, the guru of all sports writers, were all dead. Duncan Edwards was clinging to life and Matt Busby was on a respirator. They'd been returning from a European Cup match against Red Star Belgrade and had stopped to refuel at Munich. The plane crashed into a bank at the end of the runway following a third attempt to take off with ice forming on the wings. My tiny fragile world came crashing down. I couldn't believe it, didn't want to believe it. I ran out of our house up to Martin Carnaby's about a half mile away. Had he seen it? Was it true? He had and it was. We shed a tear.

For the rest of the term I couldn't concentrate at school. I paid little attention to what the teachers were saying and became quarrelsome with friends. This got me in hot water with my teachers and some of them I'm sure were unable to forgive me for the rest of my time there. I became more withdrawn and moody at home. No one seemed to notice and that only served to make things worse. Didn't they realise what it meant? The Babes were the single most important thing in my life. Why was I the only one feeling this way?

Later that year, when I was twelve, it was decided that in order for Mac to be closer to his job we would move to Scunthorpe. To yet another council estate. We began our lives at No. 13 Enderby Road in a strange town where I knew no one. For a shy boy this was a mountain I had no choice but to climb.

THIS TRAIN

This train was built in '32 outside of Chesterfield
No chrome, no fancy leatherette
Just good old northern steel
They christened her the Pioneer
She ran from north to south
Just a ticket man and an engineer and strictly word of mouth

She had no trouble spotting him decked out in uniform
When he got off that train some time in 1941
They hurried to her sister's house
She took him there before
He stroked her breast, he kissed her mouth
He closed the bedroom door
His train was running

This train blew no warning
This train sacrificed
This train keeps on humming, humming

This train became a runaway in 1948
There was no way to stop it until he applied the brake
Just a little common decency
Is that so much to ask
She said I beg to disagree and ran upstairs to pack
Her train was running

This train she runs on confidence
This train she is a rock
This train pulled into Destiny and shuddered to a stop
He stepped onto the platform with his teenage attitude
He was hoping for direction
He was searching for the truth

She was no longer Pioneer, but Southern Crucifix
When he got on that train again in 1966
But it didn't feel the same as when he'd ridden her before
As if that change of name had ripped the heart right out of her
But this train keeps running

This train she's got stories
This train's compromised
This train keeps on humming, humming

This train ran out of steam some time in 1983
They said that she was obsolete
Though I would not agree
I believe what put us here is gonna take us in
And no amount of kick and shove
Will change a God damned thing

This train was built in '32 outside of Chesterfield
No chrome, no fancy leatherette
Just good old northern steel

2. SEARCHIN'

When we moved to Enderby Road in 1958, Scunthorpe United were in the second division of the English Football League. They played their home games at the Old Showground, opposite the Baths Hall in the town centre. Living directly opposite us on Enderby Road was a lad about our Neil's age called Pete Haller, a Scunthorpe United fan whose big brother took him to home games. One Saturday, Pete and his brother came over and said they were going to the match and asked if I would like to go. It was my first real football experience and I loved it. It was good quality football and I quickly became a Ronnie Waldock fan. Waldock was the first of several muscled, bullying centre-forwards. The team had enough talent to gain promotion to the top division but couldn't quite do it. In the early sixties they had Barrie Thomas, a brilliant old-fashioned, bruising centre-forward; Peter (Noddy) Neal a dynamic, blond-haired centre-half tipped for national honours; and the goalie Ken Jones had been part of the Welsh squad for the World Cup in Sweden. They beat some great teams but could never quite find that special something to move into the upper tier. At that time some of the top sides – Liverpool, Sunderland and Sheffield Wednesday – were second division teams.

From my second year at Riddings Secondary Modern I was right-winger for the school football team. I thought I was the Bobby Charlton of North Lincolnshire. I lived and breathed the game and swapped my *Eagle* comics for copies of *Charles Buchan's Football Monthly*. I began spending what pocket money I had on collecting football programmes, occasionally even using the money my mom gave me for school lunch. I'd starve from breakfast until tea just to buy a copy of the Arsenal versus Liverpool FA Cup Final programme of 1950, which features the Compton brothers in the Arsenal team – Denis on the right wing and Leslie at centre-half. I still have that programme.

My greatest passion though was reserved for Manchester United. Many were the times I stretched out under the summer sun on our front lawn to read about my heroes. When I was fifteen, I worked up a plan to get Matt Busby, the manager of Manchester United, to take me on. I would start with a low division team and through skill and sheer hard work I would work my way through the divisions until my reputation as a world-class winger soaring to undeniable heights would mean he absolutely had to sign me. I wrote to Jimmy Scoular, ex-Newcastle United star and current manager of Bradford Park Avenue. In 1962, Bradford Park Avenue had recently been promoted from the bottom division and it was my duty to help them on their way up. I explained to him that I was a young, up-and-coming winger, just the sort of player he might need in order to progress. What I hadn't considered was that Jimmy Scoular might write back to me. I panicked a month later when an envelope bearing the initials 'BPA' flopped through our letterbox. 'Jimmy Scoular would like to extend to you an invitation to a try-out for the Bradford Park Avenue Football Club on Sunday April 3rd. Please phone.'

I told my dad about it and asked if he'd take me. He was on the afternoon shift that week, so I asked my mom's younger brother, Uncle Fred, who was a big football fan. He was excited for me and offered to drive me the 120-mile round trip to Bradford. I honed my skills in the park and practised my crossing at weekends with my local Sunday team. In from the right, in from the right, in from the right, over and over. I became more and more nervous as the day approached. Only the mental picture I'd formed of me and Bobby Charlton setting up Albert Quixall headers from both wings kept me going.

I was called into Jimmy Scoular's office when I arrived at Horton Park Avenue, the home of my future employers. He had all of his Newcastle United memorabilia on the walls and was sitting behind a huge wooden desk. It would have been intimidating for a seasoned veteran, but for a fifteen-year-old poseur it was terrifying. He had probably done this a thousand times. I was on the verge of an anxiety attack.

'So son, it says here that you are a left-winger eh!'

I don't know where the left wing bit came from, I was a right-winger, but I was speechless and simply nodded.

'Right then, get your kit on then get out on that field and report to the trainer.'

The trainer made up two sides and I could tell from the off that most of the boys already knew each other. Then it dawned on me, this was a youth team practise, most of the lads were on the verge of first team football and I was an interloper. For the first half hour of the game I was fed perfect pass after perfect pass and I muffed cross after cross. The boss stopped the game and called me over. He could see I was more naturally right footed and wondered why I'd lined up on the left wing. 'I'm a right-winger really,' I said and saw his next question coming even before he shaped his lips to speak. It came at me in slow motion, a lazy, looping inswinger. I could see the words written in that brilliant Bradford April sky.

'So what the hell are you doing on the left wing?'

'Well, I've been following your recent results and thought you needed a lefty.'

His eyes rolled. If I could have found a stone on that muddy mess of a pitch I would have squeezed under it and stayed till nightfall when everyone had gone home.

Mr Scoular, God bless him, was patient.

'Right, get out on to the wing, show me what a right-winger looks like and put a bit of pace on the ball, you're 2-1 down and I need you to win this game for us.'

Sad to say I wasn't much better on the right than I had been on the left. I visualised in my mind's eye what Mr Scoular's report might say, 'Cannot kick with left, no better with right, totally fucking useless Scunthorpe wannabe.' Mr Scoular was actually a lot gentler than that, it probably wasn't the first time he'd had to dismantle a schoolboy footballer's dream. He said, 'Go home lad, work on that left foot for a year and call me back next season.'

Uncle Fred tried to cheer me up on the way home as I sat in the passenger seat sulking. When he dropped me off at our front gate he said, 'Don't worry about it, you did your best.' He said he could help me, if I wanted. But I knew already that my professional football career was over before it had even begun; washed-up at the age of fifteen. My mom was preparing Sunday dinner. She asked me how I'd done.

'Quite well. They said they would let me know in a couple of weeks.'

Brother Andy glanced up from behind his comic.

'Yeah right!' he said, 'a couple of weeks.'

I could have smacked him.

If you ever look at a biography of mine and it says I once played professional football for Bradford Park Avenue, you'll now know better.

Mom had been the piano player in a small ensemble in the military and we had an upright piano pushed against the wall in a far corner of our front room. The piano stool had a padded hinged seat which she kept all of her sheet music in. Mom could play boogie-woogie, she had a mean left hand that used to fly around the lower keys, pounding out bass notes. I was impressed and loved to listen to her play but for some reason she was reluctant to. One day however, after much pleading from me, she agreed to play something for my friends and me. We listened to her for a while and then, showing off, I pretended it was a player piano and started to wind an invisible handle at the side. I embarrassed Mom terribly. She snapped down the lid and stormed out of the room, refusing to play any more. I could never get her to play for me again, even when it was just the two of us. I don't think she ever quite forgave me for making her look silly.

The first record I ever bought was 'Searchin'' by The Hollies; I got it from the record bar at the Scunthorpe Co-op on the high street. I'd heard it on the radio and was besotted. It was the harmonies that took my senses by storm. They were tight and thick and I loved the sound they made. I took it home and played it six times in a row on our little blue and white Dansette. I say ours, it was Mom's really, but she rarely used it and I'd laid claim to it. By the sixth repeat of 'Searchin'', Mom had had enough. She blasted into the room, ripped the disc out of the Dansette and snapped it in half. 'Get that bloody racket out of my house,' she said. I didn't have to, it wouldn't play anymore. After that little incident I began stashing all my subsequent singles over at my friend Dave's house.

Dave Akid and I had become close friends around 1960 during my penultimate year at Riddings Secondary Modern. We bonded while playing football after school at Burringham Park at the end of our road. It was one of those old-fashioned parks with a huge area of grassland at the lower end and a smaller sculpted area at the top end where they'd built a children's playground. The lower end was ideal for playing football and Dave lived right opposite. Most evenings during the summer months I would walk around the corner to his house to pick him up.

We shared an insatiable passion for football, music and cool clothes. Our only bone of contention being that he was a Liverpool fan and I was already dyed-in-the-wool Manchester United. However, I held the ace because we were in the first division and he was still in the second. We spent a lot of our time together aimlessly whacking a beat-up football around or perched on the grassy bank overlooking Burringham Hill, talking music while counting the bright-red double decker buses as they came and went. We talked a lot about music, in particular The Hollies, who were just emerging and whom we both loved. We were in disagreement there too. He thought that Allan Clarke was the glue that bound them together, while I said it was so obviously Graham Nash. Some days we'd simply lie on our bellies and browse through the ad section of our *Melody Maker* or, if we couldn't find one, the *NME*. We'd fantasise about moving to London, where side by side we'd become star salesmen at Lord John's clothing shop on Carnaby Street before starting a successful pop group of our own called 'Time and The Gravy Train'. I saw Dave recently after a show and we laughed about our days in Burringham Park. He reminded me that I always had the cleanest footy kit he'd ever seen because I refused to tackle in case my shorts got dirty. Some things never change.

Dave lived in an old house, considerably older than ours, and I felt a little uncomfortable going there to visit him. It always seemed to be a messy place with a fully-loaded clothes airer hanging from the ceiling like a display of prayer flags. I'm a short guy, but I'd always have to stoop and duck under the clothes. The front room, at Dave's insistence, was kept spotlessly clean and reserved exclusively as a retreat for him and his visitors. His mom was a tiny, grey-haired, round-shouldered old lady and Dave was forever shouting at her for one reason or another. She would ignore him, sitting in her easy chair smoking and reading. I took away the impression quite early on that Dave, while only a teenager, was very much the responsible adult. He took care of his mom, his kid brother Johnny and his little baby sister Denise. The dad never seemed to be there. We didn't talk about it.

It didn't happen overnight of course, but it seemed that one day we were kicking that leather ball around in the mud, with us both in rags, and the next day Dave was knocking at our front door dressed like a prince. I answered the door and there he stood in a beautiful, charcoal-grey pinstripe suit, a white shirt and tie, and a pair of highly-polished black brogues. Dave had tired of school and had somehow managed to land a job at John Colliers, a prestigious tailor's on Scunthorpe's high street. From that day on, I don't think I saw him dressed anything short of impeccable.

I left school at the beginning of the summer holidays of 1962. I'd just turned sixteen and work crept up on my blind side. The houses in Enderby Road were laid out in such a way that our back garden, separated by a wire fence, backed onto the garden of the houses on the street that ran parallel. Our parallel street was Somerby Road. Our neighbour over the fence was a man we called Jed, short for Gerald. He was a foreman for J.D. Tighe, the largest painting and decorating firm in North Lincolnshire. My mom and Mrs Jed knew each other from hanging their washing out on the same day. (It's funny how the memory works. I can name the entire front five for Bristol City that year, but I can't accurately recall the name of my closest neighbour.) They'd spend time gossiping and smoking cigarettes over the garden fence. One day, as I was about to leave school for good, Mom must have mentioned to Mrs Jed that I didn't have a job. My plan had been to extend my education for a couple more years, preparing for a higher learning. My teachers had other thoughts. They'd convinced me, much to my bitter disappointment, that I'd be wasting my time staying on and should simply find a trade. That evening, unbeknownst to me, Mrs Jed told her husband about that nice young lad down the garden, Dorothy's son, who might make a willing apprentice. The next day Jed shouted over the same fence to my dad that there was a job for me if I wanted it. Mac didn't bother asking me, he simply accepted on my behalf and told me later. I was a painting and decorator's apprentice, like it or not. The following Monday I became a wage earner and my dubious career in painting and decorating began.

My first eight hours on the job involved being taken to a building site and told to heave huge pine boards from one pile to another. I was told to 'prime' them. Primer was a nasty smelling, pink, oil-based paint used to first coat and effectively seal the wood. I was a messy primer. No one had bothered to tell me until I was covered with the stuff that it could only be removed by lathering myself in turpentine. During my first week on the job I rubbed my hands, arms and face raw. At this point I was advised to buy myself a pair of overalls and some protective gloves. Initiation they laughingly called it. The art of priming consisted of applying the pink liquid to all the wood's surfaces – front, back and edges – until the pile of planks on my left became the pile of planks on my right. I would then be moved to another area of the building site to begin the process all over again. It was like painting Scotland's Forth Bridge. I had no idea that so much untreated wood existed and after the first month of this 'apprenticeship' I was starting to wonder if this was my lot in life.

Not long after I began my sentence with J.D. Tighe, I was taken to a local pub one lunchtime by some of the craftsmen. Up until then I'd never tasted alcohol, so when asked what I wanted I chose a glass of orange juice. My workmates gave me the evil eye. I caved and said that perhaps I might try half a pint of beer. I took a tentative sip and hated the dull, sour taste and its thick, malty consistency on my tongue. I asked if I could put some sugar in it. Non-stop laughter erupted and echoed around the establishment, drawing mean stares from the locals. Words like 'mama' and 'titty' were uttered. I knew even then I would never be a serious beer drinker.

By some small stroke of good fortune, I was not to be alone in my world of wood and pinkness. After only a couple of weeks on the job I was introduced to a fellow apprentice, a lad called Johnny Doughty. I liked Johnny because, like me, he was a football person; he liked playing and watching it. We went to many a game together at the Old Showground and commiserated with one another after yet another poor outing by our beloved 'Iron', as Scunthorpe United was affectionately known. It was Johnny who suggested that maybe we should pool our meagre resources and buy a cheap and cheerful transistor radio. It was an inspirational suggestion. From that moment on, from our 8am arrival to our 5pm departure, our world of pinkness became remotely bearable as we tuned into the BBC Light Programme on the long wave, developing a taste for the available pop music of the day. Listening to the radio became my saving grace as I progressed through the wilderness of painting and decorating.

I graduated from priming on building sites to priming indoors, to sanding, second coating and then one day, without fanfare, I was taken to the signwriting shop, where I began to feel like a true apprentice. In the paint shop they refinished with spray paint the entire bodies of commercial vehicles, including the undercarriages and wheels, and then wrote the company name on the doors and sides. We dealt mostly with big 16-wheelers, oil and petrol tankers. We also worked on grocery and hardware delivery vans from small, independent local companies. They would come to us as shabby, oil-stained wrecks and leave as shiny rejuvenated beasts of the road. Occasionally, an old horse-drawn carriage or coach from someone's private collection would come in to be refinished. These special assignments were only ever taken on by Arthur, the master craftsman and shop foreman. I loved to see these jobs coming in because I knew Arthur would on occasion let me 'second coat' his paintwork and then have me stand to watch and learn as he meticulously lined the body and wheels of these ancient reminders. Lining was a beautifully delicate process whereby a sixteenth-of-an-inch wide painted line was applied to circumscribe and accent the wheels and bodies. Arthur was stern, but could also be a kindly soul if he knew you earnestly wanted to learn. He took me under his wing and began to teach me the trade.

Signwriting was done with a series of brushes of different widths. The best and most expensive ones had a tapered wooden stem and a tip made of sable. The lettering itself was done with the aid of a mahlstick. This was a rounded, wooden rod about a metre long with a ball of leather at one end. If you were right handed, you held the mahlstick in your left hand, resting it on the writing surface across your body at an appropriate angle. You would then rest your right forearm on the mahlstick whilst signwriting. All painting and signwriting on vehicles involved three coats. The initial coat formed the primer, the second coat added depth to the finish, and the final coat was done in shiny gloss paint. The paint was oil-based and the brushes were kept meticulously clean by washing in turpentine at day's end. The shop too was kept as clean and dust-free as possible. We hosed the floor down before every job.

There were four of us in the shop. Derek Cottam was a motorcycle freak. He had a passion for opening up his Vincent Black Shadow on the country lanes on his way to and from work. Derek would call me 'Um' because every one of my answers to his questions would start with 'Ummm'. Colin, the other craftsman, was a decent man but somehow frustrated by life. He was very judgemental and had an insatiable need for always being right. Being the youngest, I usually bore the brunt of his daily frustrations. He constantly corrected and ridiculed me in front of the others. If I questioned why, he said it was for my own good. It would make a man of me. In the shop I laughed it off, but in time I began to take it personally and the sting became a hurt. I once steeled myself to tell him how I felt, but this only served to accelerate his unsolicited opinions.

We always had the radio on playing pop music. Now and again Arthur would shout at us to 'turn that muck off' but most of the time he indulged us. I developed a natural inclination to sing along and after a while needed no prompting. Derek used to say

I had a really good voice and told me that I should join a group. His favourite line was, 'You're better than that twaddle.' The more he'd say it, the more I convinced myself that maybe I was.

I quietly asked around town and discovered that The Rebels, an old-fashioned three-piece rock'n'roll band, were looking for a singer. They played mostly American music: Chuck Berry tunes augmented by standards of the day like 'Rockin' Robin', 'Little Egypt' and 'Under the Boardwalk'. I learned the lyrics and auditioned. I don't think anyone else was particularly interested in joining The Rebels so I got the job. We played the occasional weekend village hall gig, but in general we worked very little; we spent more time in the drummer's car talking about being in a band than we spent actually playing. We used to get together and drive the 60-mile round trip to Doncaster and back for something to do in the evenings, just fooling around. They would do that thing where you swap drivers without stopping. They thought it hilarious but it terrified me. Shortly after I joined, the group decided to try and raise their profile and took on a manager, a local up-and-coming hairdresser, John Stevens. He suggested we change our name to something less 'aggressive' and came up with the highly inspired 'Classics'. He gave each of us a tiny identifying curl that fell neatly across the left side of our foreheads, then had us photographed and business cards were made. I felt it was all a little embarrassing and effeminate, but hey, I was the new boy and he was our big time manager with only our best interests at heart.

I wasn't long in the Classics before I was headhunted by a higher profile band. Someone approached me and said they were from a group called The Imps. Their singer, Freddy Havercroft, was leaving and was I interested in taking his place? I went to a rehearsal to listen to them and was deeply impressed by what they were doing. It was very different to the Classics and more modern sounding. They were covering songs by The Hollies and had a rendition of The Everly Brothers' 'Sleepless Nights' in a beautiful two-part harmony. I thought wow, that's what I want to do, so didn't hesitate in accepting their offer. Once I'd said yes there seemed to be some kind of friction triggered in the band; some of them wanted me in and others didn't. Bill Gibson and Craig Austin played guitar and bass but were also the two main singers. They wanted me to stay, but the others were against it. This escalated and I can't have played more than a couple of shows with them before leaving. Still, I saw it as an important experience for me. I was flattered that they had asked me and enjoyed the attention of being on stage. It gave me the idea that this was something I could pursue. A later version of The Imps would eventually morph into Methuselah and sign to Elektra Records.

One Saturday, there was familiar face at our back door. It was Dave Akid and his pal Charlie Cromack. They told me that they were going to London for a few days to 'check out' what all the fuss was about. They were going to see Carnaby Street and wanted to know if I was interested in going with them. Of course I wanted to go with them. The only thing was, The Iron had a League Cup tie against Stoke City. Stanley Matthews was coming towards the end of his career and I thought it might be my last chance to see him play so I said no. However, I did ask Dave to bring something back for me. Ever since I had seen The Beatles and the Stones on *Thank Your Lucky Stars* I'd wanted a pair of boots like theirs: black Cuban heeled, with a chisel toe and a long criss-cross stitch from heel to toe. They were very enticing. A shop in Tottenham Court Road called Anello & Davide was advertising them for sale in *Melody Maker*. I asked Dave if he could find me a pair, size seven-and-a-half, and gave him a pound.

On the Monday after work I banged on Dave's door anxious to claim my new boots. He ushered me into the front room where a number of trendy looking shopping bags were scattered across the sofa. One of them bore the initials A & D. The boots were everything I'd hoped for. I had never been near anything like them. I set them on the rug before me and gazed at them, stroking and turning them around as if a new angle might enhance their beauty even more. Exactly as *Melody Maker* said, they had the sexy curved Cuban heel and the fancy stitched line all the way up to the perfectly chiselled toe. Not only that, they fitted perfectly.

The only problem I had was balancing in them. I'd never worn such a high heel before, but if you want to be trendy, you suffer and you learn fast. I still have those boots today. When I stopped wearing them, I wrapped them in plastic and archived them.

Just as I was thinking how uncool and suburban my old jeans looked with them, Dave opened up a second bag and pulled out a pair of maroon-velvet, Lord John hipsters.

'If these fit you,' he said, 'you can have them. I bought two pairs.'

I made them fit. He was slightly smaller in the waist than me, but it was nothing a quick intake of breath couldn't fix. I put them on and felt very cool. Dave had all sorts of clothes in his bags: shirts, trousers, a suit, he must have bought up half of Carnaby Street. I decided there and then I wanted to dress that way too. The only problem was Mac. I knew he would have a fit if he saw me wearing clothing like this. I decided to leave my things at Dave's house and whenever we went out I'd change in his front room. It was frustrating having to do it this way, but rather than getting into an argument with my dad I went along with it. I know what he would have said: 'As long as you are living in my bloody house, you do what I bloody well say and wear what I bloody well tell you to!'

Scunthorpe in the mid-sixties was a boring place for a teenager. Dull doesn't begin to describe it. There was not much on offer by way of entertainment and the town was slowly becoming the butt of national jokes. The council came up with the brilliant idea of enhancing Scunthorpe's profile. They decided, in their wisdom, that the town needed to get hip and change its name. They proposed what they saw as the more enticing 'Sunthorpe'. Needless to say, the locals were having none of it and Scunthorpe it remained.

I began attending the local youth club. They played great music and had dance contests there. Charlie Cromack's girlfriend, Sheila, offered to teach me to dance. After a half-dozen lessons, one Saturday night we entered and won a youth club dance contest together, jiving and twirling to Del Shannon's 'Swiss Maid'. There was also a small folk club in Scunthorpe called

The Folk Cellar. It was in Ashby, about three miles up the road towards Scunthorpe town centre. We convened there once a month with our friends. It was called a folk club but it wasn't a folk club in the strictest sense, more a music club. They booked all sorts of music, but more often than not it was local or regional rock bands. If we were lucky we got to see some of the B-league national acts, maybe a band from Sheffield or Doncaster or, at a push, Manchester. I once got to see an early version of Joe Cocker and his Grease band there, but most of the bigger acts were booked into the Berkeley Hotel or Baths Hall in town. The acts I liked were mostly soul bands and they didn't come any nearer than the bright lights of Sheffield and that was 50 miles away. I went there a couple of times on bus trips organised by The Folk Cellar. I saw Wilson Pickett backed by a band with Elton John, who was still Reg Dwight back then. They played at the King Mojo Club on the Pitsmoor Road. We saw James Brown do his famous cloaked falling down 'I can't get up, I can't go on' act at the Mojo Club. It was a coffee bar and dancehall owned by Peter Stringfellow. Many big stars played there including Ike and Tina, Martha and the Vandellas, Stevie Wonder and Jimi Hendrix.

If we took the 123 bus from the corner of Enderby Road and Burringham Hill to the top of Mary Street in town, we could visit The Buccaneer coffee bar. During the day it was a soup and sandwich café that catered for the local retail sales people. In the evenings they threw caution to the wind and allowed the Scunthorpe mods and scooter boys and girls to congregate there. A friend of mine we called Little John had innocently gone in at lunchtime for a cup of tea and a bite to eat, met some friends and arranged to see them there again that same evening. He loved the feel and ambience of the place and went back a couple more times just to be sure. He told Dave about it who in turn told me. It was as near to Bohemian as Scunthorpe got in those days. It was hip in a poetry-and-candle, finger-snapping sort of way, where people talked quietly and sipped frothy hot drinks while perched on tall stools at room-length tables built into the wall. There was no live music or an alcohol licence, it was strictly beverages and a juke box. In the way some gravitate towards pubs, we made The

Buccaneer coffee bar a place of our own and a cosy place to meet. It's still there, a tiny place sandwiched between an estate agent's and a recruitment office on Oswald Road.

One evening in The Buccaneer, Dave introduced me to a couple of girls he knew. They were from Scunthorpe but had moved down to London the previous year and were home for the weekend. They had a flat in Highgate in North London. One of them worked at Chanel on Bond Street in the West End. They talked about the music, the fashion, the shopping, the culture, the people and the need to escape from small-town mentalities. I listened intently, quietly excited by the conversation as Dave encouraged them to talk more. By the lilt of their voices and their confidence I could tell that the girls were probably ex-grammar school and middle class, not the sort I was used to, but I was drawn to them, though not in a sexual way. I saw them as adventurers and admired that in them. I was intrigued by their naive worldliness. By the end of the evening I felt convinced that I had to go down to London and find out for myself what all the fuss was about and told them that. They said if I was serious about going I could stay with them a while and check out job possibilities. If it didn't work out I could always come home again. On the outside I remained calm and nonchalant, but inside I was bubbling with excitement. It was exactly what I wanted to do, but I told them that I needed to think about it.

I was only halfway home before I knew for certain what I was going to do. The next day I told my parents what I was contemplating. It came as a huge surprise to them and there was some initial concern and resistance, but they must have spoken about it together and to my surprise they became quickly supportive of my idea, to the point of being encouraging. My brother Neil hadn't enjoyed his time at grammar school and had left as soon as he could to join the navy, Andy wasn't going to be far behind him on the same path, so I can imagine that the prospect of finally having the house to themselves must have been appealing.

A couple of evenings later, Dave and I went back to The Buccaneer. We met the girls again and I told them I'd like to take them up on their offer. We arranged a date. That week I gave a fortnight's notice to Arthur at the paint shop. As best I could, I began to mentally prepare myself for my big life change. In reality, I had no idea what to prepare for, or how to do it. I was very nervous, it felt akin to jumping into the deep end of a swimming pool without knowing how to swim. The one thing I knew for certain was that I couldn't wait to get the hell out of Scunthorpe and down into the centre of all that action.

Dad was at work when I left and didn't say very much to me the night before. Mom gave me what little money she could spare to help with the train fare and a little extra for emergencies. As I left she made me promise to buy a return ticket and to change my underwear every day. I packed the one bag I had, took a bus to the railway station, bought a one-way ticket and was gone.

IN LONDON

The London that I used to know
The one from thirty years ago
Declares its lifeless status quo
And so it goes

In London they've got subway trains
The House of Lords and acid rain
The Albert Hall, it still remains
In London where I spent my prime
Where youth was king that summertime
I thought I'd pulled the perfect crime
Being there, sleeping by your side

In London we were scatterings
When consciousness meant everything
Now we choke on bigger things
And who said grow them wings and fly

In London where the city jeers
At architecture's golden years
Where no man steps or interferes
In London

In London we had high ideals
A sense of style and Cuban heels
You don't forget how good that feels
In London town the money screams
At long forgotten kings and queens
From strike intensive union teams
And who said grown men never cry

In London where she hung her head
I only work here sir, she said
I didn't weave this tangled thread
In London where you feast your eyes
As dreams are born and passions fly
But brother, are you satisfied
And who said dreams they drift like snow

In London where commandments drool
Like wisdom from the mouths of fools
They didn't learn that stuff in school
In London

Oh London that I've grown to hate
I've seen your class evaporate
Signed, disillusioned, sad expatriate

3. LET THE MUSIC BEGIN

Stepping off the train at Kings Cross station, smack dab in the middle of the London hustle and bustle, I felt very small and insignificant. Momentarily, I wondered if I'd done the right thing. As I reflect back on it, I'm amazed at how I managed to take that huge leap of faith. I must have been incredibly desperate to get away. For a careful, shy boy from Scunthorpe, to leave my friends and the relative safety of home behind, without so much as a how's your father, was completely out of character. It was the spring of 1965, I was just 18.

I was met at Kings Cross by the older girl from The Buccaneer, the one who worked at Chanel. I was grateful she was there. We took an underground tube train up to Highgate and that night, as I went to sleep on a sofa in a strange new world, surrounded by an air of great adventure, I felt strangely peaceful and confident. The girls went to work while I stayed around the flat for a couple of days trying to get my bearings. Occasionally I'd wander as far as the local tube station to look at maps and figure out how to get to the West End.

On the Saturday morning, I ventured out. I'll never forget that first nervous journey. Carnaby Street was exactly where Dave had said I'd find it. Out of the underground station at Oxford Circus, turn right along Oxford Street to Argyll Street and then right again down Argyll and past the London Palladium on the left. Liberty's department store with its imposing Tudor facade was blocking my path. A quick jog around it onto Great Marlborough Street and right again into Carnaby Street. I was there. I nervously sidled down Carnaby Street, taking it all in. It was an incredibly emotional moment for me and even now, as I think about it, I have to catch my breath.

I was looking to find a job. I reasoned to myself that everyone would want to sell clothes and jobs could be scarce, so I decided on shoes. I walked into a shop called Topper, which appeared to be the most fashionable shoe shop on the street. As I entered, a young man about my age nodded towards me and smiled. I asked him who I should talk to about a job. He pointed out his manager. There I was, a naive, wide-eyed young boy approaching the manager of one of London's top fashion stores.

'Do you need anybody?' I asked.

'Have you ever sold shoes before?'

'No I haven't, but I'm a quick study.'

'I'm sorry, we really need someone with experience,' the manager said and turned away.

As I left the shop, the boy who'd nodded at me followed me outside and stopped me.

'Let me give you a bit of friendly advice. I know for certain they're looking for someone at Ravel's next door. Go in there and if they ask you about previous experience, just tell them you worked in a shoe shop back home. Where are you from?'

'Scunthorpe.'

'What's your name?'

'Ian MacDonald.'

'Right then Ian from Scunthorpe. My name is Paul.' We shook hands. 'When you go into Ravel's and they ask, tell them that you worked in a shoe shop in Scunthorpe and you are looking to make a fresh start in London.'

I walked into Ravel's and did what Paul had told me. Before I had a chance to say more, the manager asked, 'When can you start?' I was ready to take my jacket off there and then and get stuck in. 'Monday,' I said. 'Great! See you here at 8:30 Monday morning.' As I walked back passed Topper's I gave the thumbs up to Paul who came outside and said, 'Let's meet for a sandwich at lunchtime and I'll tell you all you need to know about the art of selling shoes.'

I'd been in London for just a few days and I had my first job. It was a huge boost to my confidence. It's indescribable the elation I felt at that moment. Just a few weeks before I had only dared to dream about London and Carnaby Street, and now I was actually going to work there. Paul and I became good friends and within days of starting my new job he and I would meet up after work to eat and explore the London music scene. It was great fun but exhausting too. On more than one occasion I'd have to drag myself to work the next day.

One night Paul pulled out some blue pills.

'Here, take one of these. It'll make you feel good and you won't get tired.'

I asked him what they were and he said he just knew them as French Blues. He'd bought them from someone in the West End and they really worked. On a Saturday night we would go clubbing, sometimes until three or four in the morning, and I saw bands that I'd actually heard of before.

There was so much music in the West End. The Flamingo and the Marquee clubs were on Wardour Street. The 100 Club was on Oxford Street, but our favourite spot was a new place on Oxford Street next to the Tottenham Court Road tube station. It was called Tiles and it quickly developed a reputation as a mod club. Many emerging young bands played there. We saw Manfred Mann, The Who, The Animals and Mike d'Abo's Band of Angels. It was such an exciting time in my life and the city was so vibrant, even at three in the morning we'd walk out onto the street and there were people everywhere, partying, still going somewhere. London began to ease me out of my shell.

I'm not sure what the girls made of my quick adjustment to city life. After I started my job I hardly saw them. I had only known Paul for a couple of weeks when he invited me to abandon my couch in Highgate and share his basement flat in his parents' home south of the river in Merrick Square, Southwark, quite close to the Elephant and Castle. The houses there were all three-storey town houses, built in a big U-shape around the square with a community garden in the middle. On our way to the station in the morning we could see into the basement windows and had to pass Len Deighton's house, the famous author who wrote *The IPCRESS File*. We could see him sitting at his desk, already hard at work on his next best seller. He seemed to be there every morning, pounding away at his typewriter.

Ravel's was situated at the corner of Carnaby and Ganton

Street. On the opposite corner was Lord John's where Dave Akid had bought my velvet hipsters. In 1965, Carnaby Street was beginning to be the 'in place'. The word was out and everyone went there to buy their garb. John Stephen had a famous shop, Mary Quant was there, I Was Lord Kitchener's Valet, Mates, Gear and Lady Jane. Pretty soon the publicity people realised it was the ideal backdrop for photo shoots. I saw pop groups such as The Koobas and John's Children have pictures taken there, and the French singer Françoise Hardy. Tom Jones came by one day with a model holding a leopard on a chain. Of course Hendrix had to have his photo taken there after he bought his military jacket at Lord Kitchener's. Pretty soon the mod bands would come down for their publicity shots, gazing at our window display, ogling the shoes they wanted to buy. The Small Faces were regulars as was Marc Bolan. I sold shoes to him. Some of our best customers were The Dave Clark Five. Dave himself, I can tell you from experience, had some of the sweatiest feet in music. His keyboard player Mike Smith was probably our best customer. If he liked a particular pair of shoes he would instantly buy a half-dozen pairs. That's when I first realised there was a decent living to be made in music.

One of the first important rules I learned at the shop was to never let a potential customer get away. If they seem to want to buy, keep them hooked until they either buy or you run out of sales pitch. If the shoes were pinching we'd tell them that we could put them on the 'stretching machine'. This involved going down into the basement where we kept the broom. We would then stand on the brush head and push the handle into the area that was pinching the customer's foot, easing the end of the handle around firmly but carefully. It worked every time. Even now, if my girls Luca and Madelief tell me that their new shoes pinch, we have our little joke about using the stretching machine and I reach for the broom handle.

I'd been working in the street for about six months when a Liverpudlian about my age came into the shop to try on shoes. He introduced himself as Johnny Hayes. He had been a drummer in a band back home called The Trends. They'd come down to

London to make it and hadn't. Johnny had stayed. To make ends meet he got a job in a nightclub called Brad's on Duke of York Street. He worked there as a DJ and eventually joined a resident band called Colors. With him in Colors was Steve Hiett, a singer, guitarist and songwriter, and Albert Jackson, also a singer. Johnny told me that Colors were disbanding and Steve and Al were looking for a third vocalist to form a new group based around vocal harmony. Johnny called it South London Surfing Music. He asked me if I could sing. I used Paul's method and told him I'd been in a couple of bands back home. He said if I was interested he would introduce me to Steve and Albert. I flashed back to my first joyful experience with harmony in The Imps and told Johnny I'd like to meet them.

Steve and Al had first worked together while attending the Royal College of Art in Central London. They shared a flat in Bromley with two other people. Our vocal blend instantly felt good. Steve was a big fan of Brian Wilson's writing and had begun composing in that style. I liked Steve's songs a lot and quickly agreed to be part of their soon-to-be band. I began visiting Bromley regularly to learn more songs and work out vocal harmonies. Before too long a manager came into the picture. His name was Jonathan Weston. Jonathan claimed to be a saxophone player; he'd originally applied for a job with Colors but it transpired that he was a terrible sax player. Not wanting to alienate him, the band told him he could be their manager instead. In truth, he wasn't too good at that either. We became The Pyramid and later just Pyramid. Jonathan paid me a retainer of £10 a week to stick around. We played a dozen or so shows as Pyramid, but I don't ever remember seeing any money from them. The one solid thing Jonathan did for us was to find us a recording deal. He somehow managed to convince a new Decca boutique label called Deram that we were the next big thing and they signed us.

Jonathan came from a wealthy upper-class English family. After he became our manager we'd sometimes stay at his family home in Much Hadham in Hertfordshire, rehearsing in one of the big rooms. I remember we were there the day that England won the World Cup. Jonathan had managed to make a few connections in the industry, mostly because he had money. One of his connections was a man named Tony Hall, who had recently been put in charge of Deram.

I handed in my notice at Ravel's one Saturday morning. The manager wasn't too pleased, Saturday was a very busy day for us. He said, 'Fine, you can go now if you want to.' I said, 'Right, I will then.' I put my coat on and walked out onto Carnaby Street towards my new future. It was raining. I then realised that I had left my umbrella in the basement next to the 'stretching machine'. I had to eat humble pie and went back into the shop. My ex-manager was helping a customer and as I walked past I said, 'Excuse me, I think I've left my brolly.' He rolled his eyes, gave a sigh of resignation and went back to attending his customer.

Moving out of a world of shoes and into my new world of music was a frantic period for me. I was rarely in the West End. I moved out of Paul's family home and back north of the river to Paddington to lodge with my new friend Johnny Hayes. Paul and I slowly lost touch. I would visit him on the street whenever I needed to be in the West End, until one day I went to Topper's to see him and he simply wasn't there. The manager told me he'd quit. I called Paul's house and his brother told me he had gone away on holiday for a month.

Tony Hall listened to some of the demos that Jonathan played him and decided to pair us up with an emerging young producer named Denny Cordell. Denny had been working at Decca with The Moody Blues. Tony was impressed by what he'd heard and had him produce a single for Deram by a singer called Beverley. She would later be known as Beverley Martyn, John Martyn's wife.

I had been in London less than a year and was in a band about to make our first record. It was a heady realisation and a lot to take in, so it was with a great sense of anticipation that we entered the studio with Denny to make our first single for Deram in the winter of 1966. The A-side was 'Summer of Last Year' and on the flip was 'Summer Evening'. Both were Steve Hiett compositions. We had top, young session musicians playing on these songs. John

McLaughlin played rhythm guitar, John Paul Jones was on bass, and Nicky Hopkins on piano. Clem Cattini, who was the go-to drummer at the time, was also there. He'd played on everything from The Tornado's 'Telstar' to a record I had actually bought, 'Shakin' All Over' by Johnny Kidd & The Pirates. Big Jim Sullivan was also part of our recording and played the beautiful guitar riff on 'Summer Evening'. He had a difficult time figuring it out and Steve had to sit and teach it to him. Steve said that by the time he was done teaching Big Jim the riff, he might as well have done it himself. It was an indescribable moment for me when our first 45 came out. Holding it in my hand and realising that I'd just made a record which had been released commercially. It did quite well for a debut disc, making it into the Top Ten on Radio London but not a ripple outside of the capital. Regardless, we were a happy bunch.

We became a very eclectic band. Between the three of us we liked everything from John Sebastian to Curtis Mayfield to Brian Wilson. We had a top-notch musical director in Mike Lease, a Welshman who played the Hammond organ. We'd met and bonded with Mike on our Deram recording sessions. Together with him we developed a non-stop, sixty-minute live show, weaving from song to song with the aid of a slideshow put together by students and friends of Al at the RCA. They created moving images that were projected onto a drop-screen that the three of us stood in front of, with the band behind it in silhouette. Mike led the band from the Hammond. It was an efficiently conservative line-up consisting of a bass player, a drummer and if the money was decent, a lead guitar player.

We had decided to dress nice on stage. I wanted to emulate all the pop acts I'd seen performing on *Ready Steady Go!* and *Top of the Pops* and began by wearing a turtleneck under a dark-grey, double-breasted suit with a light-blue pinstripe that I'd bought while working in Carnaby Street, but soon discovered how hot it can get on stage and looked for an alternative. Jonathan also had connections in the clothing world and sent us down to Old Compton Street in Soho to be fitted for matching, cream-coloured silk suits, custom-made by a man named Dougie

Millings who was known as 'The Beatles Tailor'. He'd made the famous collarless suits that The Beatles wore on their first American tour in 1964. We were quite a sight.

We didn't have a booking agent, but between us managed to arrange a handful of shows, mostly art school dates in and around London. Our biggest claim to fame was that we opened for The Move at the legendary Marquee Club in London's West End. This was during The Move's destruction period when they would have the shell of a car on stage. During the show, their singer Carl Wayne stood on its roof, took out a big axe and chopped it to pieces. I was more puzzled by how the hell they had got it into the club than why they smashed it up. Our other prestige date was an arts festival out on the pier at Brighton where Keith Moon saw us and came backstage to speak to us. We'd just come off stage and hadn't thought much of our performance. He popped his head around a curtain they'd put up as a makeshift dressing room and said, 'That was great guys.' Someone replied that it was crap and told him to fuck off. Mike suddenly realised who he was and quickly said, 'Oh, thanks man.' Whereupon Keith replied, 'Oh, now that you recognise me you wanna speak to me.' We explained that we didn't think it had been much of a show compared to what we could do and he mellowed somewhat, raving on at Steve about his guitar playing.

During a soundcheck for a show at the London Royal College of Art, something was earthed wrong in the onstage wiring. Steve had his Telecaster on and when he grabbed the microphone stand, the electrical current surged through him and he couldn't let go. He bounced around the stage like a rag doll. We all thought he was messing about until he fell off, separating him from the mic stand and mercifully breaking the circuit. Steve was in hospital for quite a while. Apparently he'd told the nurses that night to hurry and fix him up as he had a show to play. But Steve's trauma was essentially the end of the band. Or at least one of the contributory factors. Our producer Denny Cordell had by this time moved on to his next project, producing Procol Harum's 'Whiter Shade of Pale'. Jonathan too had elected to manage Procol Harum, leaving us clueless and in the lurch. He became embroiled in a legal battle with Procol Harum and his bank assets were frozen. Having funds cut off was truly the end for us. My retainer disappeared at a moment's notice and I survived on the goodness of friends. He'd bought us quite a bit of equipment while managing us and, as Steve was recuperating in the hospital, Jonathan gave away his beautiful white Telecaster to Ray Royer, Procol's lead guitarist. Steve never forgave him.

Steve recovered, but didn't professionally return to music. In that short space of time we'd been together, he'd had enough of the hypocrisy and uncertainty. He drifted into graphic design and eventually into photography. He was a friend of Jimi Hendrix and took his famous backstage Isle of Wight photographs. Steve was dedicated and driven and by 1970 was one of the top ten fashion photographers in the world, working for *Vogue Paris*, *Elle* and *Marie Claire*. He later moved to Paris, where he lives to this day. He published a number of coffee-table photo books and still freelances for *Vogue*. He likes to dabble in songwriting, recording his music at home on his little two-track recorder. I spent time with him in Paris a couple of years ago. We played together a bit, reminiscing about our Pyramid days. Al finished his degree at RCA and went to work for *Reader's Digest*. He became an expert in antique furniture restoration. In the 1980s he had his own programme on BBC Two teaching people to renovate furniture. He too has written books, including the famous *Collins Care and Repair of Furniture*.

I had been living with Johnny Hayes in a rented one-room apartment in Sussex Gardens, Paddington. The house had four floors and each floor was broken down into various sized flats, the smallest being a single-room bedsitter and the largest a two-bedroom flat with a kitchen. A party was being held in one of the bigger flats and we were invited. The renter, another Paul, was the building manager. He was a friendly, educated, well-spoken, red-bearded bohemian type; a self-proclaimed artist. When Johnny and I walked into the party there was music playing the likes of which I'd never encountered. It was a type of instrumental music that begins with a riff. The band slowly but deliberately disown the riff to slide seamlessly into what I later learned was called improvisation. The music was played in this case by what sounded like a quartet consisting of drums, bass, electric guitar and saxophone. I was mesmerised by the sound and structure of the music and the guitar player in particular who I would discover from our host was a Hungarian-born jazz guitarist called Gábor Szabó. Paul noticed me standing motionless by the stereo, eyes closed, and he sidled up next to me.

'Do you like this music?'

Yes I did, very much. 'What is it?'

'It's the Chico Hamilton Quintet,' he said, 'and the album is called *Passin' Thru*. When it's over I'll play you something else you might like.'

When the Chico Hamilton LP finished, Paul pulled out another album with a dark, sultry picture of a man playing a trumpet on the cover. In white letters it said 'Miles Davis' and in a smaller light-blue print it said 'Kind of Blue'. He put it on and the needle came down on that first moody riff of 'So What'. Ba dah dad dah dad dah dad dahh dad, dahhh da. I was transfixed. The entire album, all forty-five minutes of it, came down on me like a musical rainstorm. I don't know how else to express it, but it simply blew my mind. Even now I don't fully understand why. It hit me on a deep emotional level I didn't even realise was inside me. I had no idea this genre existed. It was recorded eight years previous, in 1959, and had completely passed me by. A whole new world of music had been set before me and my musical education began in earnest.

Johnny was letting me stay with him at Sussex Gardens out of the goodness of his heart, but he'd met a lady he would eventually marry. There just wasn't enough room for all of us and we knew it. With Pyramid no more, in the summer of 1967 I found myself jobless, penniless and homeless.

I'd befriended Tony Hall's ex-wife, Mafalda, and her boyfriend David. They lived in a luxury flat in an exclusive part of Chelsea. Mafalda reminded me of Mama Cass. She was a big lady who liked to wear long flowing robes with her dark, almost waist-length hair. She had a kind, motherly vibe to her. They knew I was a struggling musician and whenever possible would invite me to eat with them. The flat above them was unoccupied and Mafalda had the key for it. Although the flat was empty, it was carpeted and heated. I made a deal with Mafalda and in the evening she would feed me and give me a blanket, a pillow and the key to upstairs. I'd go up and sleep, snug and warm on the thick pile carpet. With my suitcase and a small collection of LPs under my arm, I made the most of it.

I thought back to my days as an apprentice painter and decorator, those freezing cold December mornings when the paint was a useless frozen lump that refused to adhere to any surface, no matter how well I prepared it. My fingers would burn with the intense cold and be so painful and stiff that I couldn't hold a brush. I decided that I must have been paying a price for not paying enough attention at school. I thought there was no escape and some mornings I simply painted and sobbed with the frustration of it all. Then the escape came with the signwriting shop and Derek telling me, 'You're better than that twaddle.'

At eight in the morning I came back down from my squat and went out to walk the London streets for the day. I had no idea what I might do next. I felt that I needed to figure it out myself and bother as few people as possible. Fortunately, this period didn't last too long and besides, I didn't feel homeless. It seemed more like a big adventure along the road to something better. Something would turn up, I felt it.

One evening I got back to Chelsea and Mafalda said I was to call her ex, Tony, at Deram Records. I phoned him and he said, 'I've just been having a conversation with a young man called Ashley Hutchings. He plays bass guitar in a band called The Fairport Convention. They are looking for a singer. They saw Pyramid and were interested in Steve, but he doesn't want to do it. I told Ashley that you were looking around for something and he's agreed to meet with you and talk.'

And there it was.

PART TWO
THE SUMMER OF LAST YEAR

EVEN THE GUIDING LIGHT

Even the guiding light of days in the loving underground
Would find it shady weather here today
I went up on the ledge and didn't find a soul around
But that's just me and who am I to say
When it's all the same, so many miles away

Now we're falling over all these chiefs
And running out of braves
It's getting hard to know just what to say
There was a time when I could find belief in Jesus Saves
Till something came and took it all away
I reckon he was saving for a rainy day

Now there's no way to touch upon
This understanding had we known
How close it was to being a sea of sand
Heaven knows, we had the time
And as I see the only crime
Was being just a little short of land

Send me home with a country song
And leave it ringing round
Ask my friends, they know which one to play
Even the guiding light of days in the loving underground
Would find it shady weather here today
Then it's all the same so many miles away
So many miles away

4. LEARNING THE GAME

I arranged to meet up with Fairport Convention at Sound Techniques Studio in Chelsea on 10th August 1967. I arrived with my suitcase in one hand and my collection of LPs under my arm. Ashley Hutchings met me at the door and asked if he could have a look at the records. He went through them one by one. I had an eclectic mixed bag including The Impressions, The Byrds, The Kinks and Tim Hardin. Ashley seemed quite impressed.

I thought the invitation was to just meet the band and an audition would follow. When I arrived they were already working on the recording of their first single. Joe Boyd, their manager and producer, called down from the control room and introduced himself before saying, 'Okay guys, let's do something.' Ashley and the band had recorded a 1930s old-time jazz tune by Maxine Sullivan called 'If I Had a Ribbon Bow'. Joe put me to work with an American friend of his, Tod Lloyd, who had been appointed vocal coach. We worked out some 'Oooh's and 'Aaahh's and I was asked to do a spoken word part: 'All my live long days, by the stars above me.' The recording was finished by teatime and mixed later that same evening.

By the end of the session no one had told me if I was in the band or not. There were smiles all around. I was shown the stage repertoire and asked to begin learning it. I thought 'Oh! Okay, I must be in the band.' Two weeks later I stepped on stage with Fairport Convention for the first time at the Middle Earth Club in Covent Garden. Judy Dyble and I sang; 'Lay Down Your Weary Tune', 'Chelsea Morning', 'My Back Pages' and 'Let's Get Together'. The band will have ended with an extended jam on the Paul Butterfield Blues Band's 'East-West'.

Richard Thompson, Simon Nicol, Ashley, Martin Lamble and Judy had been a band for a couple of months when I met them. Ashley had previously been in a blues jug band called The

Ethnic Shuffle Orchestra. I remember thinking what a cool name that was. They rehearsed in a room in Simon's mom's house in Muswell Hill. The house was called 'Fairport'. Judy came from a group of her own called Judy and The Folkmen. Richard, the lead guitarist, came fully formed at the age of just eighteen; he was able to channel Django, Charlie Christian and Barney Kessel. At that time he was training to be a stained-glass artist, just in case this music thing didn't work out for him. He would regularly nick the ends of his fingers, yet never complained and still managed to soulfully bend the strings.

A couple of weeks before I appeared, somewhere towards the end of July, Fairport Convention had played their first official show at the UFO, London's first psychedelic club run by Joe Boyd. They supported Pink Floyd, who Joe was producing, and at the end of the night he approached Fairport to talk about management. He had been impressed by what he'd witnessed, in particular Richard's guitar playing on 'East-West'. He offered them a management and production deal on the spot.

On joining them I was immediately put on a £12 per week retainer, which was about what I'd been making in Carnaby Street and two pounds more than in Pyramid. I was happy to have the security of a weekly wage again.

In the 1960s, the process of converting large houses into flats had begun. Houses all over London were being divided into flats and single rooms with plywood partitions. Directly after joining Fairport and with financial stability again, I moved into a cramped little room in Earls Court, or Kangaroo Valley as they called it back then as it had a large Australian community. It was like a mini West End, crowded and action-packed twenty-four hours a day. But it wasn't long before I realised that I'd be better off closer to the band in North London, and moved to a bedsitter in Crouch End. Soon after that I swapped my bedsit with Ashley for his room in the 'Fairport' house at 33 St. Marys Road in Brent. He said he needed more privacy and quiet. I craved just the opposite. Richard and Simon were both living there and Martin and Judy were only a stone's throw away.

Simon Nicol was the quick-witted one of the band. He made

us laugh with his lopsided know-it-all grin and smart response to anything anyone would say. He was also the compassionate one. I would go to see Simon first if I wanted to talk, or have anything explained, particularly musical things like, 'I can't seem to find my place to come in, can you show me where it is?' Technical stuff. Simon could also be the quiet and pensive one, at which point Martin would become the wit. Martin was the youngest in the band, smart, quick to respond and very funny. He was an avid reader, the most eloquent speaker and the sloppiest dresser in the band.

Ashley was rightly called 'The Guv'nor'. He seemed to be the one who willingly took care of business, the guiding light, the instigator of new ideas. He was the lifeblood and driving force who could be devil or angel, sometimes both at the same time. I was never sure how to take him from one minute to the next. We might be travelling in the van, I'd say something to him and he'd snap back, 'Can't you see I'm reading a book!' And that would be that for the rest of the journey. But then he could offer personal advice when everyone else seemed incapable. I was never close to Ashley in the way I became close to Richard and Simon. We were bandmates, but I wouldn't go so far as to say that we were close friends.

Richard and I got along quite well and it wasn't long before I made my tentative start as a songwriter under his tutelage. Richard had a lyric he was struggling to finish, probably because it was such a silly sentiment. It was a little country song called 'If (stomp)'. It wasn't a difficult task for me to finish the song, I just had to be as silly as he'd been. While it's not the pinnacle of songwriting achievements, it did open up the possibility of us writing together more. Although just eighteen at that time, he was already a wonderful musician. He seemed very worldly, sharp-minded and quite studious. He gave off a quiet, unassuming vibe but could also be playful, bohemian and off the wall. One afternoon we were due to play at the UFO in Covent Garden and had agreed to do an interview. Richard, Ashley and I met a writer from one of the music papers in a nearby coffee shop. The journalist took out his notebook and at the same time Richard pulled from his bag an alarm clock with Mickey Mouse hands on it and huge ear-like bells. Richard set the alarm for forty-five minutes. When the alarm went off everyone in the coffee shop swivelled around to see what the commotion was as Richard announced, 'Right that's it!' then promptly slammed down the alarm button, dropped the clock back into his bag and all three of us stood up and left. We weren't exactly your normal band from Muswell Hill.

One thing that truly launched Fairport was having John Peel talk us up on his radio programme, *Top Gear*. He must have seen one of our shows as he began inviting us to record sessions for his programme with his producer Bernie Andrews. The sessions were recorded during the week and played on John's show on Sundays. We usually did four to five songs at a time. The studios were still old-fashioned places with wires running everywhere and lots of union rules about what we could and couldn't do without assistance. Our first session took place in November 1967. We recorded Chet Power's 'Let's Get Together', Jim & Jean's 'One Sure Thing', Dylan's 'Lay Down Your Weary Tune' and Joni Mitchell's 'Chelsea Morning'.

No one in the band was writing in earnest at that point and almost our entire repertoire consisted of covers. John Peel would occasionally come down to listen to us record. He didn't have to, the sessions were the responsibility of the producers, but he was a good friend as well as a fan. Occasionally the sessions overran and we'd bump into other acts coming in for their slot. All the visiting American songwriters wanted to play for John. His show was innovative and extremely popular and they knew that if John liked what you did, he could break you in the UK. In this way we got to meet the likes of Tim Hardin, Leonard Cohen, Tim Buckley and David Ackles; songwriters from across the Atlantic whose tunes we were covering. From my perspective they were glamorous and highly impressionable times.

When our first *Top Gear* radio session was broadcast, we were driving to Birmingham for a show. We had the radio on and when it came to our session, we pulled over to the roadside in order to hear it clearly without the constant hum of the engine. It's an amazing experience to hear oneself on the radio for the very first time and the overall feeling in the van was one of excitement and elation, but as soon as we set off again the post-mortems began. Judy and I tended to stay out of these discussions, but the others would analyse and pick apart their performance. Richard usually felt he could have played a better solo or have been more innovative. I felt Martin could be overly critical of his drumming. He had a knack of pinpointing the exact moments when he could have played something better or different.

Our first single was released on the Track label in February 1968. On the B-side was the song I had written with Richard – my first recorded composition. Our debut album, *Fairport Convention*, came out a few months later. In April 1968, we flew over to Paris for a TV show called *Bouton Rouge* and performed three songs: Tim Buckley's 'Morning Glory', Emitt Rhode's 'Time Will Show the Wiser' and a Richard Fariña song called 'Reno Nevada'. It was my first trip out of the country and I had to hurriedly have a passport issued. On 'Reno Nevada' Richard pulled out a finger-blistering five-minute guitar solo that people still talk about to this day. Richard was already being spoken of as a guitar genius. The film of that performance is readily available these days on YouTube. We travelled straight back from France to play a show that same night at the London School of Economics.

Once every couple of months we were invited to play at an after-hours club in London's West End called Speakeasy. It was a members-only affair and some of the more famous musicians would go there after hours to relax, unsolicited by fans. Eric Burdon of The Animals, Eric Clapton, Zoot Money, Jimi Hendrix and Graham Nash were constantly there. The band regularly performed the Paul Butterfield instrumental 'East-West', but its form changed so much that it became unrecognisable from the original. Whenever someone asked Richard what it was, he'd respond with something silly. One night at the Speak, Graham Nash asked Richard what it was called. Richard said, 'King Midas in Reverse'. Now wouldn't that have made a great song title.

Judy and I were the non-musicians in the band. By that I mean we didn't play an instrument. We were simply the singers. Most songs had been set in keys suitable for the players rather than the singers. We had to adapt. When Richard soloed, Judy and I would get out of the way and sit on the side of the stage while he and the others 'stretched out' as they called it. Sometimes the instrumental sections went on for twenty to thirty minutes. I would close my eyes and listen while Judy would sit and knit. One night while we were playing at the Speak, Hendrix dropped in, as he often did. We were in the throes of yet another 'experiment' and he saw and heard what was happening. He asked Simon if he could borrow his guitar to jam along with Richard and the band. These were special moments for me, Richard and Jimi going at it side by side.

The band was unique in style and choice of material and that got us loads of attention, with Richard carrying us along on his wide young shoulders. Our double-pronged vocal approach made us stand out; we were the only band around with male and female lead vocalists. We played music that no one else in the UK was attempting and this was before Fairport developed their folk-rock tag. A lot of people thought we must be American because of the name, the repertoire and the line-up. We were heavily influenced by American music at the time, but we would borrow the songs and shake them up a little. We made every song our own. Leonard Cohen's 'Suzanne' for instance. No one was playing Cohen the way we were. Come to that, hardly anyone in the UK was attempting Leonard Cohen songs. We were really the first. Richard loved jazz. Ashley was a big fan of The Byrds and blues. We all loved the contemporary songwriters: Phil Ochs, Fred Neil, Richard Fariña and the songs of Jim & Jean. We heard 'Lay Down Your Weary Tune' on a Jim & Jean album. In the early days, Joe Boyd was very much part of the team. Joe had been working at the Newport Folk Festival in Rhode Island and knew a lot of influential people. He was a festival producer there when Dylan went electric. He found us Leonard Cohen songs and Joni Mitchell tunes on publishing acetates before anyone else in the UK had heard them. He brought us 'Chelsea Morning' when it was still a publishing demo. If there was a record or band we wanted to hear, he would get it for us. We were listening to bands like Moby Grape and Buffalo Springfield at the same time as the music-business people in California were getting to know them. Joe was a facilitator in the truest sense of the word. Through him we had music coming at us 24/7 from the cream of North American songwriters. I learned of so many American West Coast songwriters and bands through Joe. Some songs I still play to this day.

We played the length and breadth of the country when many of the towns were still only approachable by A roads and the M1 was the only real motorway. Driving down to the Van Dike Club in Plymouth was an all-day event, and the same coming home, which we often did straight after the show. We played quite a lot of the big universities: Leeds, Sheffield, Exeter, Oxford, Cambridge and Manchester were all on our radar. That's where the money was. But we never forgot the clubs. They were the ones that helped put us on the map and we stayed faithful to them, most of all the wonderful UFO. We loved playing there. With the universities, you never knew until you arrived who would be on the bill with you. At one university show, we arrived to find that our friends The Family were headlining, we were on second and Joe Cocker and The Grease Band were opening. Those were the days.

Whenever we travelled north, we made a habit of stopping on our way home at the Blue Boar services on the M1 at Watford Gap. At any time after one in the morning you were almost certain to meet a band you knew, and if you didn't know them, you'd get to know them. This way we got to catch up and swap stories with our friends, bands like Heads Hands & Feet, Yes, Blossom Toes, and singer-songwriter Al Stewart. The Blue Boar became a highly anticipated and established meeting point.

We carried our own sound system with us. During those early days in the development of sound systems there were no such things as onstage monitors – at least not in our band. We began to notice in live situations that for some reason Judy was starting to sing sharp, she would push the note above pitch, which for anyone who knows anything about singing is quite a difficult thing to do. It became an issue for all of us and particularly for me. The more it was pointed out, the more the poor girl became self-conscious about it and the more she was unable to correct it. It's incredibly difficult to sing harmony with someone who is singing sharp and I struggled to know what to do. Because we didn't have monitors and Judy, being unfamiliar with singing in a loud band, couldn't really hear what she was doing, we decided to turn the speakers in a little bit. With each successive concert the speakers would be pushed in a little bit more until there was a danger that the audience wouldn't hear us properly. Moving the speakers in didn't make much difference to her pitch and there was a band discussion. My heart went out to her. It was emotionally painful for everyone and particularly Ashley, Richard and Simon, because they were all close friends of Judy's, they had started the band together. Joe came in to the discussion and I believe it was him who suggested that Judy ought to perhaps move on. Judy left just before the first album came out. We had a concert in Rome on the same bill as The Byrds and that might have been Judy's last. Ashley took the lead and volunteered to tell her, sitting with her on a bench to break the news. It was incredibly difficult for us all.

After Judy left, she began working with Ian McDonald of King Crimson. I didn't want people to think I had also left Fairport and came up with the ingenious plan of changing my name to Mom's maiden name. Unbeknownst to me, it wasn't as tricky as I thought it might be; on my birth certificate I was registered as Ian Matthews.

   For a couple of months I was the only vocalist as we searched for another female lead. We approached Heather Wood from The Young Tradition. She didn't want to be involved in contemporary music but mentioned that she had a friend, Sandy Denny, and that she would tell her that Fairport Convention were looking for someone. Not long after, Sandy walked into the rehearsal room and blew all of our minds. She sat on a high stool with her big Gibson acoustic guitar and everyone in the room was slack-jawed because of the sheer power, authority and intensity of her voice.

The decision to ask her into the band was a no-brainer and she joined us there and then.

I liked Sandy a lot. She was very straightforward and more seasoned than the rest of us. She'd played the folk clubs as a solo act and had been in an early version of The Strawbs. She was a drinker, a smoker, and told things the way she saw them. She wasn't afraid of reactions and could handle contradiction – 'Deal with it' might as well have been her mantra. I was in awe of her and intimidated by her at the same time. She was such a huge talent, particularly when it came to songwriting. She wrote mostly at the piano and her chords were always fat, unpredictable and in your face. Sandy also had an undeniable musical presence, seemingly unafraid of anything or anyone, whereas I was timid and still feeling my way as a singer and as a person, intent on keeping myself small. After she joined the band I always felt that I was singing in her shadow, yet our voices blended so effortlessly.

Not long after Sandy agreed to be a member of the band we were playing an open-air festival on Hampstead Heath. At soundcheck, she was nowhere to be found. With ten minutes to go until stage time, still no Sandy. The minutes ticked down and she still didn't materialise. By stage time the promoter simply said, 'You'll have to go on without her.' And we did. With Fairport I had started to sing with my eyes closed. My eyes were shut tight and we were halfway through 'Reno Nevada', approaching Richard's guitar solo, when I heard applause building. The applause turned to cheers and I thought 'I'm really doing well today'. It culminated in a huge cheer as I finished my vocal and Richard launched into his solo. I opened my eyes and with a huge smile I glanced across the stage. There was Sandy, strapping on her twelve-string, waving merrily to the crowd, not a care in the world. She'd arrived and that's all that mattered.

We were a sight to see on stage. Sandy could look good, but she could also look like a Salvation Army shopper. We all could. On stage, she either wore beautiful long gowns, or mini-skirts with her trademark fringed suede waistcoat. I was still into nice clothes, an overlap from my Pyramid days. In my first months with the band I wore velvet suits and a tie, usually black, bought at the Kensington market, and of course my boots were from Anello & Davide. Somewhere along the journey the suits made way for jeans and leather-fringed jackets. A sign of the times I suppose. I took to wearing sunglasses with round wire granny frames, just like the bands in San Francisco. I preferred indirect light to bright light and they gave me a nice shady place to hide. I'm wearing dark glasses in most of the photos and film you see from those days. Ashley preferred knee-length boots and Martin almost always could be seen in a knitted scarf. Richard, it seemed, wore whatever was at the foot of his bed when he got up. Like me, he favoured a fringed jacket. We played in what we travelled in, but that was irrelevant, we were far more about the music than the clothes.

I was still friends with an ex-girlfriend Julie Chapman. Julie and I had met during my Pyramid days while she was working for Denny Cordell and we'd had a brief on-again, off-again relationship. Julie arranged a birthday party for her kid brother Steve and invited her friend Christina Deane. Her plan was to put the pair of them together. No one had told me about the plan. I walked in, spied this lovely young thing and made a beeline for her. I only later learned after Chris and I had begun dating that I had been the fly in the ointment.

I wrote my first decent lyric about Chris shortly after we met. It's called 'Book Song' and appeared on the second Fairport album. I used to take Chris along to the Fairport shows whenever there was space in the van. In the song I wondered if she understood what it was I was doing and what she thought about while we played. I took my words to Richard's room with a vague melody running through my head. He liked the lyrics and played around with chords until he found the right ones to perfectly accent the melody. I felt like a proud father when the song was complete. Richard played guitar and I think sitar on the recorded version. Mine and Sandy's voices blend as well as they ever did on that track. It was a long, long way from my first effort, a lyric I scribbled down for The Rebels back in Scunthorpe, 'The Man with the X-Ray Eyes'.

One night we were playing at the University of Essex and before the concert Martin and Sandy began scribbling on a blackboard in the dressing/class room. Soon everyone took up the chalk until the board was covered with characters, fireworks, the uni itself. Even our roadie Harvey and his dog Bradford featured. The next day someone must have realised it would make a good album cover and a photographer was dispatched to take a photo of our 'artwork'. Fortunately it was still in tact and it became the cover for our second album *What We Did on Our Holidays*.

I'd been uneasy and feeling a little like a fish out of water in Fairport Convention ever since Sandy had joined the band. It wasn't enough for me to want to leave, but I was never sure where I stood, or even sometimes where to stand. Sandy brought a wealth of unsung traditional material to the table and I was both puzzled and threatened by that. The music was alien to me and the band were embracing it wholeheartedly, absorbing it, while I had been perfectly happy with the direction we were moving in. Sometimes Sandy would begin to play and sing a traditional tune and the others would join in playing. I wasn't an instrumentalist back then, I only had my voice to fall back on. The music was strange to me, I didn't care for it without knowing why and I didn't know where to go with it. It became more and more apparent that the band was quietly but positively morphing towards that style and it started to become a bone of contention for me. One night, Sandy played something backstage before a show, it could have been 'She Moved Through the Fair' or 'A Sailor's Life', and the rest of the band said, 'Let's put it in the set tonight. Sandy knows the song and we can all busk around it.' The band had no fear of improvisation, so it was left to me to thump around on a conga drum, trying to contribute something of my own to that alien music. The cracks and the writing on the wall were beginning to appear.

When we travelled to concerts we'd usually meet at the Witchseason management offices on Charlotte Street in the West End. One day I arrived at the agreed time, but I was the only one there apart from Joe Boyd. It later transpired that I had been told one time to arrive and they had been given a different one. Joe asked me to come into his office and sit down.

'We need to talk Ian,' he said.

He didn't beat around the bush, that's how Joe was.

'The band have asked me to tell you that they want you to leave.'

It was a huge shock, I didn't see it coming, after all I was singing with them most nights and sharing a house with two of them and no one had implied anything of the kind. As uncomfortable as I was with the direction, deep down I loved being in the band and in my naivety when Joe said leave, I presumed he meant soon. It never occurred to me that I was expected to leave immediately, within the hour.

While Joe and I were talking, the rest of the band began to arrive. When they went down to the van, naturally I followed and took my usual seat. There was a hushed silence until Ashley turned to me.

'Where do you think you are going?' he said.

'With you of course.'

'No you're not, you're out of the band.'

Sandy swivelled in her seat and narrowed her eyes at Ashley.

'You cruel bastard,' she said.

I sat there for a moment or two, stunned, trying to take it all in, before climbing back out of the van. I heard the door slide shut and off they drove. I stood rooted, trying to make sense of what had just happened. In the blink of an eye I was out of the band. I took a walk around the West End to let it all sink in. It was raining. Then I went home.

We were young and ambitious. I see now that they did what had to be done and I had become expendable. For the band, it was about forward progress and it needed to be made at all costs and as quickly as possible. As far as I'm aware, there was never any malice intended. We were in a musical dogfight to be recognised and to quote a well-worn phrase, 'When the going gets tough, the tough get going.' Fairport Convention were tough and going places.

Thinking about it now, fifty years later, I still feel that same huge, gut-wrenching sense of disappointment and failure that I felt at the moment of impact on that chilly February afternoon. It's the first and only time in my long career that I've ever been asked to leave a band. I silently vowed there and then that it would be the last.

When I had moved into the house we rented in Brent, next to Golders Green, Paul Ghosh and Andrew Horvitch, who I believe were two of Richard's old school friends, lived downstairs. We lived upstairs where there were two rooms at the front of the house. Richard had the smaller one and Simon Nicol lived in the other larger room. Down the hall was a communal bathroom and at the far end, a step-down kitchen. Across from the bathroom was a mid-sized back bedroom. That's where I lived with my girlfriend, Chris. I was quiet and non-confrontational in those days and after being ejected from the band, I simply carried on sharing the house with Richard and Simon. When we'd pass each other in the hallway, or end up in the kitchen at the same time, we'd never talk about what had happened. I was hesitant to stir the waters. Being out of the band was bad enough, I didn't want to be out of the house too. Even though I was no longer a member of the band, I was being paid £20 a week until I could find my direction. Work had already begun on recording the third album, which became *Unhalfbricking*. I had vocals on just one song, the Dylan tune, 'Percy's Song', the first track recorded for the album.

I hadn't played an instrument on stage while I was in Fairport Convention, except for the odd thump on a conga drum or a twang on a Jew's harp. After I left the band I told Richard that I'd like to buy a guitar and learn to play and asked if he would help me choose one. When I worked for J.D. Tighe, I'd seen and bought a cheap solid-body electric from a pawnshop in Scunthorpe but had never learned to play it. The fact that I needed a tutor had completely evaded me. I had no idea where to look for guidelines and I'd simply leaned it against my bedroom wall for a few weeks and stared at it in a mixed state of awe, bewilderment and despair before selling it back to the pawnshop at a loss. This time, however, I had Richard. He took me to the Rose-Morris showroom on Shaftesbury Avenue where I bought a relatively inexpensive Framus acoustic. He then gave me a few lessons in chord shapes. We began with an E minor, a simple two-finger chord, followed by an A minor, a three-finger chord, and then a step up to C major that still only required three fingers. I played those three chords over and over and over until I developed painful little blisters on the tips of my fingers. Richard said to not worry, they would subside and turn into calluses and calluses were good for a guitar player. I took a week off before picking it up again to learn a D chord and then a G, which is in fact a four-finger chord and a tad more difficult but essential as quite a few of the songs I would initially write would be in G. Once I had mastered those half-dozen chords I was up and running. I knuckled down to the process and began writing songs in earnest. Occasionally I'd hit a wall and go back to Richard with the problem, whereupon he'd show me an F shape or a B minor. My playing and writing simply built from there. Playing the guitar isn't necessarily difficult, it's about commitment and consistency. Once you get beyond the blisters and hand cramps and master a few chords, you'll begin humming melodies and once you have the melody, lyrics usually materialise and voila, you're writing songs.

On 12th May 1969, Chris and I were asleep in the house on St. Mary's Road. At around two or three o'clock in the morning, we awoke to what sounded like a fight downstairs. There was a lot of banging and thumping, as though things or people were bouncing off the walls. As I wiped the sleep from my eyes and gathered my senses, I realised it was someone hammering with a fist at the front door. We hastily threw on some clothes and emerged sleepily from my room. Chris was more awake than me and ran down the stairs to open the front door. There were two young policemen standing there. They asked for me and made their way past Chris to the top of the stairs. One of them asked me if Simon Nicol and Richard Thompson lived here. I told them they did, but they were not home. They were making me terribly nervous, I could tell that something was very wrong in the way they glanced at each other in their hesitance to respond.

'Your friends have been involved in a serious accident, their vehicle left the motorway and we're led to believe some of the occupants may have died. At this point we have no further information,' one of the policemen said.

I found myself hanging onto the banister rail for stability, my legs were crumbling beneath me and my eyesight began fading to black. One of the policemen eased me up off the floor and sat me down on the top step. I said I couldn't see, I thought I'd gone blind. He reassured me that it was natural in these circumstances to experience shock and that's what was happening to me.

'Just keep your head up and breathe deep,' he said, 'you'll be fine.'

They stayed with us for a while and gave Chris a phone number for the hospital. They told us that enquiries would continue through the night and that we were to phone in the morning. It was already morning.

When we did call, no one at the hospital would tell us anything about the band. At which point I was frantic and phoned the Witchseason office, where a friend of the band, Anthea Joseph, answered. She told me they were all in the hospital. She said that Simon was relatively unhurt. He'd been asleep in the back and was the only person or thing not thrown from the van as it rolled. Richard and Ashley were quite beat up. Ashley in particular had lots of cuts around the head. Everyone was in deep shock. I asked after Martin Lamble our drummer. Anthea told me that he'd been seriously injured and had passed away during the night. He was just nineteen. Richard's then girlfriend, an American, Jeannie Franklyn was killed too. She'd been living with us in the house for a short time and was known as Jeannie the Tailor. She sewed rock'n'roll clothes for famous musicians. Jack Bruce later dedicated an entire album *Songs for a Tailor* to her. Fortuitously, Sandy had decided to ride home after the show with her boyfriend, Trevor Lucas.

Two days after the accident, I went with Simon's mom to see them in the hospital. We walked through the door of the ward and I passed out at the sight of my battered and bruised comrades. I came around, horizontal, on a bed next to them.

The crash stopped us all in our tracks. A once carefree bunch of young musicians grew up that day and until recently on a television documentary I had never heard any of them mention it. You can never quite forget these things. After that day, everything changed. The band seriously considered packing it all in. I started to think in earnest about what I should do.

I went to see our friend John Peel. He had championed Fairport Convention and was a sounding board for us all. He was living in a mews house in the West End. When I got there John was busy working on his programme in his office. I was asked by his assistant if I could wait in the living room until he was done. On a couch opposite me sat Marc Bolan. He was reading a book and had barely acknowledged me coming in. Not being confident enough to initiate conversation, I reached into my shoulder bag for my book and we both sat there opposite each other, silently reading. Then, as if it had been scripted, at exactly the same moment, we both laughed out loud. We lowered our books and looked up at one another in amazement. It broke the ice and transpired that we were both reading Kurt Vonnegut's *Slaughterhouse-Five* and had reached precisely the same funny paragraph at exactly the same time. I felt comfortable enough to tell Marc of the time in Ravel's when I sold him shoes. He reacted as though he remembered, but I don't think he did. Just then, John popped his head around the corner, smiled hello to Marc and invited me into his inner sanctum. I explained what had happened and how confused I was as to what I should do next. We talked about music in general and he asked me what I was listening to. I told him that I had a passion for the emerging contemporary American singer-songwriters. He replied, 'Well then, follow your heart.' He suggested that I take all the craft and knowledge I had learned with Fairport and use it to my advantage. 'You know what it's like to be on a stage, you know how to sing and you have studio experience, don't let any of that go to waste.'

I took the tube back to Brent, mulling over what John had said. It occurred to me that he was right about all these things and that I'd like to make an album. I just needed a way to facilitate it.

KNOWING THE GAME

This here's a song about the brightness in the flame
A song I want you all to hear
You may be taken down, you may be written off
It's knowing how to stay the same
Knowing how to play the game

I am the old eternal optimistic fool
You only see before my eyes
There is another time, there is another way
It's knowing how to hold the sign
Knowing when to cross the line

There's an awful lot of people I should know
But most I wouldn't recognise offhand
Did you ever take to running, did you find it on your own?
I've seen it in your eyes
Beyond a shadow of a doubt I realise

This here's a song about the vision in the night
The voice to make you all believe
You may be rising now, you may be wondering
It's knowing how to hit your stride
Knowing when to buy the ride

This here's a song about the brightness in the flame
A song I hoped you all could hear
You may be criticised, you may be drifted by
It's knowing how to lose the ties
Knowing when the fallen rise

5. SUDDEN DISCOMFORT

I needed to find a manager. In 1969 I was relatively new to the manager game and wasn't sure what to look out for, I'd already had two and both had unceremoniously dumped me. A friend introduced me to a successful songwriting duo who were also managers – Ken Howard and Alan Blaikley. Ken and Alan lived opposite the Holly Bush pub in Hampstead and ran a company called Axle Enterprises. At the time they were writing pure pop songs for most of the acts they managed. They'd written numerous hits for Dave Dee, Dozy, Beaky, Mick & Tich and a Top Ten single, 'From the Underworld' for The Herd. They'd also had a big number one hit with 'Have I the Right?' by The Honeycombs. I decided to cautiously approach them and see how things felt. I needed someone who believed in who I was and embraced my musical vision. Ken and Alan appeared to tick those boxes. We had a long discussion at their house.

'Okay Ian,' Ken said, 'here's what we think. We've never been involved with anyone from your musical background before, so we believe it could be advantageous to both parties. It could broaden our horizons, give us an alternate type of credibility and possibly give you the launching pad you appear to be searching for. We'll manage you and get you a record deal.'

It seemed like only weeks, but was probably far longer, before a recording contract was signed and sealed with Uni records, a boutique label and a division of MCA. This label was home to the likes of Elton John, Neil Diamond, Rick Nelson and Desmond Dekker. I was proud and excited to be in such exalted company. Ken and Alan wanted to write the songs for the first album, but I was also keen to write myself, so we compromised. They wrote six of the songs, I contributed five and Richard Thomson gave me a brand-new composition about his post-accident feelings called 'A Commercial Proposition' – 'Alright, everything's alright. Everything's all, all right now.'

Ken and Alan were nervous about putting their real names to the songs they had written for me. They were primarily known as pop writers and desperately wanted to appeal to a more progressive audience. Working with someone from my background was a whole new universe for them. We talked it over and they hit upon the idea of using a pseudonym. For the purpose of my album they became Steve Barlby. I've often wondered about that name and where it materialised from.

One of the songs they wrote for my album was called 'I've Lost You'. It found its way into a package they pitched to Colonel Tom Parker for Elvis Presley to sing. As mine was the only existing recording, I can only imagine that Elvis must have listened to me singing it as he learned the song. Years later I asked Norbert Putnam, Elvis's bass player, if he remembered learning the song. He did, but had paid no attention to which version it was. Elvis had a big hit with it and it featured in his Las Vegas shows. The recording also appeared in the MGM film *That's the Way It Is*. I once dreamt about being introduced to the King and him asking me on stage to duet the song with him.

We recorded the album at De Lane Lea studios in Central London in the autumn of 1969 with a cast of stellar musicians. I was unfamiliar with the who's who of session musicians and approached my Fairport friends about working with me. They were still recovering from their accident traumas and recording gave them a focus. I also asked Richard Thompson to produce it. He accepted but inexplicably backed out at the mixing stage so I had to finish it myself. I had Gerry Conway on drums, Dolly Collins on the flute organ, Roger Coulam from Blue Mink on the Hammond organ and Pete Willsher on lap steel guitar. Add to that my Fairport friends Simon, Ashley and Richard. Thanks to a heads-up suggestion from Ashley, we added a man called Gordon Huntley on the pedal steel guitar.

Uni Records were ready to commit substantial amounts of money to promote my first album. The recordings were mixed and the sleeve art was finished. I was shown a mock-up of the design and it was stunning, but it said 'Ian Matthews'. I thought, 'My God, that's me.' I panicked, suddenly realising that I wasn't yet ready for a solo career. At the eleventh hour I had an emergency meeting with Ken and Alan and asked if I could have my name replaced by a band name. 'But Ian,' they said, 'everything's been paid for, you cannot simply change things now.' But we did. They gave in to my insecurity and agreed with Uni that if I could come up with a good name within twenty-four hours they would make the necessary changes. Around that time I was listening to quite a lot of music by a Canadian folk duo called Ian and Sylvia. They were the first to record Gordon Lightfoot's song 'Early Morning Rain', and Ian Tyson famously wrote 'Four Strong Winds'. On one of their albums they had a song Sylvia Fricker had written called 'Southern Comfort'. A clanging bell went off in my head and I thought, 'Hey, I can call the album *Matthews Southern Comfort*.' It was a name that rolled off the tongue effortlessly, it sounded like a band name and, most of all, it got me out of a huge dilemma.

The folks at Uni loved the name and decided they could get sponsorship with it. When the promotion began we were gifted box upon box of the sickly liqueur, Southern Comfort. The makers of Southern Comfort also saw the wisdom in using our name for their promotion. By the time the second album was released we were even using a slightly altered version of the Southern Comfort logo as an album cover. I never had the nerve to tell them that I had an intense dislike for their sweet aromatic drink. I still do.

The first album was released as *Matthews' Southern Comfort*, with an apostrophe. It met with reasonable critical success and didn't do too bad commercially, entering the lower reaches of the UK Top Fifty albums chart. I was up and running and the pressure was then on to form a touring unit.

Towards the end of my Fairport days, I'd met and been drawn to Marc Ellington, a transplanted American songwriter from Eugene, Oregon. We'd met at a BBC session where he was chaperoning his old acquaintance Tim Hardin around to his promotional commitments. At the time Tim was quite strung out on various stimulants and Marc had been hired by Verve to get him safely to his appointments. Marc and I became good friends. Chris and I would quite often spend time with him and his wife

Karen, listening to music at their flat in South East London. Marc was a solo artist with an album on the Philips label and had become friends with a young rock band on the same label called Harsh Reality. Marc told me confidentially that due to insufficient sales, Philips were about to drop Harsh Reality even though they were all extremely good musicians. He thought I should consider them as potential band members and took me to hear them rehearse. Mark Griffiths played lead guitar, Carl Barnwell was a singer-songwriter and rhythm guitarist, and Roger Swallow was the drummer. These players became the core of my new band Matthews Southern Comfort, to which we added session man Gordon Huntley on pedal steel. A young student, Pete Watkins, was our first bassist, but because of his study commitments, was quickly replaced by Andrew Leigh, who'd just left the hugely popular Spooky Tooth. Quite soon after that, Roger our drummer left and we held auditions. Of the half-dozen or so drummers we auditioned, Ray Duffy, who'd just left the pop group Marmalade, stood head and shoulders above the rest and was an obvious choice. This then became the final version of Matthews Southern Comfort.

We rehearsed incessantly, getting ourselves road ready, until the songs and arrangements were coming out of our ears. The first show we did was at a popular club in Birmingham called Mothers, where Fairport had played the night of the accident. We were part of a triple bill with Fairport Convention and Fotheringay, the band Sandy Denny had formed after leaving Fairport.

For one of our shows, we were booked on a ferry to the Isle of Wight. We were an hour early and decided to relax at the water's edge. Before we got out of the car, a joint was passed around and I had one of those 'What the hell, why not?' moments. There were six of us. We got out of the car and instantly I became lost. I didn't know where I was and couldn't recognise anyone. I panicked and freaked out, running around at the water's edge looking for someone I knew. The band, meanwhile, were standing by the car howling with laughter. They thought I was just messing about, entertaining them. When they realised I wasn't, one of them came and got me, took me to the car and stayed with me until normality resumed. But that was the last that hash and I saw of each other.

Including my first 'solo' album, we recorded and released three records in the space of a year. There was quite a musical leap from the first album to the next one, *Second Spring*. I've never been one to look back to analyse, I move on very quickly. I viewed the first album more as a Howard and Blaikley project and a stepping stone towards what I had in my head, but definitely not what I wanted to do. I'd kicked the door open with the first album and slammed that same door shut behind me with the second one, leaving my Fairport era on the other side.

During the entire period of creating *Second Spring* I became a musical sponge. I wanted to know as much as possible about the developments in the contemporary singer-songwriter world. It seemed to me that apart from a select few, almost everything good that I was hearing was coming from America. I was absorbing and being inspired by everything, even as far back as the classic country writers like Hank Williams and Johnny Cash. But now this brilliant new wave of songwriters was emerging. I was learning from the likes of Joni, Tim Buckley, Leonard Cohen, Tim Hardin, Fred Neil, Fariña, Neil Young and one of my all-time favourites, Eric Anderson. I still believe Eric Anderson's beautiful *Blue River* album is one of the most important records of that era.

I wanted to rediscover that contemporary American singer-songwriter feel and sound that I had liked so much while I was with Fairport Convention, before they became infatuated with electrifying traditional folk. I was captivated by albums such as The Byrds' *Sweetheart of the Rodeo* and Ian and Sylvia's *Great Speckled Bird*. Matthews Southern Comfort, particularly Mark Griffiths, who already was a fine arranger and explorer of unusual chord shapes, helped me to reimagine and reinvent that material, bellying up to the sound I thought I was hearing in my head.

We recorded another Ian and Sylvia song, 'Jinkson Johnson', Richard Fariña's 'Blood Red Roses', Steve Gillette's 'Darcy Farrow', the classic 'Something in the Way She Moves' by James

Taylor, plus three of my own songs. This was the music we took on the road.

I loved the *Second Spring* album, it was a pure group effort. Nevertheless, I was still the nominal leader who didn't really want to be because of the pressure I felt from it. I was the face and the name and consequently had to deal with the barrage of press that followed. I still had the feeling of wanting to be smaller, an invisible part of something bigger.

In the summer of 1970, Matthews Southern Comfort supported Fairport Convention at a summer fair in Maidstone, Kent. It was a traditional English country fête with kids eating ice cream, mums, dads, grandparents, balloons and dog shows. The entire event was filmed by the famous music documentary maker, Tony Palmer. The story goes that Tony Palmer was a friend of Sandy Denny and he'd been down to the Fairport house to discuss making a film about Fairport. Then the accident happened and not long after Sandy left the band, so the project was shelved. Then out of the blue Richard Thompson got in touch with Tony to see if he would like to film them at the Maidstone festival. Tony secured money to make the film from the most unlikely of sources: the actor Stanley Baker was being chased by the tax man following his massive success with the film *Zulu*, so in order to offload some of his money he agreed to fund the Fairport film. The film got a cinema release, paired with *Pink Floyd: Live at Pompeii*. Those were heady and bizarre times for creative people. The film is available on DVD these days. We are seen performing 'My Front Pages' and 'Southern Comfort'. Fairport ran through a series of electrified jigs and reels. By that time Ashley had moved on and both Dave Pegg and Dave Swarbrick had become permanent band members.

I had been able to buy a decent hi-fi set-up by the time Neil Young put out *After the Gold Rush* and I hustled down to my favourite record shop, Musicland in Berwick Street, to buy it on the day it was released in the UK. I took it back to the flat on the top floor of the rambling old house I was sharing with Chris on Rosecroft Avenue in Hampstead. From the very first listen I was hooked. I played it three, possibly four times, before waking up in the middle of the night with the song 'Cripple Creek Ferry' steaming through my head. I got up and played the album three more times. I couldn't believe what I was hearing. It was so cutting edge. The songs were so well constructed and the instrumentation was perfection on a disc. What a massive talent this man was and what a career he must have before him. That record was a pivotal moment in my own musical development.

Three years later, while sat waiting for an appointment with David Geffen up in the Geffen Roberts management offices on Sunset Boulevard in LA, Neil was sitting opposite me, waiting to see his manager Elliot Roberts. What I wanted to say was, 'Hi Neil, I'm Ian Matthews. I once recorded your song "Tell Me Why" with Matthews Southern Comfort. Can I tell you what an honour it is to meet you and how much I greatly admire your work.' He'd most likely have responded, we could have had a nice conversation, he must have been aware of my work. But I said nothing. I stayed small and let the silence beat me up again. I was still too shy. Neil didn't instigate any conversation either and we left as strangers who'd sat in the same room together, being small. All I had to do was open my mouth and let the words tumble out, but I couldn't find a way to do it.

By the time we began recording *Later That Same Year*, Matthews Southern Comfort's third album of the year, the cracks were beginning to appear. The band were on a wage and I paid them a fair weekly amount as our profile grew, but still they wanted more. They came at me through Howard and Blaikley, believing the work they were doing deserved more. Maybe it did, but I didn't have more to give. Ken and Alan thought they were a very good band and that I should hold on to them at all costs. I understood the thought behind that. They were my managers and I was paying for their managerial wisdom and trusted in them. They wanted me to consider giving the band a share of the action. I listened patiently and eventually agreed to give each of them a ten percent share of my royalty. Fifty percent in total. In hindsight it was far too much and the outcome should have been predictable. They still complained. It was a lose-lose situation. By then Carl Barnwell, a more than decent songwriter, had visions of being a lead singer. His songs were included on the album and, as a gesture of faith in his talents, I also let him contribute a couple of lead vocals. He was already ahead of the others financially and visually, but he seemingly wanted more. At a certain point, in order to bring sanity back to the band, I reluctantly let Carl go. We played a couple of shows without him and spent the entire evenings looking across the stage at each other wondering what the hell we'd done. There was a piece of the puzzle missing and we all knew what it was. Mark Griffiths said, 'I think we've made a mistake letting Carl go. Do you think we can ask him back?' We asked him the question and thankfully he re-joined us.

Gordon Huntley was considerably older than the rest of us. He tried to hide his age. We were in our twenties and he was supposedly in his forties. He was an experienced session musician playing a specialised instrument and because of this he had, shall we say, been round the block a few times. He presumed this gave him the right to a bigger opinion. Gordon was also a good storyteller, I don't know if his tales were true or not, but he spun a great yarn. On the road I shared rooms with him. One time I woke up in the middle of the night with him screaming, 'We're in a spin, we're in a spin.' Naturally he frightened the hell out of me. I shook him awake and he apologised, telling me that during the war he'd flown in Lancaster bombers as a navigator. He'd apparently been shot down three times on missions and many of his comrades had perished. From that moment on, I insisted on being the one to room with him. Protecting my flock I suppose. I didn't want them to have the same experience I'd had and thought it a secret best kept.

Gordon was from the town of Newbury in Berkshire. He told me that once while on leave he went to a dance. Outside the dancehall a fight had started and was getting nasty. Gordon claimed to be a karate black belt and decided he needed to break up the fight. He joined in trying to separate the fighters when, unannounced, three others jumped into the action and set about Gordon. This triggered his martial arts instincts and what he saw as a need to protect himself. He threw two of the interlopers down the stone steps of the dancehall, finding out later that they were in fact plainclothes policemen. According to Gordon, one of the policemen broke his neck and died from his injuries. Gordon was sent to prison.

Apart from his tall – or true – tales, he was an amazingly innovative pedal steel guitar player. He'd hand-built his first instrument by attaching clutch pedals from a tractor and a bicycle brake cable. By the time he joined us he was playing one of the famous Buddy Emmons pedal steels. The problem I had then and now with the instrument was that it is a remarkably dominant sound and one can very quickly tire of it. It was inescapable and soon became the identifying sound of Matthews Southern Comfort. It appeared on everything we did and to me it screamed 'this is country' all of the time. Even when Gordon was being inventive, and he was a very inventive player, it still had an undeniable country vibe and I did not want that. I suppose there's a case for saying that once you have a good formula you should accept it and embrace it, but I wasn't then and never will be that way inclined. I wanted a progressive, contemporary sound but didn't know how to realise it. Instead of finding a way to verbalise my dilemma and look for a solution, I began to get sulky and irritable. I became unpredictable and at one point left the stage in mid-show. Not in a malicious way, or to wreck the performance, but simply because I really wasn't enjoying it and didn't know how else to express that.

The BBC had a policy called 'needle drop time'. It was a Musicians' Union rule that meant they were only allowed to play a certain percentage of commercially released music in any given period of time. In response to that rule they had acts come into the BBC sound studios and record extra songs from their repertoire that the BBC could then give airtime to. An ingenious plot. We were invited to do a BBC session. We had three songs rehearsed and ready to go, but the powers that be wanted four. That week I had been to Musicland yet again and bought Joni Mitchell's *Ladies of the Canyon*. I took the album to the rehearsal room and said, 'Guys, listen to this. You'll love it.' I played them a song called 'Woodstock'. They instantly liked it and thought it would make a perfect fourth song for our session. We spent the rest of the afternoon working on an arrangement. Everything you hear on the recorded version of the song, the pedal steel, the chiming tremolo electric guitar, the delicate picked acoustics, was all conceived that day. We arrived at the BBC radio session, played our four songs and that was that, until a couple of weeks later when it aired. Ken and Alan called me asking for the name of the song we'd played on the BBC. Uni had apparently been inundated with hundreds of phone calls asking where they could buy the record. They in turn had phoned Howard and Blaikley, who, being just as baffled as they were, called me.

Between the management and the label they decided that the song absolutely must be added to the new album we had just finished making, *Later That Same Year*. In typical Ian fashion I dug my heels in, firm in my conviction that the album was perfect the way it was. Remarkably, they caved. I can't believe I got away with it, but I felt the album had to stay as it was. The songs, the sequence, everything was perfect. Ken and Alan went along with it on the condition that I compromise and record 'Woodstock' as a single. We went back into Morgan Studios in Willesden with our engineer Robin Black and recreated our BBC recording. Of course, the American label, Decca, had other ideas. We had absolutely no control over what they did. In their infinite wisdom they blithely and randomly removed the song 'Jonah' to create space for the hit. I wasn't happy about it, but also knew that no amount of fussing would change their minds and, after all, we had eyes on the same goal.

Morgan was my favourite studio. It was a relatively small complex comprising of three separate studios. There was a huge upstairs room that seemed to be permanently occupied by Led Zeppelin. Every time I'd ask who was upstairs, it was Zep. Around the corner from the front door was a medium-sized room, and there was a smaller, more intimate room at the back. Of course I preferred the smaller one. It had a tight, cosy sound to it. We were in there one day when I saw Sandy Denny traipsing up the stairs. She told me that Led Zeppelin had asked her to sing a song for them. It was of course 'The Battle of Evermore', later to become a classic.

The Matthews Southern Comfort recording of 'Woodstock'

entered the charts quite a while after a Crosby, Stills, Nash and Young version. Ours was a slow burner. Uni were reluctant to release it while CSN&Y were hovering in the lower regions of the Top Fifty, threatening to move higher. But they didn't, it just sort of fizzled out and that was when the Universal machine flew into action. At first it took its time charting and then completely out of the blue one of the BBC's flagship jocks, Tony Blackburn, made it his record of the week and it took off like a sky rocket. It eased its way up to number ten in the charts and I thought, 'We're there, we've done it, a Top Ten hit.' But the best was yet to come. It began selling in what I considered silly numbers. Management told us that it had gone from selling 1,000 copies a day to 10,000 a day; in its best week it was selling upwards of 30,000 copies a day. Ken and Alan called me and said, 'Hang onto something because it's going to make a significant leap next week. Quite a bit higher than number ten.' When the chart was announced we'd flown over everyone else to the number one spot.

That week we were invited to appear on *Top of the Pops* and it was a surreal experience. The kids in front of the stage were anticipating dancing to Freda Payne's 'Band of Gold' which had reached number one the previous week. When suddenly the DJ announced, 'It's number one, it's *Top of the Pops*, it's Matthews Southern Comfort with a song called "Woodstock",' all of the kids immediately stopped chatting mid-sentence and swivelled around to gape at us, with a look of puzzlement on their faces, as if to say 'Who the hell are these people?' By our second week on *Top of the Pops*, they knew who we were and they were dancing.

I still believe Joni wrote a beautiful song with a wonderful message. Lyrically it's a little idyllic and naive, but if you truly believe in the sentiment, it stands up to this day. I maybe should not say this, but I've always preferred the Crosby, Stills, Nash and Young version to ours. It has muscle and a certain necessary aggressiveness to it, whereas ours is a little too serene. We simplified Joni's chorus and left out the bits about 'billion year old carbon' and 'caught in the devil's bargain'. CSN&Y included them and in retrospect I wish we had too. Now when we play it live those lines are included.

I met Joni briefly backstage when we opened for James Taylor at the London Palladium with 'Woodstock' at number one in the UK charts. At the time Taylor was her significant other and she was travelling with him. She had her photograph taken with us without a word about our recording. We circled one another for a few minutes, wondering who would be the first to give in and say 'thank you'. It slowly became apparent that she wasn't going to say anything and I was damned if I was. She just did her PR bit and smiled for the camera. I heard later through the grapevine that she had in fact told a journalist that she preferred our arrangement.

With 'Woodstock' at number one it felt that everyone wanted a little piece of me and very little of it had to do with music. By everyone, I mean press and radio. It became all about promotion, when in my mind it should have been about creation. Of course, I understand that promotion is an important part of the overall package. Record companies need to see returns from their investments, but at the time I lived in a fantasy world where I thought I could just write, record and play. If I could have hired someone to do the talking for me I would happily have given them the job. I had Howard and Blaikley telling me I needed to do this, do that, go there, say this, don't say that, don't worry you can do that later. Ad infinitum. As it turned out, there would be no later. I became so disillusioned and frustrated by all the extracurricular activity that I found non-existent faults in the music and the band to the point where I convinced myself that my only option was to get the hell out. I then began taking those frustrations home with me at night. I became dark and moody with lots of deep unresolved anger and that in turn affected my relationship with Chris. She couldn't seem to comprehend what I was feeling when everything appeared to be going so well and began to back away from me. I had no one I could speak to about it and what should have been a joyful period in my life became an unbearable load. In hindsight, I should have taken a step back, called a meeting, sat everyone down and looked for solutions. But I had neither the experience nor the tools. In my head, making changes wasn't an option. Of course it was and years later I realised that.

It all came to an ugly conclusion one night at Birmingham Town Hall. We had a hit record and a sold-out show. At the soundcheck I was in a deep, disagreeable funk. We did the soundcheck. The band was happy with it, but to me something was very wrong. It sounded and felt like a countrified mess, as if no one cared, and I couldn't, wouldn't or didn't know how to verbalise it. I made a snap decision and without telling anyone I put my guitar in its case, walked down to the station and caught the first train back to London. I went home, closed the door, locked it, got into bed and pulled the covers over my head. When Ken and Alan called I insisted that Chris answer it and refused to speak to them. I let Chris do my talking and when she'd eventually had enough, we stopped answering the phone altogether. We knew who it was and what they wanted. I wasn't interested. They reverted to slipping messages under my door, to which I didn't or couldn't respond.

I was in a very dark and confused state. I saw no light. That was more or less it for Matthews Southern Comfort. I couldn't face the band. Remarkably, all this was happening with 'Woodstock' still in the Top Ten. Mark Griffiths later told me that the rest of the band let it go and moved on, but apparently Gordon had told them he was going to kill me. Knowing of his physical abilities, I believed it and that scared me.

It was well and truly over and the band made the decision to carry on without me. I would have done the same in their shoes. They signed a deal with Harvest records, eventually changed their name to Southern Comfort and made three more albums. I didn't bother listening to them, I simply wasn't interested. I needed a fresh start, with a clear head and new surroundings.

We had toured endlessly, released three albums, done numerous BBC sessions and more press and media than one could shake a stick at. We'd also had a worldwide hit single. I know all too well now that I dealt with it in an incredibly immature way by abandoning the band and pulling those bed covers over my head, but I didn't know what else to do. I didn't realise I had options. I meant no ill will or malice towards my bandmates, I simply couldn't cope with success. I was just a scared young boy from Scunthorpe.

In one of my scrapbooks there's a cutting from my local paper, the *Scunthorpe Evening Telegraph*. It appears that a journalist went around to the house to speak to my mom and dad when the record got to number one. The article says, 'Steelworker Allan MacDonald and his wife Dorothy, who live at Enderby Road, can feel justifiably proud of their lad.' They then quote my dad, 'A lot of people won't know that our son is a pop star,' he said, 'because he changed his name from MacDonald to his middle name Matthew.' Not strictly true. The *Telegraph* also mentioned that Matthews Southern Comfort were due to play a show at The Winter Gardens in Cleethorpes on November 17th. I must have played one of my last performances with the band right in my own backyard and was too preoccupied to even realise it.

After I left the band I stopped singing all of the Matthews Southern Comfort material for quite some time, including 'Woodstock'. It just didn't feel right once I was no longer fronting the band. It was all a bit too close to home for me and it would be a long time before I began performing the song again. Even then it was usually an a cappella version. The song has been very good to me over the years, I have no problem throwing it in as an encore. Over time I've learned to embrace my success and I can now reinvent the song to suit the occasion. I would estimate that song has probably extended my career by a good twenty years.

ROAD TO RONDERLIN

Oh the night it is so very cold
And I fear the mist is closing in
Should we hesitate once more
Our natural life is over
And we'll never find the road to Ronderlin

Oh my wife I am so much a fool
And the victim of a wandering mind
From the path I let us stray
With the sunrise far away
And the mist is of the deepest kind

Oh my dear I fear so for my life
For my soul and for our children three
Do you hear the night birds call?
Do you here my voice at all?
Oh road, sweet road where can you be?

6. A CHILD IS BORN

In the space of less than two years I found myself out of two highly successful bands. I was disillusioned and disappointed but unbroken – should the truth be known I was a little angry at myself for allowing it to happen. Nevertheless, I was eager to carry on with my singing and songwriting. Ken and Alan realised early in our relationship that I was a fragile soul, but they had missed the warning signs and now I'd been overloaded. They suggested that maybe it was time to launch my solo career and assured me that I didn't need a band around me making demands.

The problem was I was still officially contracted to Uni with Matthews Southern Comfort. Ken and Alan said not to worry, they would fix it. They pored over the contract with their solicitor and miraculously found a loophole. They discovered a clause that said when we were ready, Uni were responsible for the funding of an American tour. When they were confronted with it, Uni's response was that they were not in a position to honour the clause because of a current executive problem. Ken and Alan argued that if Uni could not support a tour then the contract was null and void. Amazingly, I was released from my deal without further discussion. This left Uni in the bizarre situation of having had a number one single in the charts with the artist out of contract.

Ken sent out a press release that said we were looking for a solo deal. It instantly made front-page music weekly news. So, nothing much had changed there. Apple showed an immediate interest, as did the Rolling Stones label. Ken and Alan called me one day.

'There's a new label called Vertigo, a subsidiary of Philips and they are very interested in signing you. They already have Rod Stewart and we think it might be a good home for you too.'

We went to the Vertigo offices for a meeting and they made me a very good offer to record three albums for them. I liked the vibe there. We went back to Holly Mount to discuss our next move. Ken and Alan thought that Vertigo felt right. We accepted their offer and consummated the deal.

My friend Marc Ellington had played me Cat Stevens's album *Tea for the Tillerman* and I loved the sound of the record. I noted that it had been produced by Paul Samwell-Smith. Paul was one of the first musicians I was aware of who had made the transition from player to producer. He had been the bass player in The Yardbirds and had now built a solid reputation as a producer. Cat Stevens was his current and most impressive calling card. I asked Ken and Alan if there was any way they could convince him to produce me. They said to leave it to them and once again they somehow worked their voodoo and Paul became my producer too.

My first solo album will always be special to me simply because of the way it came together so effortlessly. I wrote practically all of the songs for it behind closed doors in my flat on Rosecroft Avenue, and although I revealed a lot of my feelings in a somewhat shrouded fashion, some of them contain very personal revelations. Apart from two songs by my hero Richard Fariña and one by an unknown New York writer, Jake Jacobs, all of the songs were mine. Something had been triggered inside. I wrote about everything I was feeling; about losing Martin, about being misunderstood, about my inability to communicate. It all came out in the songs. A therapy of sorts. A diary made public. Meanwhile Chris and I were going through a rough period in our relationship. She'd told me that she was pregnant. I wasn't ready for it but immediately suggested we get married. We made wedding plans before she told me that she'd discovered she wasn't pregnant after all. I took it as an honest mistake. These things can happen.

In general my songwriting for that first Vertigo album is quite opaque. I thought I was being creative when in fact I was being elusive. I searched for ways to say something simple that would leave the listener puzzled. I seemed to be resisting showing my true naked feelings. But it was a process I had to go through to be the writer I've become today. The one song where I feel I truly opened up and simply stated what I wanted to say was on the song 'Thro' My Eyes' and it came to me fully formed in a dream. I woke up in the middle of the night with it running through my head. I got out of bed and wrote all the lyrics down on a piece of paper. In the morning I'd forgotten about my dream until I found the paper on the coffee table. I read it through thinking, this is great, I need to tap that source more, but I never could. When a song comes through you rather than from you, it's a magical feeling.

During preparations for the recordings I told Paul that I desperately needed a right-hand man, someone who'd listen to me and could express my ideas to a band in the studio and lead them through an arrangement. He told me he knew a guitar player from a band who'd recently had an accident on the highway. He was taking some time off to 'get his head together'. The band was called Everyone and the guitarist was Andy Roberts.

Andy was born four days before me on 12th June 1946 in Stanmore. At the tender age of twenty-four he had already experienced enough of the music business to last a lifetime. He'd gone to Liverpool University to study law and bumped into Roger McGough, a poet. They began working together in a music and poetry band in 1966. They called themselves The Liverpool Scene. The ensemble lasted until 1970, at which point Andy left and formed his own band, Everyone. Then came the accident and rehabilitation. Now here he was. I liked him instantly. He and I connected on both a musical and a personal level.

Between Paul, Andy and I, we put together an excellent core unit of musicians for the recordings: Gerry Conway on drums, Pat Donaldson on bass, Keith Tippett on piano, and a guitar duo of Tim Renwick from Quiver and my old pal Richard Thompson.

A couple of weeks into the sessions it became clear to me that Paul was not completely focused on the recording. He began arriving late to work and one day called in wanting to cancel the session. At that point I had to put my foot down. I had an album to make, an important one. I had a career to be getting on with and had little tolerance for setbacks. I felt we were already on a particularly fast track and this train was unstoppable. It was puzzling to me that Paul was seemingly disinterested until I found out that he was having severe domestic difficulties but didn't want to confide. It later transpired that he was also under pressure to get back into the studio with Cat Stevens. Just a quick word in my ear could have fixed it and saved us both a lot of confusion and disappointment.

I soldiered on with assistance and advice from my engineer Robin Black. I was testing my skills at production when Andy said to me, 'Listen, I have a good friend, Sandy Roberton. He's a budding producer, and a good listener, you'll like him. He's already told me he's willing to sit in and guide you through this. Interested?' Andy's instincts were spot on. On his own time and at his own expense, Sandy was invaluable on my first production. He came down to Morgan at the drop of a hat and solved whatever quandary we were in. In hindsight, I wish I'd thought to credit him as co-producer.

When we came to record the song 'Thro' My Eyes', I knew I wanted something sparse and acoustic, yet emotional and intense. As we eased into the recordings I also thought of Sandy Denny. I asked her if she would come in and play some piano for me. It was a simple song and I felt her understated style would complement it perfectly. She was a little insecure at first until I explained that I just needed her to play those big fat chords she was so good at creating. She came in and navigated her way through the song with the end result being exactly what I'd envisioned. At the end of the take we were all blown away by the feel of the song. It was painfully simple, yet incredibly moving. I thanked her and told her how beautifully she'd played and that it was a keeper. She felt good about herself and I took that moment to ask if she would consider adding a vocal harmony. What she gave was such a soulful, heartfelt performance that it moved me to tears. I think we all knew immediately that we had something special. All these years later it still sounds and feels fresh and deeply emotional.

Lyrically the song is a cry for understanding. While I'm not a religious person, I do consider myself to be spiritual and 'Thro' My Eyes' feels like a spiritual of sorts. The song is a prayer: a prayer of guilt, a prayer of confusion and a prayer for understanding. We played it recently at my wife Marly's mother's funeral and the sound of both mine and Sandy's voices filling that huge church sent shivers up my spine.

It was only months before I had my first solo album out. I'd left Matthews Southern Comfort in November 1970 and by May 1971 *If You Saw Thro' My Eyes* was released. The cover of the album features a candid shot of me taken by my old Pyramid bandmate Steve Hiett. In it I'm pensively looking through the window, chewing on my thumbnail, with Tessa the cat on my lap. Who knows what I'm thinking. Probably worrying about doing more promotion.

No sooner had we finished *If You Saw Thro' My Eyes* than Vertigo were asking for more and we soon began work on a follow-up, my seventh album in less than three years. This time the songs were less personal, including some leftovers from my previous writing spree. I hadn't had time to conceptualise my thoughts and experiences; I was still easing myself away from the previous album and these new songs were more a collection than a concept. Nevertheless, they have a theme of perseverance and trust running through them. A few of my tunes are about the struggles to come to terms with balancing a soaring career and a relationship; 'Morning Song' and 'Hope You Know' are blatant relationship songs.

Chris told me again that she was pregnant. This time it was true. I had a two-month American tour booked with Richard Thompson and Andy Roberts. Again, I felt the tension inside me building but had no time to catch my breath. Do I cancel the tour and stay with Chris or should I honour my commitments? She and I talked about it and I decided to do the tour. Knowing that I was soon to become a father should have been a joyful experience, but for some reason I felt torn and once again it made me edgy and hard to be around.

We had completed roughly half of the album before Richard, Andy and I went off to tour America. I told Andy that I wasn't too happy with what we'd done and that I might begin again after we return. I tried to convince myself that I needed to make a better album than *Thro' My Eyes*, but knew deep down that it was virtually impossible.

Ken and Alan recruited a temporary manager for me while I was in the USA, a New Yorker named Bob Schweid. Bob had worked with Van Morrison during his Bang years. He assigned a young Brooklyn kid, Bobby Ronga, to tour manage us. Mercury Records were the American parent company for Vertigo and we began our final rehearsals in one of their cramped Manhattan rehearsal studios. Young Ronga was a funny guy, full of East Coast wisecracks and witticisms. One night at rehearsal he was watching us play and out of nowhere said, 'I can play bass.' We turned and stared at him blankly. I said, 'Go and get your bass then.' Off he went, coming back an hour later with a bass and a small amplifier. He plugged in and he was good.

'I can't pay you any more Bobby, but if you want to tour manage and be a part of the band the job's yours,' I told him.

He played with us and took care of business the entire tour, never once complaining about his workload. God bless Bobby Ronga. That's how a Brooklyn boy became a bass player with three English folk singers touring America. Strangers in a strange band we laughingly called ourselves. We discovered the following year that Bobby wasn't simply a good bass player, he could also pick a mean guitar.

The tour in 1971 consisted mainly of three- to five-night residencies. One of the early residencies was at the Los Angeles Troubadour. We flew out to the coast and set ourselves up in yet another rehearsal space for a couple of days, preparing for our Troubadour experience. Somehow, two young guns from Linda Ronstadt's band found out we were there and turned up unannounced at the rehearsal. My name was on the Troubadour facade so naturally I thought they had come to see me. They watched for a while and asked if we'd play something with a guitar solo in it. It quickly became apparent that they had very little interest in me and Andy, they just wanted to hear Richard. We gave them a smattering of 'Please Be My Friend' and afterwards they took Richard aside for a quick chinwag. They apparently told him they were forming a band and searching for a lead guitar player. They knew of his reputation and wondered if he'd be interested in joining them. They were Glenn Frey and Randy Meisner and they named their band Eagles.

The Troubadour club seated around 350 people and our show was sold out. I call it 'our show', but in actuality we were opening for Donny Hathaway, a Chicago-based R&B/soul singer. It was all a bit daunting really. That first and soon-to-be last night, we walked into the spotlights to be greeted by a club packed with the Los Angeles soul community in all their Friday night finery. Three skinny, soft spoken, white English boys and a long-haired Brooklynite. Richard playing his dulcimer, Andy and I with our acoustic guitars and Bobby Ronga on bass. We stuttered our way through maybe two songs, 'The Poor Ditching Boy' and 'Genesis Hall'. The crowd quickly became restless and began talking, then there was some gentle catcalling, interspersed with booing, which escalated pretty fast. The crowd noise grew louder until it was overwhelming the music. Realising it wasn't working, I didn't deal with it too well. I was disappointed and angry. I stood up and slowly slouched off the stage, dragging my guitar behind me. The others realised I'd gone and followed suit. Richard, who was bolder than the rest of us, strolled to the front of the stage holding his dulcimer in front of him.

'Ladies and gentlemen,' he said, 'contrary to popular belief, this (meaning his dulcimer) and not the saxophone is your national instrument.'

I thought we'd well and truly blown our chance to shine on the coast, but Doug Weston, the owner of the club, God bless him, realising his faux pas, was incredibly nice about it. He took full responsibility for the mismatch and proposed that we come back at the end of the tour and play a week with Randy Newman. Meanwhile, I was reading reviews in the press of shows on the East Coast by Southern Comfort. They had continued touring without me and their shows were getting awful reviews, but what made me furious was that I was the one taking the beating in the press. It was bad enough having a difficult time out west, but at least I was actually there on the stage.

When we returned to the coast for the Randy Newman shows

at the Troubadour we shone. The type of crowd Randy drew was perfect for us. I loved his music and he was a kind and courteous man to work with. We stayed at the famous Tropicana Motel on Santa Monica Boulevard. Underneath the motel at street level was a small diner called Duke's where we would usually eat breakfast. One morning I walked in to find a crowd gathered around one of the tables. I squeezed through the melee to find Moe of The Three Stooges holding court and handing out signed press photos. I joined the queue but by the time I reached him they were all gone. He said he'd be back the following morning, but he never reappeared.

While we were out west, Joe Boyd was there too working for Warner Brothers Records and he invited us over to visit. Richard, Andy and I sat in his back garden one afternoon, singing and messing around, when someone began to play the Crystals hit 'Da Doo Ron Ron'. I light-heartedly suggested we try it a cappella and put handclaps to it instead of guitar. It sounded and felt so good, as though we had been performing it for years. We had one more show to play at the Troubadour and were feeling pretty loose at that point so I said, 'What the hell, let's put it in the show tonight.' It proved to be such a popular addition that when we got back home, I didn't hesitate to record it for the new album.

The first thing I had to confront when I got back from America was a visibly pregnant girlfriend. When I'd set off on my tour in early August, her belly had been almost flat, but when she came to meet me at the airport in late September it caught me completely by surprise how big she had become during my absence. Of course we'd spoken by telephone while I was Stateside, but I'd no previous experience with visualising the stages of a pregnancy. On seeing her again, the realisation immediately hit me that music would have to take a temporary back seat while I focused on more important matters.

Chris and I were married at the Hampstead registry office on 28th September 1971, shortly after my return. It was by choice an intimate gathering. My mom and dad drove down from Scunthorpe, my dear friend Johnny Hayes and his wife Bridget were there – Johnny as my best man. Ken and Alan came and Chris's mom. A small, select group. We had a lunchtime reception at a local Greek restaurant before Chris and I jetted off for our honeymoon in the Portuguese Algarve. We took a ten-day rental on a tiny white bungalow perched on a hillside overlooking a sleepy fishing village. It felt idyllic waking up every morning to complete silence broken only by the occasional bird call. Even the salamanders creeping across the walls like moveable art couldn't spoil the tranquillity of it all. Chris had more than a mild phobia about reptiles and her first reaction had been to run from the house. But she quickly realised that these gentle creatures were neither threatening nor harmful and accepted them as part of the package.

I had developed a habit of taking my guitar everywhere with me in those days and I saw no reason why a honeymoon should be the exception. Whenever inspiration hit I needed to be there at the ready, guitar in hand.

On our return home, when I had a few days breathing space, I went back into the studio and listened to what I'd recorded before the tour. I made the decision not to scrap anything we'd already done but to keep going and add to it instead. What I'd thought to be average work at best now sounded quite good. I had simply been too close to them. It had been a blessing to be able to let them lie and hear them again with a fresh ear.

Chris and I had been going over possible names for our child and so far had only one. We both wanted and hoped for a girl. One of my favourite songs at the time was the Steve Gillette composition I'd recorded with Matthews Southern Comfort, 'Darcy Farrow'. We both loved the name Darcy and decided that if our baby was a girl that would be her name. If the baby was a boy then we'd have to improvise.

While we were awaiting our baby's arrival, I fleshed out lyric ideas I'd begun in Portugal. I commandeered the living room and figured out chords and melodies to 'Never Again' and a dirge-like, Neil Young-sounding tune called 'Midnight on the Water'. Along with the three or four covers I'd found, one of them being 'Da Doo Ron Ron', we recorded the second half of the album, mixed it all and effectively put the new album to bed. The finished record reflected my attempt to make sense of everything going on around me at the time and that's why it's called *Tigers Will Survive*. I put Chief Satanta of the Kiowa on the cover in contrast to the title. He had believed and trusted in the system and the people running it and was ultimately betrayed.

Before you could say Jackie Robinson, Vertigo wanted to release 'Da Doo Ron Ron' as a single. The track that almost wasn't had become a commercial proposition. Shortly after its release Howard and Blaikley told me that Vertigo had secured me a spot on *Top of the Pops*. Everyone was excited about the possibilities, everyone except me that is. The thought of another hit gave me the horrors and I put my foot down.

'I'm not doing it!' I told them.

As soon as I heard the words *Top of the Pops* I saw the writing on the wall and panicked. I thought, 'What if it does well and that whole Matthews Southern Comfort scenario repeats itself?' I really couldn't cope with the thought of that happening. What I did want, and had tried many times to explain to my managers, was longevity. I wanted to be taken seriously as a singer and more importantly as a songwriter, not some kind of toy that is wound up and trundled onto a stage to mime on the telly. Howard and Blaikley were of the opinion that I was sabotaging my career. I'm not sure that was exactly their concern, but I was definitely obstructing the flow of cash in their direction. However, I was adamant that I would not give in to the demands. The truth was that I still wasn't equipped to handle the disruption that could come with having a hit record. Time has taught me that musicians are defined by one or two songs, when in fact they have a lifetime of material that's equally good or better. I only have to look at my own catalogue to see that. I feel that some of my best work has been ignored. I want people to relate to my music for its creative and emotional merits, not by how many units it is shifting. I believe to this day that I made the correct decision to turn down what everyone around me saw as a unique opportunity.

The worry I had about whether to appear on *Top of the Pops* with 'Da Doo Ron Ron' was nothing when compared to what was happening in real life. Now I had to seriously consider that my first child was about to be born. Both Chris and I felt that with the baby's imminent arrival we needed more space. The flat was very small; two rooms, a kitchen and a bathroom really. Once there were three of us we would need a bit more room to breathe. We hurriedly made the decision to try and move before the baby arrived and contacted an estate agent. She showed us several places in and around the Hampstead area. One house in particular was a gorgeous little two-storey mews cottage right in Hampstead village and well within our price range. As much as both of us liked its old-world charm and convenience, we knew we would outgrow it very quickly and had to turn our backs on it. These days that tiny space sells for more than a million pounds. We found a bigger two-bedroom flat on the second floor of a newer building in Altior Court on Highgate Hill. It was ideal. We swiftly closed on it and moved in.

We were now attempting to become accustomed to a new home and struggling to keep our relationship evenly keeled. We wholeheartedly believed that the arrival of our child would significantly improve things. In the early hours of 5th February 1972, 3:30am to be precise, at the University College Hospital London, our little Darcy, or Darcey as it was misspelled on her birth certificate, made her grand entrance. I wish I could say it was a magical, emotionally charged and awe-inspiring moment for us, but I can't because I wasn't in the room to see it. Chris had gone into labour late the previous night and I'd phoned a taxi to take us to the hospital. On arrival she was hustled off to the delivery room and, despite my protestations, I was left to simmer in the chilly confines of a dark and inhospitable waiting room. I was the only person in there. In my naivety I had presumed that I would be next to Chris throughout Darcy's birth, but it was not to be.

'Out of the question,' they said. 'We have a policy that requires prior notice and you did not give it. We are not prepared for your presence in the delivery room and I'm afraid you will have to wait here until your wife has given birth.'

I didn't remember such notice being requested but presumed we had simply missed it in our preparations. They told me that if Chris insisted on me being there, they could try to facilitate it, but I decided in the moment that she had enough going on. She was already in labour and rather than make a fuss I opted to keep the peace and stay put in the bleakness of the waiting room. At some point I must have fallen asleep and the next thing I knew there was a gentle tapping on my shoulder.

'Congratulations Mr Matthews,' said the nurse, 'your wife has given birth to a beautiful baby girl. They are both well and resting. You should go home and get some sleep. Come back tomorrow morning and you can visit them.'

Reluctantly I left. It was already tomorrow. I couldn't find sleep when I got home and by 10am I was back at UCH to see Chris and for the first time my little girl, with the heady realisation that I was now a father.

IN SPITE OF MYSELF

I was a mill town boy at the start of my life
I was a mill town boy at the start of my life
I heard voices whispering and they kept insisting
That my heart was a different place

I've had a weight on my shoulders all of my life
I've had a weight on my shoulders
And though I could not shake it, I've refused to hate it
And I've carried it in spite of myself

I've had a guardian angel most of my life
I've had a guardian angel most of my life
Sitting on my shoulder, so I would not falter
And I felt him watching over me

Mill town kid's got a right to sing
Breaking away on borrowed wings
This kid's seen everything in spite of himself
He's got a story to tell in spite of himself

I've been a reckless wanderer all of my life
I've been such a reckless wanderer
But I don't regret it and I'll surely bet that
I'm a wiser man in spite of myself

I've seen black clouds hovering over my life
I've seen them black clouds hovering
When I've hit rock bottom and I've been forgotten
But now my head is in a different place

Mill town kid's got a right to sing
Stealing away on borrowed wings
And this kid's seen everything
In spite of himself, he's got a story to tell
In spite of himself

I lay my head, I close my eyes
I slip into the night
Then I say a little prayer from where I lay
I've heard that when a memory fades
A tiny bead of light escapes and leads us to a brand-new day

Mill town kids don't know how to sing
Stealing away on borrowed wings
This kid's heard everything
The warning bells
But there's a story to tell in spite of himself

7. ALONG CAME PLAINSONG

While we were on tour in America, I'd mentioned to Andy and Richard that our little musical unit felt so good that we ought to consider forming a band when we got home. Richard instantly declined as he was already into the planning of a solo career and wanted no distractions. Andy was interested and we decided to discuss it more back in Blighty. I left it at that.

During the completion of *Tigers*, Andy and I discussed what the two of us might possibly do together. We compared music we liked and tried to visualise what that something could be rather than diving in unprepared. We decided it should be an acoustic affair, possibly a quartet that featured vocal harmony. Andy mentioned a bass player he thought would fit, David Richards, who had been a member of his Everyone band. Andy said that David was also a decent piano player and the idea of a bass player who could alternate on piano greatly appealed to me. In the interim, while I'd been a homebody anticipating Darcy's arrival, Andy had contacted Bobby Ronga about him flying over for them to do some road work together. We'd had such a positive experience with him in America that it was possible that Bobby could also fit into our loosely-sewed plans. We decided to give it a try by setting ourselves a task.

One afternoon the four of us got together in the living room of my new flat and took a song we all liked, a Tandyn Almer composition that the Association had recently had a US hit with called 'Along Comes Mary'. It's a relatively complex song with an unusual chord progression, a wide vocal range and quite bizarre lyrics. It was a silly stunt really, but we agreed that if we could come up with a creditable version by dinner time then we'd become a band. The end result was effortless, surprising and very encouraging. By dinner time we shook hands on it.

Now we needed a name. That same evening over a glass of

wine and on a whim, we randomly opened a copy of *The Concise Oxford Dictionary of Music*. Its pages fell open at 450-451, Pizzicato to Plainsong to Planets. Imagine if we'd been of a different mindset, we might now be talking about a band called The Planets or, God forbid, Pizzicato! It felt like a very significant moment for us. We had become a band. We were Plainsong.

Meanwhile, Howard and Blaikley were again busy boys on my behalf and made yet another appointment with Vertigo. They wanted to offer the new band to them. It would effectively kill two birds with one stone, but the record company were in no mood to comply the way that Uni had. They made their stand: 'We don't have to make an offer for Plainsong, we already have Ian Matthews under contract,' they said. Ken and Alan came back deeply disappointed. I thought it over and came up with an idea. They might go for it and they might not. My plan was to say, 'Okay guys, Ian owes you one more album. You are contractually obliged to give him £75,000 to make that album. What if he delivers it to you for a fraction of that, say, £5,000! Then will you let him go?' Basically, I was offering to buy myself out of my own contract for £70,000. I felt incensed that they believed they owned me. They did own my recorded work until the contract ended and that's what they were in fact saying. Miraculously they went for the deal and we were set free to go fishing for a Plainsong contract.

As Plainsong galloped along we seemed to utilise Ken and Alan less and less. Between the four of us in the band, along with Sandy Roberton our producer and unofficial advisor, plus Gemini, our booking agency, there was very little for them to do and I was still handing over twenty-five percent of my earnings to them. We were a self-contained unit and more than able to function without managerial help. Axle Enterprises were quickly becoming expendable, there was nothing for them to be involved in and far less to control than when I was a solo artist. More to the point, the rest of Plainsong had no interest in being managed by Ken and Alan. We had a meeting and reached an agreement for me to buy them out, whereupon Plainsong became a legal partnership.

Howard and Blaikley had been an inspired and fortunate choice of management for me. They had written and produced a lot of huge hits and knew practically everyone in the UK music community and that had worked in my favour. I'm not sure that I ever truly understood them, or how their decision making worked, or even how they ran their enterprise. But I didn't particularly care, that wasn't my motivation. It never occurred to me to wonder if they were honest brokers. I must say I had my suspicions about some of the business dealings they'd done on my behalf, but the results were to my advantage and I was upwardly mobile.

After 'Woodstock' was a smash, I walked into their house and saw two silver discs hanging side by side on the wall. They'd been awarded to Ian Matthews by *Disc* magazine and by the *NME* for sales of over a quarter of a million copies.

'Ken, these awards have my name on them, why is it that I don't have one?' I asked.

He was a little sheepish but finally conceded that I could take one, despite the fact that both had my name on them. There was also the somewhat questionable deal they made with the drink company Southern Comfort on Matthews Southern Comfort's behalf. No one in the band seemed to know just how many cases of that stuff Ken and Alan had been given under my name, but it must have been considerable as it just kept on materialising.

Those incidents paled in comparison to what I discovered years later concerning my Matthews Southern Comfort royalties. Their company Axle Enterprises managed me and took quite a hefty percentage of my earnings. From my share of the royalties I then gave the band half. Since I'd left Axle they had been withholding my royalty cheques and I wasn't quite sure why, or how to go about getting them back. It took me years to resolve, but in the end it was simple. During a conversation with Sandy Roberton at Rockburgh Records in 1979, the topic came up and Sandy said, 'Do you want me to call them and sort it out?' Within a week he had it all ship shape. My statements were brought completely up to date and a fat cheque was deposited in my bank account. Just one of a number of issues that Sandy helped me with during our working relationship and I'll be eternally grateful to him for it.

Howard and Blaikley had been a persuasive force though. Whatever they went after, they seemingly got. I'm not sure how they persuaded Paul Samwell-Smith to produce my first solo album, but I wasn't surprised that they had. The way they got me into and out of binding contracts was magical by any standards. Sure they were in it to make money, what manager isn't? In my book, the ones who say they aren't doing it to make money are the ones you need to watch out for. I may not have even had a career had it not been for their involvement.

Chris and I decided to move yet again. We'd been presented with an opportunity to buy an older house in Gospel Oak, an area of London that sits in the Borough of Camden at the south end of Hampstead Heath, slightly north-west of Kentish Town and only twenty minutes by tube to the West End. It was a three-storey Victorian building next to a major railway line. When we first viewed it, the owner thoughtfully warned us that there might be a lot of noise from the trains. The big diesels had just been brought in and were quite loud. He said that a century of thundering steam trains was bound to have loosened the foundations and he felt it his duty to tell us. But it didn't matter, we already loved the house and bought it regardless. It was a no-brainer really and would mean no extra outlay after selling the Highgate flat, plus we gained an abundance of space. The house had a wonderful feel to it and it became our first real home. Chris took care of all the moving while I knuckled down and made my obligatory album for Vertigo, which I named *Journeys from Gospel Oak* after the daily trips I made from my new home to Sound Techniques studio in Chelsea.

My pals Andy Roberts and Jerry Donahue agreed to work on the recording with me, along with drummer Timi Donald, who would soon feature on the new Plainsong album. We also had Fotheringay's Pat Donaldson playing bass. Because I didn't want to use any of the material I was writing for Plainsong, the songs were mostly culled from my current listening collection. I recorded a

Mickey Newbury song on it called 'Mobile Blue'; Paul Siebel's 'Bride 1945' from his brilliant *Woodsmoke and Oranges* album; 'Sing Me Back Home', one of my favourite Merle Haggard tunes; and 'Met Her on a Plane' by the incomparable Jimmy Webb. I contributed two of my own, 'Knowing the Game', another of my anti-music-business songs, and 'Franklin Avenue', a Hank Williams eulogy. The recording took three days, after which Sandy Roberton and I took two more days to mix it. By now we were coming towards the winter of 1972. The album should have been released the following summer but because of our legal hassles Vertigo quickly lost interest in it and in me. They went as far as to issue an outtake from the album on a sampler of upcoming releases called *Suck It and See*. I can only imagine that after all we'd been through, I wasn't exactly their flavour-of-the-month artist. *Journeys from Gospel Oak* surfaced a couple of years later on an independent label called Mooncrest. I have no idea what sort of deal they made with Vertigo, but it had to have been better than the one Vertigo made with me.

Andy Roberts was very fond of an establishment on Kensington Church Walk called Turret Books. It was owned by a man named Bernard Stone. The shop was a big favourite of the Liverpool poets, many of whom Andy had worked with. He told me that Bernard always kept a bottle of Merlot open for them. It was a great place to browse and listen to the daily literary discussions. One day the bookshop assistant, whose boyfriend was an amateur flyer, suggested a book to Andy by a San Francisco writer called Frederick Goerner. The book was called *The Search for Amelia Earhart*. Amelia was the first woman aviator to fly solo across the Atlantic before disappearing in mysterious circumstances over the Pacific in 1937. Goerner had made four trips to the Marshall Islands in the Pacific Ocean in search of the truth about Amelia. Andy read the book and then excitedly told me all about it. He was full of facts and quotes about what Goerner claimed really happened and eventually passed his copy on to me. It was a fascinating read, hypothesising that Amelia was captured after crashing her plane while spying for the Americans on Japanese controlled islands. By the time I reached the end of the book, Andy had discovered a song by an old-time cowboy songwriter called Red River Dave McEnery. The song was called 'Amelia Earhart's Last Flight', but the lyrics didn't jive at all with Goerner's book, in fact it supported the American government's version of the story and was quite romanticised.

Red River Dave's song said, 'A ship out on the ocean, just a speck against the sky, Amelia Earhart flying that sad day; with her partner, Captain Noonan, on the second of July, her plane fell in the ocean, far away.' I felt we needed to tell Goerner's story, it was far more believable than the official version. So I wrote my song, 'You take it or you leave it, but I'm telling anyhow, there's a story you should know. Amelia was a hero in all of your hearts, and that's all they want you to know,' and called it 'The True Story of Amelia Earhart'.

A lot of people thought at the time, and some do to this day, that the Plainsong album *In Search of Amelia Earhart* was a concept album. But it wasn't. The album garnered a lot of press under that assumption and, to be fair, we didn't do much to discourage it. The fact is, the album is a collection of songs inspired mostly by the music we were listening to at the time. Because we were fascinated by the book about Amelia, we accentuated the album graphics far more than was necessary. The art deco cover has the image of a tiny plane flying across a Japanese-style setting sun. The lengthy sleeve notes go into great detail about Amelia and her disappearance, simply because we were bursting to share the story. It never occurred to us that it might be perceived as a concept album. There are two songs that deal with her directly, Red River Dave's and mine, plus some unintended innuendo in a song called 'I'll Fly Away', which was written in the 1930s by the gospel songwriter Albert E. Brumley.

Concept album or not, I was starting to learn that it's impossible to know who is listening to your music and who likes what it is you're doing. A year after the album was released, I was in New York and a writer friend Karin Berg took me to a club called The Bitter End in Greenwich Village. John David Souther was playing. I knew him but had never seen him play. There were six or seven of us seated on a bench angled sideways to the stage. During the break in JD's performance, Karin told me she wanted to introduce me to her friend. I was sitting on her right and she leaned back to reveal the grinning face of Lou Reed appearing from behind her left shoulder. He looked at me and began to sing 'If you're gonna try, you gotta face the music. If you wanna dance, you gotta call the tune.' I was astonished. My mouth hung open, gaping.

'You know my song?' I managed to stammer.

He leaned into me as if to make a point.

'Ian,' he said, 'I know your song, I know all your songs and I love this damn album. It's a wonderful piece of work. I'm a fan.'

Lou Reed had just told me he's a fan, incredible. Some days it's like that. It's part of what makes this troubadour life so unpredictable and fulfilling. It's always a humbling surprise to me when someone from another genre tells me how much pleasure and inspiration they get from my work. The diversity sometimes astounds me.

I'm told the album sold around 60-70,000 copies worldwide. This did not go unrecognised by our label Elektra and they asked for a second. It hadn't had as good a result as *Later That Same Year*, the last Matthews Southern Comfort album, which sold 165,000 copies in the USA alone, but nonetheless a decent showing for an album that did not have the hit 'Woodstock' on it. Consider that in those days you had to sell upwards of 100,000 to achieve a reasonable chart position and in a relatively short period of time. So I would have understood Elektra's stance had they chosen to not give us the green light for a second album.

One evening, Andy Roberts and I were invited up to Elektra label boss Jac Holzman's hotel room at the Savoy. He was in London on business. It was late. We had a couple of drinks and talked a little Plainsong business. Jac said, 'Would you like to do a line?' I didn't know what that meant. He took a folded white packet from his pocket and tipped a small amount out onto a glass-topped table. With a razor blade he separated it and made three short lines. He rolled a pound note up tightly and leaning over the table, drew one of the lines into his nose. I wasn't sure. Andy said, 'Trust me, I think you'll like it.'

We were encouraged to take Plainsong on the road more. We didn't need much encouragement to be honest. Looking back, it seemed that we were constantly touring. Our booking agency, Gemini, based in London, had a Dutch booker called Frank van der Meijden working for them. We consequently made quite a few trips to the Netherlands that year. Our style of music was very popular there and we did in fact play on a bill with Argent, The Incredible String Band, Focus and The Strawbs at one of the very first Pinkpop festivals. Today it's one of the bigger weekend Dutch festivals. Back in 1972 it was a small, one-day affair.

After the album came out we started to have problems with Bobby Ronga. He had a good heart and was an important member of the band, but for some reason he began drinking quite heavily. It started to affect his and, in turn, our stage performances. It came to a head one night on our way back from a somewhat average show in North Wales. We'd travelled together in one vehicle and somewhere along the return journey Bobby drunkenly called out from a rear seat, 'Stop the car, I have to take a piss.' We were on a dark country road and pulled over. We asked Bobby to go into the nearest field to take care of his business. We waited. Ten minutes slipped by and he hadn't come back. Considering his state, we decided to give him a while longer, but after twenty minutes we went into the field to look for him. He was nowhere to be found and after much discussion we had to decide what to do. Do we wait, do we search some more, do we report him lost or should we just leave him to it and go home? We eventually decided on the latter. It was late, we were tired and cranky, rightly or wrongly we just thought 'fuck him' and drove off. We got back to London feeling incredibly guilty about our decision and stopped at the house Bobby shared with his girlfriend Jill to tell her. By this time it was almost three in the morning. We banged on the door until Jill came down to open it. We told her sheepishly that we had some bad news, we'd lost Bobby. 'What do you mean?' she giggled. 'Bobby's upstairs in bed. He's been home for more than an hour.'

He had apparently taken a piss and in his drunken haze had lost his way out of the field and arrived back at the road around the corner from us. Confused as to why we would have left him and apparently angry too, he began hitchhiking home. By some huge stroke of fortune he had managed to get a lift from a passing car all the way back to London. As Jill was telling us, we remembered seeing a car go by while we were waiting for Bobby, but it never occurred to us that it would stop and he would get in it. Needless to say, we were not happy. We decided as we drove away that he was becoming too much of a liability and something had to be done. Sadly, Bobby had to go.

We struggled on after he left but, just like the Carl Barnwell situation, it wasn't the same without him. The dynamics always change when a member leaves and I felt incompetent as the lone rhythm guitar player. I seemed unable to consistently provide the solid swath of acoustic wash necessary for Andy to play over and we made the decision that one way or another it really had to be a quartet. We speculated as to who might replace Bobby and someone hit upon the idea of asking Paul Siebel. We all loved his music, we'd recorded his song 'Louise' and his 'Any Day Woman' was solidly in our stage repertoire. He was also on the same label as us. But did we really want to go through the process of integrating yet another American into the band? The more we discussed it, the less it appealed to us, but we needed to do something for band morale. I was dispatched to New York to find Paul and ask him.

I tracked him down with the help of Keith Sykes, a southern folkie I'd befriended on an earlier visit. He and Paul were old friends and he knew where to find him. I phoned Paul and we set up a get-together in my hotel room. I had MIWS or, Mild Idol Worship Syndrome where Paul was concerned and desperately wanted it to work. I wish I could say our get-together went swimmingly and that he readily agreed to become part of Plainsong, but that's the stuff of fairy tales. Once we sat down to jam, it became quickly apparent that his once heart-wrenchingly seamless tenor was all but shot. His range was practically gone, his playing was unsteady at best and he hadn't written a new song in quite some time. I left Manhattan bitterly disappointed and daunted at the prospect of having to go through the stress and boredom of auditions once I got back. We decided to soldier on as a trio, but we had to devise a game plan. David thought that maybe if we committed to making a new album it could solidify us. Andy and I had been writing, plus we had a few stage songs we wanted to try putting down on tape, so we booked ourselves into Sound Techniques.

With Sandy Roberton again at the controls, we launched ourselves headlong into our second album, as a trio, temporarily calling it *Now We Are 3*, with the three written backwards. We discussed the kind of album it should be. After my struggles with *Tigers Will Survive*, I wanted to make it sound as different as possible to *Amelia*. Different and simpler. I think we succeeded in both respects.

It was mostly a drum-free album, quite sparse and definitely more lo-fi than the first one; there were no double-tracked acoustic guitars the way we had on *Amelia*. The problem was, we just couldn't get it to gel. No matter which song sequences we tried, it just wouldn't hang together. There was no real cohesion or flow to it. The songs seemed quite diverse. Andy and I were being influenced from opposite directions. I was writing about more personal matters and listening to contemporary songwriters, while his contributions to the album screamed country. It was confusing for a listener. I don't know about the others but I was disappointed with the result. In retrospect, I think maybe we second-guessed ourselves too much, our version of the old sophomore jinx, trying to make a different album than the last one rather than simply agreeing on a style and getting on with it.

We were preparing to deliver the album to Elektra when I received a phone call from Jac Holzman in America. He suggested that at his expense, maybe I could bring it to him rather than send it and we'd listen to it together. I thought it a strange request but nevertheless flew to New York with a test pressing in my bag. Jac picked me up at JFK and we drove upstate to his house. We were sitting down together to listen to it when he said, 'Before we play it, tell me what you think of it.' I didn't want to lie.

'To tell you the truth Jac, I'm not that crazy about it. It isn't as good as *Amelia* and that disappoints me.'

'If you don't like it, then I'm not interested in hearing it.' And that was that.

Over the weekend I learned the real reason for him bringing me all the way from London to his home in Upstate New York. He went on to tell me that he was forming a new label out west called Countryside Records. It was a joint venture he'd entered into with Michael Nesmith, late of The Monkees. Michael had become a solo artist and created a persona for himself called The First National Band. Jac asked me what I thought about flying out west to speak to Michael about the possibility of him producing a solo album for me. It sounded to me like an exciting development in my career and I agreed to go. Before I left, Jac said, 'I want to play you something. I'm thinking of signing this band and I want to hear what you think.' Then he played me the first Queen album. I had never heard anything remotely like it and told him, 'Sign them up!'

I headed to Los Angeles to meet with Michael. I liked him instantly. He was a cross between a grown-up version of the character I'd laughed along with on The Monkees' television series and the serious songwriter I'd heard on record more recently. He was funny, engaging and a zero-tolerance-for-bullshit sort of person. He seemed like someone who had been through the music-business mill and learned a few important lessons along the way. I felt that we made a solid musical connection and that I could work with him. We spent a few days sitting in his Countryside Studio ranch discussing music and tastes and the logistics of such a project. It would mean me leaving my family again to be in Los Angeles for an extended period of time.

We eventually got around to talking about who I would like to play on the record. This was beyond my wildest dreams and I gave Michael a list of players I had recently been listening to and admired. Leland Sklar, the bass player with Carole King; Danny Kortchmar, guitar player with James Taylor; Jimmy Gordon; Sneaky Pete; Larry Knechtel, keyboard player with The Wrecking Crew; Chris Etheridge, the Flying Burrito Brothers bass player. The list went on and on. Michael said, 'Leave it with me. I'll make some calls and do my best to get them for you.' This was not long before Christmas in 1972 and we made plans to begin recording in January 1973.

It was all so exciting. I envisioned it being not just a temporary thing but a real opportunity to possibly live and work in California, a chance to become part of the music scene I'd so greatly admired and occasionally emulated from afar. But I had a family to consider too. I would somehow have to convince Chris that this was an opportunity too good to miss for both of us. It meant moving her and baby Darcy to California and I wasn't sure she would be up for it. Her mom lived just around the corner from us in Palmers Green and was the security and safety net she so desperately craved. I would effectively be taking that away from her and it would then just be Chris, Darcy and me.

As well as the personal considerations, I had the professional ones too, not least of which was the small matter of Plainsong. Without me, I knew there would be no band. Andy and I were the core, the driving force, and the last thing I wanted was to lose my best friend in the process. But the possibility of a career on the West Coast had a solid grip on me and I was unstoppable. When I told them, no one was happy, but David Richards in particular was enraged by my decision. He was convinced that it had been my plan all along to use Plainsong as a vehicle to further my own career. This was far from the truth and I denied it. He called me at the studio in California when I was recording with Michael and let his still festering feelings be known. 'I'll get you back,' he said, 'I'm gonna fuck your wife.' I laughed it off but I knew it would be just like him to try.

I was hesitant about broaching the idea of moving to California with Chris and with good reason. Chris was devoted to her mom and vice versa. She visited her mom every Sunday and Grandma was besotted with baby Darcy. I knew that a move to Los Angeles several thousand miles away would not be well received. If we moved, it was going to severely dent that mother/daughter relationship. I was constantly touring and recording, which meant I was rarely home. Moving to Los Angeles would be no different, but I so desperately wanted to go. I had been listening to contemporary North American singer-songwriters since the late 1960s and it had long been my dream to go to California and be a part of the scene. I naively thought a fresh start in California might be just the cure for us.

Chris had a hundred reasons to not go. 'What about the house?' I thought we should probably hang on to it and try to rent it out. 'What about Mom, my friends, my life.' I was torn. The musician in me simply had to go. The husband and father in me understood and felt her concerns. Was I being selfish and opportunistic, or was I being realistic about our future? The voice in my head kept telling me, 'This could fix things. This could make things right again.' Chris was resistant and for a while we sparred around it. I explained that apart from it being a wonderful career move, it could also be a new beginning for the two of us. We'd leave our mounting problems behind us in England and begin again. Darcy could grow up with wall-to-wall sunshine. I knew I'd be tearing her away from her home and friends but, selfishly, my career was my main concern. I felt that Europe had run its course for me and I needed new musical challenges. Finally she agreed and I prayed I'd done the right thing convincing her. We made plans. I would leave in January, make the album and set things up for them to follow on. Rather than sell our lovely house, we agreed to keep all of our belongings and rent it out as is, on the off chance that things didn't work out…

PART THREE

CHASING RAINBOWS

JIVE PYJAMAS

Nose up, wheels down, coasting into Angel Town
Far as the eye can see an ocean of humanity
So tired, for God's sake, adrenalin, keeps me awake
It's springtime '73, I'm changing my philosophy
Let's go, say when, can it be that late again
First thing, crack of dawn
I'll make peace with that LA morning
Surf's up, so fine, echoes of a different time
Strange days, best forgotten
Man this desert town is getting hotter

Hey there Angel Town, tell me all your dirty secrets
I wonder do you even see me, cruising in your Lamborghini
Say there Angel Town, show me all your dirty laundry
Wet dreams and psychodramas
Where'd you get them jive pyjamas?

Eased down, blended in, such a foreign discipline
Ground shakes, heap big fun, I wonder should I turn and run
Ventura Boulevard sparkles like a Christmas card
Strange days, remembering, how nothing felt quite genuine

True love, or not, I gave it everything I got
Top Ten, flat broke, Jive Town, she's a cruel joke

Dark times, so alone, someday soon I'm going home
Big plans, long, thin rope, I'm humming like a gyroscope
Bad trips, made some, all my best friends, tagged along
Tight-lipped, highly strung, just one more line and then we're done
Boundaries, yeah we crossed em, inhibitions gone, we lost em
Bean Town she's my muse, free transfusion can't refuse it

Nose up, wheels down, coasting into Angel Town
Far as the eye can see an ocean of humanity

Hey there Angel Town, tell me all your dirty secrets
I wonder if you even see me, posing in your cheap bikini
Say there Angel Town, show me all your dirty laundry
Shattered dreams and psychodramas
Where'd you get them jive pyjamas?
Hey there Angel Town, turn me in the right direction
Wet dreams and melodramas, why'd you wear such jive pyjamas?

8. VALLEY HIGHS AND LOWS

I returned to Los Angeles in early January 1973, ready to start recording. It felt like a new beginning for me. I was buzzing with excitement at the prospect of making an album with THE Michael Nesmith.

Michael's wife Phyllis picked me up at LAX and drove us north on Interstate 405 where we joined what seemed like the entire community of southern California creeping towards the beach exits of Santa Monica and Mar Vista. Half an hour later we were making the winding climb out of the LA Basin before descending into a smoggy San Fernando Valley where the 405 turned slightly east towards Sepulveda and the North Hills. It was as if I was seeing Los Angeles for the first time through a kid's eyes as we swept past the mighty Anheuser-Busch brewery on our left and onto the Nordhoff Street exit into what seemed more like a residential area than a setting for a recording studio. The Countryside Ranch rested unassumingly a couple of hundred yards back from where Tupper Street almost came to a dead end. Maybe it was the perfect spot! Easing down through the gears, Phyllis took a cautious left into a long, dirt driveway leading up to the ranch house. The studio itself was a sprawling, stuccoed bungalow with an Olympic-size swimming pool in the back garden. It looked and felt like someone's home but with a studio in it. The two main bedrooms had been converted into the studio; the larger one had become the playing room and the smaller one the control room. The living room was still a living room but when we arrived it was clogged with musicians lounging, swigging coffee, writing charts, comparing musical ideas and banging away on acoustic guitars. I was at ease in the creative atmosphere the moment I walked in.

There was a slight hitch. Michael had tried to get the musicians I'd requested, but most of them were unavailable.

'Which ones?' I asked.

'Well,' he said, 'to tell the truth, I couldn't get any of them, but no worries, I have a terrific house band and they're excited to be working with you. What do you think?'

What did I think? I'd been duped, that's what I thought. I didn't verbalise it because what choice did I have? I was here, the studio and band were booked, my house in London was being rented out and my family were making plans to join me. I don't believe Michael was being malicious in his planning – opportunistic maybe – but it was done with a good heart and in his position I may have made the same play.

All things considered, I was still in southern California and about to make a new solo album. I would make a good one, regardless of the disappointment. I knuckled down and began recording with the Countryside house band. Michael did manage to bring in a couple of my heroes; the incomparable Roland White – Clarence's brother – played some mean mandolin, while Byron Berline, originally of The Dillards, brought his inimitable fiddle sound to the party.

I aptly named the album *Valley Hi*. As good as the album is, stylistically it was not the one I'd planned to make. I had flown the Plainsong coop to get away from a country sound and here I was compromising myself yet again towards that style of recording with a genre I was loath to explore yet once more tentatively dangling my foot in. Over the years my displeasure with *Valley Hi* has been well-documented and I see no reason to create yet another post-mortem. I had the power to dictate the direction the record went in, but I didn't use it. Instead, I was a good boy and went with the programme, making the best of an uncomfortable situation. Had I stuck to my musical ideals, rather than wanting to please everyone by showing my cooperative side, it could have – and would have – been a significantly different album.

One song we recorded for the album was a rearrangement of Steve Young's 'Seven Bridges Road', which inadvertently created folklore history. A few years later I found myself at Don Henley's house. In his sparsely furnished living room he had a simple, unassuming sound system with a stack of LPs leaning against the wall next to it. At the front of the stack was a copy of *Valley Hi*. In 1980, the Eagles released a live album and on it was an almost note for note version of my arrangement of the song, but the sleeve notes claimed that it had been 'learned from their friend Steve Young in San Diego'. I knew that they hadn't and they knew it too. None of the band ever acknowledged their sourcing of the song until twenty years later on a greatest hits package where in the sleeve notes Glenn Frey talks about how they took the arrangement from me. In a way they did, but let it go on record that up until now I've all too easily taken credit for that arrangement, when in fact, had it not been for Michael Nesmith's acoustic flatpicking skills, it could have been a completely different kettle of fish. Michael was equally responsible for birthing that version of the song. Possibly a different version wouldn't have appealed to Don Henley the way it did and the ensuing controversy may never have happened. Steve Young later confided in me that of all the numerous covers of his song, mine was always his favourite.

Chris and Darcy followed me out to California that spring. Phyllis Nesmith had found us a house on Vesper Avenue in an area called Van Nuys in the San Fernando Valley. It was a little wood-framed bungalow with yellow stuccoed walls and a front door that opened up straight into the living room, a California feature. When it was built it had been smaller, but now a third bedroom had been added, a step-down affair into what had once been the garage. Chris and I made it the master bedroom. The house came with the bonus of a fair-sized swimming pool in the backyard that I'd just float around in as I couldn't swim.

When *Valley Hi* was released it received wonderful reviews. The foremost weekly business magazines *Billboard* and *CashBox* made it their 'Record of the Month' alongside Van Morrison's *Hard Nose the Highway* and Neil Young's *Time Fades Away*. Between the Countryside Studio and Elektra Records there was a giggling hysteria and everyone seemed quite pleased with themselves. They all loved the album. I felt that I'd failed in what I had set out to do. It lacked dignity and leaned too far towards pseudo country. I had wanted a record that would be spoken of in the same hushed tones as Jackson Browne or James Taylor, and this record would never allow me that. This was not the one. I was disappointed, but resilient. There would be another album and this time I would make sure it was on my terms. I was slowly learning the game. At day's end, *Valley Hi* was only an album, a musical statement in a world full of musical statements. And whether I like it or not, it's a good record. If we were to ask a hundred people which Ian Matthews album is their all-time favourite, I'd lay money that more than half of them would say *Valley Hi*. At that time I had trouble celebrating it, but that aside, the sun was shining, we were in Los Angeles in a cute little house with a swimming pool. How could life be any better?

Thanks to Michael and Phyllis we made friends quickly in LA and Chris and Darcy seemed to be enjoying the lifestyle. LA is a huge city but the musical community is a village. It was said of LA that once you befriended one of the budding songwriters, chances were that sooner or later you'd be friends with them all. I put myself about, made the scene as they say, wanting to be part of the songwriter community and slowly but surely I was being integrated. I already had a nodding relationship with Glenn Frey and Randy Meisner and with them as my passport, I went knocking. Their friends soon became my friends and I slowly became accepted as the new kid in town.

Having the opportunity to work with Michael was a big feather in my cap, which I displayed with pride. It feels good when you can casually name-drop a legend. Had it not been for meeting Michael, I might never have had one of my most memorable Sunday mornings ever. Imagine eating breakfast in a luxury hotel in Estes Park, Colorado and being serenaded by the Edwin Hawkins Singers with a belting rendition of 'Oh Happy Day'. And had I not worked with the Countryside band I may never have met guitarist and songwriter Jay Lacy, who was to become an important collaborator for me.

Skip Van Leeuwen, who was Michael's business partner and dealt with the finances at the Countryside Studio, was a former National Motocross champion. He had somehow become my unofficial chauffer. One day he said to me, 'Ian, I'm tired of giving you rides. You need to learn how to drive and I'm just the guy to teach you.' Not only did Skip teach me to drive, he did it in four lessons and drove me to my official test. It was simple to pass a driving test in California in 1973. If you could understand multiple choice questions and you could steer, then you could drive. After I passed he took me to buy my first car, a little white automatic Mazda with one of those new Wankel engines. Wankel, what an unfortunate name.

Chris had initially liked Los Angeles. I could tell she liked the constant sunshine and the easy pace, it shone in her face, but she hated being away from her mother and her English friends. The euphoria of being in California slowly faded and the combination of her being homesick and me not being around proved too much for her. It's my belief that she had already made her mind up that this was only going to be a temporary move. I fully realised it one day when she told me that she wasn't going to bother making any more new friends because she'd only have to say goodbye to them again.

There was little breathing space between album release and subsequent touring. Dana Rhodes told me that she had an idea that might help with life at home. Dana was the wife of the pedal steel guitar player Red 'Orville' Rhodes. Red was an important member of the Countryside band and Michael's playing partner. Dana's Mexican maid knew of a young girl looking for work as a nanny and if I was interested she would make all the necessary arrangements for us. Los Angeles was full of Mexican girls who lived with their employers during the week and went back to their families at the weekends. Most of these girls were illegal immigrants and therefore had to be paid in cash. We agreed a weekly amount before gratefully and somewhat hastily welcoming her into our home as I put a band together and hit the road, crisscrossing the country for six weeks, playing opening slots for the group America, calling Chris whenever possible. I came home from my tour to an empty house and didn't know what to think. I phoned Michael. Phyllis answered the phone.

'Ian, you need to call Dana Rhodes.'

I phoned Dana. She said, 'I think you should come over here as soon as you can.' I got in my car and drove around to the Rhodes' house. Darcy was playing with Dana and Red's three kids.

'Where's Chris?' I asked.

'She's had a breakdown and I brought Darcy here for safe keeping,' Dana told me.

It was serious. The maid had quit and Chris had apparently phoned Dana confessing that she had become very depressed while I was away and had turned to consuming drugs and drinking herself to sleep. She couldn't handle being in a strange city alone and wanted to kill herself. Dana had immediately driven over and taken her to the UCLA medical centre to ask about medication. They assessed her and recommended that she go to a place called Camarillo for further evaluation.

The town of Camarillo has a large psychiatric facility in idyllic surroundings in the Simi Valley, north of LA. I'd heard of it. This was where Charlie Parker had recuperated. He spent six months in there attempting to recover from drug and alcohol abuse after being jailed for setting fire to his bed in a hotel. He wrote his famous tune 'Relaxin' at Camarillo' while he was there. I was very concerned and more than a little scared.

When I arrived at Camarillo, the doctor told me that Chris was under heavy sedation. They asked me to wait in the garden while they brought her out to see me. One on either arm, the nurses slowly walked Chris out. In her drugged state, I couldn't get any sense from her. I felt incredibly guilty, responsible and quite ashamed of myself. I'd moved this delicate thing away from her support system and then left her and Darcy alone in a city full of strangers and waltzed off on tour. Now I needed to do the right thing and get her the hell out of that place. I asked the doctors if I could take her home. They told me she had come in voluntarily and they couldn't legally keep her. She was free to leave any time, however, they would have to ease her off her medication first.

I went home and drove back to Camarillo the following evening. Chris was far more communicative by then but still in a foggy state. I took her back to the house on Vesper. We stopped by the Rhodes' house, picked up Darcy and brought her home with us. It was obvious that Chris couldn't cope with taking care of our daughter in her new surroundings and I was committed to going back on the road in a few weeks' time.

Chris and I sat down and discussed the choices to be made. I could cancel the tour, but it was an important time for me and if I cancelled it could mean losing face with Elektra. Possibly even my recording contract. I could do what Chris was angling for and go back to London where I could try and pick up the pieces. That would basically mean giving up on the USA and my budding career. The third option, which I didn't particularly like, meant letting Chris and Darcy go back to London without me while I stayed in California to work. It was agonising, but what realistic choice did I have? Chris agreed that as gut-wrenching as the decision was, it seemed the only practical one and had to be. I called to tell our renter Joy in Gospel Oak that Chris was coming back and she'd have to leave. Timing was so tight that she had to be out in a fortnight. She said it was impossible. I said, 'Well, you can also stay there, but you need to know that Chris is coming back with Darcy and she's not in very good shape.' Joy said she would find somewhere else to live.

To this day I get a thick, tight, emotional knot in my stomach whenever I think about that time and the decision we made. I so clearly see now that I should have cancelled the tour, stayed with them and helped them integrate. Nothing is as important as family. I know that now. But I was young and overflowing with ambition. I was selfish and chose to pursue my own dream and let my family go. In doing so, I missed seeing my little girl grow up.

I called a close friend, Mike, an aspiring singer-songwriter, and asked if he would consider taking them back to London for me. He said he'd never been there but if I covered all of his expenses and made sure he had a place to stay, he would do it for me. I agreed and a week later I drove them all to the airport, came home and had a minor breakdown of my own.

My life felt like a mess. I tried to focus on work but it was difficult and more often than not impossible. My head was full of guilt. I called Chris as often as I could. It broke my heart to hear my little girl's voice so far away, asking to see her daddy. I spoke to Chris's mom and she said that Chris was not improving and that she was concerned. Chris was still drinking heavily and regularly smoking marijuana. I told her I was on my way and flew back to London to find out what was going on.

When I knocked on the door of the house in Gospel Oak, there was no answer. I knocked louder and tried the handle. The door was locked. I went next door and found Darcy there. She was being taken care of by the neighbour. I saw that she had been given a bad haircut and her lovely long golden hair had been chopped short. The neighbour told me that Chris wasn't doing too well and she wouldn't get out of bed. 'She's next door. I have a key if you want to let yourself in.' Chris was in bed, drunk, or high. I couldn't tell which. I was terribly upset and accused her of being a bad mother. She said, 'That's rich, coming from an absent father.' Both of these things were true.

I took my coat off and went around the house looking for bottles and found them stashed in every cupboard and drawer. I emptied them all and threw everything away. I felt responsible for creating all of this unhappiness with my selfish behaviour. I became outwardly emotional and lost my temper. I told Chris I was going down to the passport office in the morning to have Darcy added to my passport.

'I'm here for ten days. You need to get help and clean up or I'm taking her back to California with me.'

I called Chris's mom and told her the same thing and she came over. She was distraught and asked me to give her a week, promising to turn things around. 'It will break our hearts if you take Darcy,' she said tearfully. It's hard to pinpoint the exact moment, but at some point during that following week something clicked for Chris. With professional help and her mom's, Chris seemed to grasp the reality of the situation. She emerged from her depressed state and began to take care of herself and Darcy. Her zest returned, she got up in the mornings and started eating properly and dressing nicely. She began looking like the Chris of old. I went back to California alone, with an ache in my heart.

Darcy began writing to me, simple little letters with child's drawings on. I still treasure them. They make me cry to look at them. I made her audio cassette tapes. I read books onto them so that she could hear my voice. It's heartbreaking to think about what we went through. I still cannot find it in me to completely forgive myself. I've tried many times. It's a physical hurt when it comes to me. I've spoken to Darcy about it often. She tells me, 'It's okay Dad, we're fine, let it go,' but I can't. California was a beautiful experiment that failed miserably.

I stayed in the house on Vesper after Chris and Darcy left until one day Mrs Kaufman the landlady came by to collect the rent.

'This place is too big for you now,' she said, 'I've got a lovely bachelor pad in North Hollywood. Why don't you think about moving there? Let me take you to look at it.'

The smaller house was fine and I took it. Mrs Kaufman was a very sweet lady, she even helped me move. The new place was within walking distance of the famous Palomino Club in a more Hispanic neighbourhood. Everyone was nice to me and I felt safe, I was simply another minority moving into a minority area.

Elektra, or Elektra/Asylum as it had now become, were suggesting I make a second album. It had been a year of changes for Jac Holzman. He had sold the company to Warner Brothers, who in turn had merged Elektra with David Geffen's label to form Elektra/Asylum. I was now on the same label as Jackson Browne and the Eagles, with Geffen running the show. There was no doubt that Geffen was a music man, but it seemed to me that his roster of Asylum artists were being favoured. With Jac no longer in the picture, I felt that I'd lost a friend. He had recently flown me to New York on the Warner's jet to attend his going-away party. I had managed to corner him briefly to voice concerns about my future at the label. He assured me that Geffen would treat all of the artists on the combined labels alike, nothing significant would change and not to worry. I wasn't the only Elektra artist feeling nervous about the future, even some of the label's bigger acts were edgy. Both Judy Collins and the Morrisonless Doors had their doubts and let it be known. Borderline acts such as myself were downright pessimistic. I felt more than a little betrayed that Jac had enticed me to California and then sold me on.

Elektra suggested that I work at their studios on La Cienega Boulevard in Hollywood. After the Countryside experience I told them I'd like to produce it myself. They agreed to it on the condition that they chose the engineer. They paired me with one of their excellent house engineers, Fritz Richmond. Fritz was a musician from the East Coast and back in the sixties had been the jug player with the Jim Kweskin Jug Band. He'd realised the limitations of what he was doing and had made the transition to recording engineer. Before moving west, Elektra had given Fritz a job in their New York studio. He was a terrific engineer and he and I were a good match. He was open to my production ideas and we saw eye to eye on most of the musical decisions. He would regale me with tales about the good old days in Boston, when John Sebastian, later of The Lovin' Spoonful, was in the jug band. He still had healthy connections to his playing past and facilitated me by bringing in the fiddle-playing legend Richard Greene from a band called Sea Train.

I wanted the album to be as different as possible to *Valley Hi*, both in sound and style, and set about selecting players accordingly. I'd recently been on a long tour with the band America. They'd had a string of international hits with songs such as 'A Horse with No Name', 'Ventura Highway' and, more recently, Willis Alan Ramsey's 'Muskrat Love'. During the tour I'd become friendly with their rhythm section – bassist David Dickey and drummer Willie Leacox. They had laid down nice fat solid grooves on stage and I invited them to record with me.

The basic sound of the record revolved around the acoustic guitar playing of my friend Steve Gillette. Steve was a dyed-in-the-wool folkie who'd written the song 'Darcy Farrow' which we'd named Darcy after. I had met Steve and become friends with him during my first year in LA. He would form the soft underbelly of the album.

With the artistic freedom I'd been given, it was an exciting record to make and I did it my way, using a much darker, less 'in your face' sound than *Valley Hi*, featuring a heavy repeating reverb on the lead vocals. I wanted to give it a trademark sound and have it be more of an LA recording. My friend from Steely Dan, Jeff 'Skunk' Baxter, laid down chunks of electric lead guitar for me. As well as writing two new tunes, I integrated a couple of tracks from the aborted second Plainsong album, plus one from *Valley Hi*, beefing them up by adding ex-Rhinoceros lead guitarist Danny Weis and his piano-playing friend Michael Fonfara. I was searching for a contemporary, cutting-edge rocky sound, yet still somehow have it reflect my acoustic roots. I chose Danny Whitten's Crazy Horse song 'I Don't Wanna Talk About It' and employed the slide guitar wizardry of David Lindley, Jackson Browne's sidekick, to play on it. Nothing felt off limits.

While we were in the studio, I discovered that Dylan's old sidekick, the infamous Bob Neuwirth, was in the big room next door recording a solo album with producer Tommy Kaye and a host of special guests. On a daily basis I would encounter the constant stream of 'famous' faces either on their way into, or out of Studio A. One afternoon I ran into the man himself and we got into a conversation in the hallway, after which he extended an invitation to me to sing backgrounds on a couple of his songs.

I arrived at the appointed time, naively believing I would be the only one there. I sauntered casually into the room to find three big voices – Geoff Muldaur, Mama Cass Elliot and Dusty Springfield – gathered around a classic Neumann microphone in the centre of the studio, already running through parts. To say that I was nervous and more than a little intimidated would be stating it mildly. I felt out of my league. They all had the power, tone and control that one associates them with and I wasn't quite sure where I could fit in. But Bob had been hearing a blend in his head and that blend effortlessly materialised. I was honoured to be standing elbow-to-elbow with three of my peers, but at the same time I realised that they were just a group of singers who, like me, had been hired to do a job. We were all in it together, to make Bob's music sound as good as we possibly could. Once I forgot about my nerves and found a place to fit in, I became at ease working with them, forgetting for the time being who they were. I laughed at their self-deprecating session humour; at one point Dusty chastised herself for screeching and Geoff, realising he was actually singing a higher part than Cass, swapped with her. It was all about the job at hand and doing what came naturally. They left an impression on me of being three easy-going people, comfortable in their skins, happy to have been asked and making sure they left no rough edges.

When I felt I'd finished my album, I played it for David Geffen. He said he liked it all except for the Richard Thompson song 'The Poor Ditching Boy'. It was a little too folky he said and suggested I swap it for something more contemporary. He gave me a copy of Tom Waits's first album and asked me to listen to a song called 'Ol' 55'. I loved the sentiment of the song and immediately had an idea for a slightly more up-tempo version, completely unaware that Geffen had already pitched the same tune to one of his premier acts, the Eagles. He was covering the bases I suppose.

I called the album *Some Days You Eat the Bear*, a phrase I'd heard my engineer Fritz use many times during the sessions. Once again, the record received a wonderful critical response and made it all the way to number seven in the 'alternative' album chart behind Zappa and Captain Beefheart but failed to sell in any significant numbers, giving David Geffen reason enough to not want to renegotiate my contract. The deal I'd made with Jac was for two albums and that's how it looked like staying. Geffen, however, by his own confession was a fan and decided to give me one more chance before deciding whether to end my stay at Elektra.

'I'll tell you what we'll do,' he said. 'We have an engineer working with us part-time. His name is Emitt Rhodes and he has his own studio in Hawthorne, down near the airport. I want you to go there and make a demo with him. Maybe three or four songs. I'll listen to it and then make a final decision.'

Emitt Rhodes! Surely not the same guy whose writing I'd admired from afar. The man who had written 'Time Will Show the Wiser'. The same person whose solo album I could not get off my turntable when it was released a few years back. This man was the stuff legends were built around and I was being asked to consider recording with him. I leapt at the opportunity.

Emitt and I recorded three songs: a pseudo reggae version of The Young Rascals' 'Groovin''; a George Harrison song that I'd heard on an Alvin Lee record called 'So Sad'; and a new one of my own, 'For the Lonely Hunter'. Emitt was inspiring to work with and I thought the demos from his small studio sounded wonderful. I was anxious to play them to Geffen. He wasn't impressed. David Geffen had a solid reputation for being artist friendly, but he was also a practical, hard-headed businessman. That day I met with the businessman. I knew I was improving both as a singer and a songwriter and had hoped that would be enough. Geffen was more interested in the numbers and didn't feel I'd done enough to convince him that one more album would significantly change anything. Selling records was his business and it was time for me to move on. However, by allowing me to make those demos, he'd unwittingly done me a huge favour when it became time to search for a new musical home.

RHYTHM OF THE WEST

You can find it, you can lose it, you can pass it on by
You can hear it, you can hold it, you can feel it in a sigh
You can fall out of favour when you're thinking you've been blessed
You can sit and wonder why to the rhythm of the west

You can love it, you can cry it, you can rock it to sleep
You can steal it, you can hide it, you can buy it on the street
You can fall out of favour when you're giving it your best
You can run yourself in circles to the rhythm of the west

You can talk it, you can wail it, you can take it to heart
You can sing it, though you hate it
And you've known it from the start
You can fall out of favour when you're thinking you've been blessed
You can hesitate for ever to the rhythm of the west
You can fall out of favour when you're giving it your best
You can sit and wonder why to the rhythm of the west

9. GO NORTH YOUNG MAN

One would think that as a musician living in Los Angeles that drugs would have made an impact on my life, but they didn't. I'm lucky in that I'm not of an addictive nature. Of course I've tried things, but never the hard stuff. Mind-altering drugs passed me by completely. I was never curious enough to want to try them.

Once in 1974 I was visiting Gary Kurfurst, who managed me briefly after I had recorded *Some Days You Eat the Bear*. Gary later went on to have success managing The Ramones. He lived in Upstate New York, not far from Sing Sing prison. One night he took me to a party in a Manhattan apartment to meet Leslie West, the guitar player from Mountain, who he also managed. Gary introduced us and Leslie asked if I wanted a line.

'Sure,' I said. 'A small line of cocaine might loosen me up a bit.'

We went into the bathroom and he cut out two lines, took one for himself and offered me the other. The weird thing was, the cocaine was pink. I thought it strange, but didn't want to appear naive so I didn't ask why. I did my line and went back to the party. Ten minutes later I started to feel dizzy and nauseous and hurried to the toilet. I locked the door behind me and, kneeling over the toilet bowl, I began to wretch and vomit over and over and over. I couldn't stop. I had the dry-heaves. Gary came looking for me, realised what had happened and went to find Leslie to give him a piece of his mind. I had apparently mistaken heroin for cocaine. Leslie had figured, 'What the hell, he's a musician, he's one of us. He's done this before.' I hadn't and never will again. Needless to say, I missed the party.

On that same trip east, an old friend of Gary who restored old cars came over one day. He'd just finished working on a 1960s Porsche 356C and invited us over to see his work. The car was a black beauty with a red leather interior. I fell in love with it there and then and offered to buy it. The only problem was that it had a manual gear shift and I only knew how to drive automatics. Gary's friend wanted the sale to happen and offered to give me some quick lessons. We went out a couple of times in his souped-up Chevrolet Impala. It was what the Americans call a muscle car and a temperamental devil. Try as I might, I couldn't seem to find a balance between clutch and accelerator. For two days I started and stalled and started and stalled that car and in the end gave it up as a bad job, but I wasn't about to be deterred from buying the Porsche.

I called my friend Joel Tepp in Los Angeles and asked him if he would consider flying over to the East Coast to help me drive the Porsche back to LA. I'd first met Joel during my early days at the Troubadour hoot nights while he was playing slide and harmonica with Bonnie Raitt. He had worked with me on *Some Days You Eat the Bear* and I knew of his love for Porches. He leapt at the chance. I bought him his air fare and within a couple of days he'd flown into JFK. Before we headed west he gave me a couple of gear changing lessons and then off we went with Joel at the wheel. He drove for the first few hundred miles and then said to me, 'Just watch me Ian. Notice where my feet are when I change gear and listen to the sound of the engine.' He went on to explain, 'It's all about feel and that's what you need to learn,' which is exactly the sort of thing you might expect a musician to say.

Joel took the Porsche almost into Ohio and then said, 'Right, it's your turn.' We swapped seats and it was much easier than I had imagined. The only mishap we had was when the fan belt broke just outside of Indianapolis. We called a tow truck and spent the night in a cheap motel while the garage ordered a new belt and installed it. We pulled into LA late on the third day. I'm guessing there are few people who learned to drive stick whilst driving across America, even less who did it in a vintage Porsche. Ironically, I only kept that car for six months before selling it on to Joel, but I never went back to automatic cars again.

My songs were being published through Island music and I took my three-song demo recording to my publisher Lionel Conway. I'd first met Lionel back in the early 1970s when he'd asked me if

I fancied producing an album for a new band called Longdancer. He had been approached by Elton John's new Rocket label who were looking for someone to work with a young folk-rock act recently transplanted from Northumberland to London. Lionel thought of me and I helped produce their debut album *If It Was So Simple*. Longdancer featured a teenage songwriter called Dave Stewart who would go on to far greater things. It was apparent even back then that Dave would at some point become a force to be reckoned with.

Lionel ran the publishing department for Island records. I'd been at Island as an artist when I was in Fairport Convention and later when I made the Plainsong album I became a contracted Island songwriter. By the time I got to LA, Lionel was still my publisher and had transferred from London to Hollywood. Lionel listened to my demo.

'I have an idea,' he said. 'I've just had a producer in here by the name of Norbert Putnam, he's making a record with the revamped Flying Burrito Brothers for Columbia and they're looking for songs. I'd like to play your song "For the Lonely Hunter" to Norbert and see what he makes of it.'

Norbert listened to my song and said he loved it and would take it to the band to see what they could do with it. He later came back and spoke with Lionel.

'This is a great song, but we can't use it. The band cannot play it. They can't find the feel the song needs.' He then added, 'But if the writer has any more compositions like this, I'd be interested in making a record with him.'

Don Ellis was running Columbia Records on the West Coast and had high regard for Norbert. Together, Lionel and Norbert went to play him the Hawthorne demos and pitch me as a potential Columbia artist. Don liked what he heard and that's how I got my next recording contract with Columbia courtesy of David Geffen and Asylum Records who had paid for my demo tape.

Since Jac Holzman left Elektra and Geffen was installed, Michael Nesmith's Countryside Records deal had disintegrated. The studio had been dismantled and the house band dissolved. After the *Valley Hi* recordings, I had stayed in touch with guitarist Jay Lacy. I'd recently set about jigsawing a touring band together and called Jay on the off chance he might be interested in being part of it. My timing was perfect. Jay was at a loose end and agreed. We began writing together and wrote a song called 'Rhythm of the West' ostensibly for the new Columbia album. I took the song to Lionel and he asked if he could play it for someone. He said he knew that Glen Campbell was looking for songs for a new record and he wanted to play 'Rhythm of the West' for Glen's producer. Several days later Lionel called me.

'Glen's producer likes the song, but he doesn't understand it,' he said.

'What's not to understand?'

Apparently he didn't understand what the title meant and had suggested a change of lyric. He wanted to know if I would change the title and the lyric to 'The Rhythm of Love'. He thought if I did that he could persuade Glen to record it. Now, I'm somewhat of a purist and once a song passes muster I'm loathe to mess with it and I told Lionel that. He looked at me quizzically in the eye and said, 'Ian, this is Glen Campbell we're talking about, think of what it could do for your career.' But I still wasn't sure and went to see Jay. Jay was pragmatic about the situation.

'Look, let's just do it,' he said. 'We have our version, let's do another for Glen and you never have to hear it again.'

I was still dubious, but against my better judgement we spent an afternoon making the changes, morphing it into 'The Rhythm of Love'. Lionel liked it and passed it on to Campbell's producer who came back a week later saying, 'Glen doesn't like it.' There and then I made a solid pact with myself that I would never compromise my songs again, for anyone. I'd gone against my natural instinct and it had backfired. From here on, I told myself, they would either accept the song I'd written or find another one. No exceptions.

We recorded my first album for Columbia at Quadraphonic Studios in Nashville. It was co-produced by Norbert Putnam and Glen Spreen, an LA-based arranger/producer. The studio was co-owned by Norbert, who had built an impressive reputation in the south as a high-profile session bass player – he was part of the Muscle Shoals set-up and was brought in from Alabama to play for Elvis in 1965. Norbert had been a child prodigy. His first session, at the age of sixteen, was when he played bass for Arthur Alexander on the studio recording of 'You Better Move On'. The other co-owner of the studio was David Briggs, a piano player who had made his mark when he was just fourteen. He was part of Elvis Presley's touring band and had played on 'How Great Thou Art'. Norbert and David were both members of Area Code 615, the Nashville-based band of crack session musicians whose best known tune was 'Stone Fox Chase'. Folks in England know it better as the theme tune to the BBC's *The Old Grey Whistle Test*.

I liked Norbert. He was warm, funny and extremely musical. One day he told me why he'd stopped playing bass. After a session one time, the group of musicians called in to a local bar. Norbert had never bothered buying a case for his bass and carried it slung across his shoulder by the strap. David Briggs once told me that if Norbert had had a few drinks he would sometimes drag it down the street behind him. Whenever he'd go into a bar, if he had his bass with him he would more often than not leave it outside, propped against the window where he could see it and everyone in town knew whose it was. Well, apparently not everyone. After the drinking session Norbert discovered that his bass was gone and rather than bothering to report it, he just went home. According to him and David Briggs, who backed up the tale, he never replaced it and never played a bass session again. When I asked him why, he said, 'Somebody stole my bass man. Fuck it.' He had a very dry sense of humour.

I told him I needed to rent a car while I was in Nashville.

'Don't rent one,' he said, 'I'll loan you one. I have a spare. Come over to the house and get it.'

When I arrived at his house I saw a pretty, light-blue 450SL Mercedes sitting in the driveway.

'You can borrow that,' he said.

'I'm afraid to drive that car Norbert. What if I dent it?'

He simply shrugged and said, 'Come on Ian, it's just a car!' I thought, yeah, just $30,000 worth of car. Nevertheless, I took it and drove around Nashville for a month feeling very cool.

I took my road band to Nashville and recorded the album tracks in just a week and then sent them back to LA. After they had left Norbert said, 'I think we could use one more track.' I told him how much I liked Van Morrison's 'Brown Eyed Girl' but the problem was, the band had gone back to the coast. 'It's not a problem,' said Norbert, 'I know plenty of good players.' He simply called his Area Code pals, who learned the song in ten minutes flat, came up with a great arrangement on the spot and had the master track recorded inside forty-five minutes. We did it in just two takes with me doing a guide vocal. What had been an afterthought almost became a hit. Columbia released it as my debut single and everywhere I went it was on the radio. Friends would call and congratulate me on my hit. I started to think that maybe it was, but for whatever reason it never quite made the transition from radio hit to sales.

After that final recording session, Norbert and Glen told me I could go home while they finished the album.

'But I want to stay for the mixing,' I said.

'Look,' they replied, 'we've spoken to your people at Columbia and you don't need to be here. We prefer to handle it with just the two of us.'

I'd never been thrown out of my own sessions before but realised they were serious and that I'd better do some fancy dancing if I wanted to stay. So I promised solemnly to be a good boy, not have an opinion, to speak when I'm spoken to and to just sit and listen. They finally agreed to let me stay. Their rules of etiquette were: 'There are musicians and there are producers. The musicians play and the producers produce and ne'er the twain shall meet.' I believe that artists should have a voice and not simply be a vehicle for production. That's why we're called the artist.

With the album *Go for Broke* finished and put to bed, I was back in Angel Town and ran into Mrs Kaufman at the supermarket. I told her I was feeling a tad cut off living in North Hollywood. I missed my old neighbourhood and asked if she possibly had a house for me back in Van Nuys? She said she thought she might have one about to be vacated, though it was bigger and would cost a bit more. It was an old two-bedroom, wood-framed house, not unlike the first one on Vesper, but without the pool. I looked, liked it and rented it.

During my LA years my association with Lionel Conway also became social. He introduced me to some of his expat friends and I began playing what the Californians call 'pickup soccer' games in Coldwater Canyon. We played on a City recreation field right where Coldwater flattens out on the Hollywood side. We'd put together teams made up of both resident and touring musicians plus record-business people to play games against each other. Amongst the regulars were Rod Stewart, Robert Plant, some members of the Average White Band and a couple of lads from Badfinger. Supertramp would sometimes stop by too. If one of the record companies was footing the bill, we occasionally got a proper referee.

Joe Bugner, the heavyweight boxer, came down one Saturday afternoon for a run out. At the time Bugner had just gone fifteen rounds in the second of his two fights with Muhammad Ali. After their first fight, Ali and his manager Angelo Dundee declared that Joe would one day be world heavyweight champ. I found myself on the opposite team to Joe and began flitting around on the wing as usual. Joe made one hell of a burly defender. I chased a ball that he was obviously going to get to first and rather than back off, just for kicks I decided I'd give him a nudge. As he trapped the ball under his right foot I ran right at him. He watched me coming, incredulous. Why would the man who stood up to Ali be concerned about some runty, long-haired musician running at him? Needless to say he didn't budge an inch and it was as if I'd run full speed into the white cliffs of Dover. I saw stars. Everyone howled with laughter as Joe grinned down at me, pulled me upright by my shorts and then good-naturedly slapped me on the back, knocking me down again.

A month later I broke my right little toe and that was my football over for a while. The doctor told me there was no way to splint a little toe and gave me pain pills. I was laid up in my house for two weeks, crawling around on all fours like a dog. I stayed in bed most of the time reading and watching TV. The problems occurred in the mornings when I woke up and wanted a cup of tea and biscuits. I had to crawl to the kitchen, careful not to bang my elevated toe on the door frames and slowly push my breakfast tray before me, back to the bedroom, feeling very sorry for myself.

I put a good band together, based around myself and Jay on guitars; him playing lead and me on rhythm. Jay had a great jazz feel and the better we became, the more I wanted to make it jazzier. We now had the players to pull it off. We had a wonderfully inventive saxophone player, Steven Hooks. I introduced him on stage as Captain Hooks. We swapped our rock organist, Bobby 'The Great White' Wright for Charlie Harwood, a far more jazzy pianist. And finally, our drummer Bobby Guidotti left us for The Pointer Sisters at which point we brought in one of LA's finest, a man named Tris Imboden. Tris was from Laguna Beach, south of LA. As was Don Whaley, our jovial, somewhat rotund bass player. He and Tris had played in a band together down there. Don had a pitch-perfect, high nasal vocal sound that slotted in right above mine, creating faultless harmonies. We toured steadily promoting *Go for Broke* and this was the band that I took into Larrabee Sound Studio in Hollywood to record my second Columbia album.

Go for Broke eventually shifted about 60,000 copies. I was fine with that, but Columbia had hoped for many more. In hindsight, there may have been too many covers on it. But we now had an identifiable sound for me and Jay to write for and we began to build a strong repertoire of blues-rock tunes that flirted with jazz. We had become a songwriting partnership that would truly hit its stride on the next album, *Hit and Run*.

For the previous two years I'd been working with a Hollywood-based management company called Overland Direction. They were competent and, as far as I could tell, honest, but after *Go for Broke* I thought they maybe lacked vision. They'd assigned me a tour manager, Johnny Palazzotto. Johnny was a Louisiana boy from Baton Rouge, around my age and easy-going with rugged good looks and a silvery tongue. Columbia liked dealing with Johnny and I decided that he might be a better option for me and that it was time to make a change. I dispensed with Overland and made Johnny my full-time manager.

Johnny's first job was to consult with Columbia and help find me a producer for the new album, someone who really liked what I was doing, respected me as an artist and someone I could work hand-in-hand with. Johnny suggested the legendary Steve Cropper and brought him down to a show we were playing at USC Irvine. I was extremely nervous at the thought of Steve Cropper being in the audience. I need not have worried. We played with great confidence and conviction that night. Unfortunately it was all a little too white for Mr Cropper, who passed up on the opportunity. Johnny then made a wild suggestion: Nik Venet, also known as Nik the Greek. Nik was in some ways part of the old guard. Older than us, he'd signed The Beach Boys to Capitol and was one of their first producers. He'd been involved over the years with many of the great Capitol acts, including Nat King Cole, Peggy Lee and Chet Baker. He'd also produced one of my favourite songwriters, Biff Rose, and was close friends with Bobby Darin. He and I clicked instantly. He felt like one of the band, easy to be around and had a consistent flow of interesting arrangement ideas.

Nik had his own unique style of producing and loved to record live. When he first mentioned the idea I kicked against it. Live in the studio made me nervous. It meant that everything we recorded became the master. I needed time to absorb a track before laying down my vocals. I had also conceived in my head that live meant a thinner, weak sounding record. I preferred a thicker sound, with fat vocal harmonies. But as Nik explained, this was not necessarily the case. Nik even wanted the solos played live. He had a persuasive way about him and soon smoothed my ruffled feathers as we reached a compromise. I'd reasoned that if you try to keep live vocals, they have a tendency to bleed into the instrument mics.

'Baffles,' said Nik. 'That's why God invented baffles.'

I wasn't used to keeping what I called guide vocals. I liked to experiment while tracking and then go back in when all the playing was done and lay down my 'keeper' vocal. Nik and I batted around all possibilities, finally reaching an agreement to record the songs live with enough separation to allow us to redo lead vocals and solos.

Nik wanted us to truly know the songs before making the record and put us into a rehearsal room for three days before we ever got anywhere near Larrabee Sound. He had us rehearse all the songs being considered, over and over again, twice a day – once before lunch and once after – for three solid days. His mantra was, 'This album is going to be recorded live boys.' We were already playing these songs on the road, but Nik honed us to a fine recording edge. He knew how to be gently persuasive while remaining amiable. He was never abrasive, offering solid constructive criticism. Nik became a big fan, once travelling all the way from Los Angeles to Phoenix, Arizona just to see us play.

During this period I was so busy, I had no time for a relationship. I was keeping in touch with Chris and Darcy. They'd sold the house in Gospel Oak and moved into a flat in Camden Town. Chris was in a new relationship and Darcy had a stepdad. I felt pangs of both jealousy and guilt when I heard this, but I reasoned that it had been my choice to stay in the USA and what Chris did with her life was her business. I followed Darcy's progress in school. She'd write me sweet, sweet letters and send me drawings and paintings of her room and little things she wanted for Christmas or her birthday. Sometimes not such little things. One year she asked me if I could send her a pony for Christmas. Chris would make me short cassettes of Darcy talking and I would respond with audio letters of my own and talking books. Maybe she thought that one day we'd become a family again. Maybe not.

In general I was in a happier, more contented state of mind. I had my music to lean on and some of my apparent happiness had to do with musical direction. I brought more elements into what I was doing, particularly jazz and R&B. Now I had the players to pull it off, they gave me more colours to paint with on a much bigger palette. They ran wild and I let them. It took a lot of pressure off me knowing I had such a great band to watch my back and it helped me as a vocalist. I could stretch out more and be inventive. I began ad-libbing, scatting along with solos. I even became semi-serious about the electric guitar, trying out all kinds of shapes and weights and sounds, eventually settling on a Guild Bluesbird. In Steven 'Captain' Hooks, I had my own latter day Roland Kirk. He could play alto and tenor sax at the same time like a one-man horn section. Audiences would go wild when he did it. He was also a wonderfully inventive flautist. I used to listen to Clarence Clemons from Springsteen's band and wonder what all the fuss was about. Steven was better and more flexible. The attack of the band came from the three instrumentalists. Jay on guitar could dazzle an audience with rock licks before switching to jazz at the flick of a switch. We also had Charlie Harwood on piano, with his long frizzy hair and fuzzy pointed beard, and a constantly lit Marlboro dangling from the corner of his mouth. He was a master of the keys. The way that Tris and Don Whaley locked in tighter than a miser's fist was mesmerising. Yes, I had a great band and yes, I was happy, but I was also lonely. Deep down, I yearned for a little tenderness and affection.

The seventies were affluent days for the major labels. It was almost obscene the way they threw money at acts they believed in. The bigger the act, the more money the label would throw. Columbia could offer what was termed 'tour support'. This made it possible for acts to visit places that were considered smaller, or B markets. Almost all of my tours at that time were done on a bus. This cut down on road costs, replacing the expense of flights and hotel rooms. If you were willing to travel in a bus the label saw it as dedication on the artist's part and were more prone to cough up support. The flip side was that there was only so much rest to be found on a tour bus with six to eight people on it with varying habits and sleep schedules.

The shows could be far apart and we'd sometimes have to drive through the night in order to get there in time for soundcheck the next day. You might play Cleveland, Ohio one night and Memphis, Tennessee, or Nashville the next. The weekends were easy to fill, but once on the road, we needed to be playing five to six nights a week. This meant going into smaller markets on 'off nights'. Every act wanted to play these rooms, promoters knew it and drove the fees down. If we were getting say $1,000 a night for a weekend show, we might play fillers for as little as $300. Sometimes the fee wasn't enough to cover the cost of getting there and band wages. This is where the record company kicked in. They simply wanted us out there and offered tour support to make up the difference. Part of the deal was that we'd also visit local radio stations and do media interviews whenever we landed some place. Ultimately it's a win-win situation for the record company. They got to reclaim their outlay, as tour support was deducted from sales royalties before anything went to the artist. We drove the length and breadth of America. I didn't really care. I was single and living the life. I knew we were developing a sound, an audience and more importantly, a sales base.

The record business in 1976 was a different beast to the one we know now. The name itself – 'record business' – spoke volumes. LPs, or records, were still the major format, with cassettes a distant second. Albums were mostly sold through FM radio play and touring. 'In-stores' were a major factor. They were not the ones we know today where the artist turns up to play a live set, most stores didn't have that capability in the seventies. We'd visit local chain stores and radio stations to shake hands with customers and thank the jocks and the sales people for their support. In order for a major label to facilitate these visits, they had a chain of regional offices across the country ready to kick in and set-up promotional visits. Columbia had them in all the big cities.

In 1976 we toured in the Pacific Northwest. We played in Portland and Eugene, Oregon followed by Seattle and Spokane, Washington before making the road trip up to Vancouver, British Columbia. In Seattle, Johnny Palazzotto and I went into the Columbia offices to meet the local staff. They had a small set-up with just four or five people: a radio promo person, a local salesman, someone in charge of the stock and a receptionist. As Johnny and I walked in that day a petite, pretty, but concerned looking girl with long, flaming-red hair was fussing around with what seemed to be a severely distressed parrot in a cage. The bird appeared to have lost most of its plumage and no one was quite sure why. This was the cause of much concern for the girl, who appeared to have a connection with the bird and was constantly, reassuringly talking to it. Not what I'd expected to encounter at a Columbia regional office. The girl's name was Judith Caldwell.

I couldn't work out exactly what Judith did at Columbia, she just seemed to float around the office doing whatever needed doing. As I waited for my day's assignments, she and I chatted about this and that and I felt an attraction to her. She was to be our designated driver for the afternoon and by close of play, she had written down her phone number for me. She was engaging and interesting and throughout the tour we spoke many times. On a day off I went back to visit her. At tour's end, rather than going home, I decided to spend more time with her in Seattle. Things accelerated quickly and after a couple of months we made the decision to be together.

It was impossible for me to be in Seattle. My base of operations and my band were all in LA. Judith had the idea to apply for a position in the art department in Los Angeles and Columbia agreed to set up an interview for her. Due to unforeseen circumstances we never made it to that interview. Driving into Hollywood in my Triumph TR7 on the day of the interview, I was distractedly making a left turn and failed to see a white Ford pickup truck coming towards me. As I turned we were hit hard on the passenger side, badly damaging both the car and Judith. At the hospital she discovered that her hip was broken.

Towards the end of one of our tours, Columbia laid on a luncheon for me in an elite New York restaurant. I probably paid for it, but what the hell. The CBS president Bruce Lundvall and his top execs were there, plus a sprinkling of A&R men and salesmen. Speeches ensued and the Columbia people spoke about how thrilled they were with my presence on the label and how well I was doing. I soaked up the praise. It suddenly dawned on me that when they were finished, I would have to get up and say something in order to reciprocate. Sure enough, Johnny Palazzotto looked over and gave me the palms up. I slowly and deliberately got to my feet, dry mouthed, mind racing, hands sweating and throat tightening as I grappled with what I could say. I looked across the table and began speaking directly at Mr Lundvall. I spoke about how happy I was to have such an incredibly supportive label behind me, how honoured I was to be with Columbia, how friendly and kind everyone was, and how much it all felt like family. I talked until I ran out of steam and sat down. Whatever I said came directly off the top of my head and as I finished there were high fives and warm, appreciative applause. Everyone left the restaurant smiling. I arrived back in LA to hear that word of my speech had beaten me there. It was two weeks before the Columbia national convention in Nashville and the whispers were that Columbia might want me to appear there and make the speech again.

When I signed with the label I'd been assigned an A&R man called Peter Philbin. His claim to fame, a dubious one at best, was that he was Bruce Springsteen's responsible go-to guy on the West Coast. I have read Springsteen's memoirs and nowhere is there any mention of the man. Regardless, he'd made his point. Philbin called me.

'I've heard about this speech you made and I want you to go to Nashville and make it again.'

'I can't be there Peter. I'll be on the road on that date,' I told him.

'Okay,' he said, 'here's what we are going to do. This week, you are going to go to a recording studio here in LA and you'll make that speech into a microphone and we'll play the tape at the conference.'

It was my worst nightmare. I couldn't for the life of me remember what I'd said in New York.

'It was just a fear-filled improvisation, Peter. If I try to recreate it, it'll sound empty and contrived.'

But he wouldn't let it go. He was an arrogant, insistent man and I don't think he gave a damn about my music. I realised I'd have to try, so asked him to help me remember what my speech had been. 'Just make it up,' he snapped. I fretted about it. It felt like such an insincere thing to do. I spoke with Johnny about it, but he seemed more concerned with keeping Columbia happy and said, 'Just do it.' No one appeared to understand how difficult it was for me, so I thought, 'Okay, I'll just do it.' Two days later I was in a recording studio.

I don't know what happened. I clammed up. I choked and sat before that microphone for almost an hour unable to speak. The harder I focused on it, the muter I became. I reasoned to myself that it's one thing to say something at a luncheon when everyone is friendly and boozy, it's a completely different kettle of fish in a cold studio trying to revive something that refuses to be revived. I motioned to the engineer to turn on the talkback and asked Johnny to come in. 'I can't bring myself to do what you are all asking,' I said and walked out of the studio into the LA sunshine.

That was essentially the end of my run with Columbia Records. Barely a week later, Johnny called and told me they'd decided not to pick up my option for another album. I would subsequently find out that Peter Philbin, in order to make himself appear more powerful, had told the company I wasn't a team player and had essentially turned my allies against me.

My deal with Columbia collapsed during Judith's recuperation period. Once she was walking again we began talking about leaving Los Angeles. It had taken some time but I'd finally realised that I had a love-hate relationship with the city. It's a transient place, most people I knew had gone there to 'make it' as musicians or as actresses and actors. The movie business was a huge attraction. In most restaurants and cafés, young people would tell you they were making ends meet, waiting for the big break. They arrive overloaded with optimism and an undeniable hunger to act. Nine times out of ten it turned around on them. They would stay a few years and go back home disillusioned.

My friend Sherwin, a New Yorker, once told me, 'LA is full of people who couldn't make it in New York.' I would take that a step further and say that LA is crammed full of people who couldn't hack it anywhere else. Johnny Palazzotto had seen no future in Baton Rouge and moved to the City of Angels. Forty years later, he's back in Baton Rouge, still involved in Louisiana music and relatively successful. The majority of the musicians I encountered during my days there were from another part of the country.

I arrived in Los Angeles wide-eyed and full of verve. Four short years later, that shine had worn off. It's that kind of place. The sun is always shining, but by the same token it's a cold, dog-eat-dog town where you have to be competitive or forget it. Some stay and get a real job. I was ready to take my leave. You don't think about it when things are running smoothly and your fortunes are on the rise, but when circumstances turn on you it can become a cold and oppressive place. It was time to move on.

Judith suggested we head for Seattle. It seemed the sensible thing to do. She was ready to go home and I wanted to get the hell out of Los Angeles. Before we left I had a few goodbyes to say to Jay Lacy and the guys in the band, my tour manager Bruce Barrow, who'd become a dear friend, and Johnny of course. After the last *Hit and Run* tour, he'd called me and asked, 'Ian, can we look at a period for the next tour.' To which I had to say, 'I'm sorry Johnny, I don't think there is going to be a "we" anymore. I think it's time for us both to move on.'

We packed our belongings and drove north on Interstate 5, over the famous Grapevine and into the California desert towards Washington State. Judith was renting a house that she shared with her younger sister Christine. It was in an area of Seattle called Ballard and that became our new home. I arrived there free of all commitments and ready to start anew.

YOU DON'T SEE ME

I can run and I can fight
Take a chance boy, take a chance
I've been thinking I just might
Now that's all history tonight

You don't even seem to care
You're not listening
You're never listening
You and I were quite a pair
You said change your style, I'll take you there
Change my style, you'll take me where?

You don't see me
You don't hear me
You don't know who we are
I've got something, I'm gonna show you
I think we'll go far
We'll go far

You say, you're so close
You're almost home
Follow me or be alone
But I can find it on my own
You say change your mind, I'll take you there
Change my mind, you'll take me where?

You don't see me
You don't hear me
You don't know who we are
I've got something, I'm gonna show you
I think we'll go far
We'll go far

10. HI-FI AND BE DAMNED

Seattle is a picturesque city built on an isthmus between two bodies of water east and west. Its western coastline is a part of the Salish Sea which connects to the Pacific Ocean by an estuary called the Puget Sound. I arrived there in the autumn of 1976. The first thing I noticed was that they actually had seasons, just like back in Britain where autumn was most definitely autumn. Seattle also has one of the best fresh food markets I've encountered anywhere in North America, it's called Pike Place Market and is situated downtown and right on Elliott Bay. For me, Seattle was about starting afresh in many ways. I immersed myself in the city and the Northwest vibe. It also gave me time to really get to know Judith.

Judith had her own unique style of dressing, shunning the popular LA jeans and sneakers look for long, flowing gowns and simple flat shoes. She had a keen mind and was a lover of culture. She loved the movies and in particular the independent and foreign language films; films I might not have otherwise become aware of had it not been for her. She came across calm and even-tempered, far more stable than I was at that time. There was a noticeable difference in our temperaments. I had just spent four crazy years in LA, while she came from the relative peace of the Pacific Northwest, with its mountains and waterways full of endangered animal life and giant firs. Unless you were travelling to western Canada, it wasn't a town you drove through on the way to somewhere else. It felt surprisingly European, with a vibe far more comfortable to me than LA had ever shown. I slowly settled in, found my Northwest feet and began writing again.

I started working with a new friend who I'd recently met through Judith, Bill Lamb. Bill lived with his wife Katy in Portland, Oregon, 175 miles south, but worked quite a bit in Seattle and whenever he did he would stay over with the Caldwell sisters. Bill and I interacted well enough that we made tentative plans to record a demo together, with the idea to become an acoustic duo. I had never considered playing in this configuration before. Bill had a powerful tenor voice and we had a similar delivery, so it was easy for us to find a natural vocal blend. He was also a very good acoustic guitar player, far more accomplished than I was at the time.

Someone in town put us in touch with a young guy named Reed Ruddy. Reed was a recording engineer at a Seattle studio called Kaye-Smith. The studio was co-owned by the actor Danny Kaye and a man called Lester Smith who owned the Seattle Mariners baseball team. Reed arranged for us to go into Kaye-Smith using downtime to make our demos. This was usually quite late at night.

We made a four-song demo tape and played it for a couple of labels, but no one bit and our planned duo was stillborn. Along the way we signed a brief and unlikely publishing deal with Thom Bell's company Mighty Three Music. Thom was from Philadelphia and his apparent fame came from producing The Detroit Spinners, The Three Degrees and The O'Jays. He had, for some reason, relocated to Seattle. I still have no idea why the man who produced 'Since I Been Gone' signed two white boys playing acoustic pop music.

I desperately wanted another record deal, but one was not forthcoming and that made me anxious and a little insecure. It made me reassess and re-evaluate myself, wondering if the mojo might have finally deserted me. In both London and Los Angeles I'd had easier access to all the right people, Seattle was a more provincial proposition and at that time would not have been considered a music-business town. Something I hadn't seriously considered.

Seattle's music scene grew steadily into the one we know today, in 1977 there was barely a scene at all. People around the country knew that the rock band Heart were from Seattle and that Richard Berry's classic 'Louie, Louie' had been written there but not much else. I was beginning to despair when Judith introduced me to an old friend of hers, Nils Von Veh. Nils had recently worked at

KZAM, Seattle's famous FM radio station, but left radio a short time before I met him and moved into artist management. He formed Beaux Arts Management with his partner John Strawn. They discovered I was in Seattle and courted me. As far as I could see, they were the only sensible game in town and we agreed to team up and work together.

Not long after Beaux Arts and I tied the knot, I took a phone call from Sandy Roberton. I hadn't spoken with Sandy since the break-up of Plainsong and I wasn't sure how he'd found my number. He asked me what I was doing.

'To tell you the truth Sandy, I'm not doing much at all right now. I've been searching for the right thing to be involved in but nothing seems to be materialising.'

'I've been thinking a lot about you lately,' he said, 'and I would like for us to work together again. Do you fancy making an album with me?'

It transpired that Sandy had recently formed his own label in the UK, Rockburgh Records. His first release had been a Gay and Terry Woods album called *Tender Hooks*. They were founder members of Steeleye Span, a group with a strong English traditional sound that my old Fairport bandmate Ashley Hutchings had put together. Sandy wanted me to be his second release. He asked if I could come to London and discuss it. Without knowing too much more about Sandy's operation I leapt at the chance, though I needed to okay it with my new management first. They were very enthusiastic, seeing it as an ideal opportunity to get the wheels back on the wagon. The Plainsong debacle was almost five years behind us. It was time to re-join forces and move on.

I flew to London and met with Sandy. We talked about the style of music I was listening to, about the sound I wanted to make and the musicians I'd like to use. It was half a decade since I'd last recorded in England and I was unfamiliar with the available studio players. I told Sandy I'd need a musical director, someone I could bounce ideas off and use as musical go-between, not unlike the role Andy Roberts had performed for me all those years ago. Sandy's response was, 'I might just know the perfect person.' That person turned out to be a Welsh songwriter with the moniker

Bryn Haworth. I knew Bryn as an electric slide guitar player who had made an album for Island called *Let the Days Go By* which I'd been listening to. When I listened to it again more objectively I thought, 'Yes I can work with this man.'

Our musical union was not without complications. I'd picked a song by New York songwriter David Pomeranz called 'It's In Everyone Of Us'. I first heard it on KZAM and instantly wanted to record my own interpretation. It's a song about having the confidence and the mindset to achieve single-handedly whatever it is you want in life. When I took my song list to London it was near the top and one of the first I played for Bryn. He bristled as he listened to it. I hadn't realised that he was a committed Christian. The lyric 'It's in everyone of us to be wise, find yourself, open up both your eyes. We can all know everything, without ever knowing why' bothered Bryn greatly, grating against his Christian beliefs. He said he didn't like it and I asked him to explain why as I thought it was a wonderful song. He was reluctant to tell me, but after much prompting he said that his belief was that only Jesus Christ had the ability and the power to do that. We were mere mortals.

'I'm not saying you can't record the song,' he added, 'I'm only saying that if you do you'll have to find someone else to record it with, because I won't do it.'

I considered my options and decided that I liked and respected Bryn enough to shelve the song and save it for another project down the road. Apart from this small glitch, he and I got on quite well and he did a creditable job. After the album was finished I extended an invitation to Bryn to be part of a touring band. He graciously declined to join our merry band of unbelievers.

We recorded the album at a studio in Chipping Norton in Oxfordshire, the same studio that Gerry Rafferty had recorded his huge hit 'Baker Street'. It's in an old converted school on New Street. The gym had become the studio and the classrooms had been divided up into small apartments. It was an all-inclusive deal, which meant that we lived there for the recording duration. The facility had a lounge with a big TV and a games room with a ping-pong table. A cook came in twice a day to prepare meals and the owners employed locals from the village to maintain the place. It was a relaxed environment to work in. We were there 24/7 and didn't really have time to go anywhere else.

Chipping Norton is a lovely village in the Cotswolds. My friend from Fairport, Simon Nicol, lived there and Keith Moon once had a pub on the high street. The studio was founded in the early seventies by Mike and Richard Vernon, who owned the famous British blues label Blue Horizon. The original Fleetwood Mac were on Blue Horizon. The Proclaimers later recorded at Chipping Norton. Fairground Attraction's big hit 'Perfect' was recorded there, as was 'Come on Eileen' by Dexy's Midnight Runners. The studio closed its doors in 1999 and in 2017 was awarded a Blue Plaque for the part it had played in British musical heritage.

Stealin' Home was an easy album to make and opened many new doors for me. Sandy is one of the best 'hands off' producers I've worked with. He has an excellent ear and has coaxed from me many of my best vocals. We used an in-house engineer called Barry Hammond who truly knew how to get the very best from the available equipment. He knew the studio inside out, it had become his room. The players were mostly Sandy's go-to guys: Jimmy Russell on drums who had played with Curved Air and later Human League; Bryn on acoustic guitar; Rick Kemp from Steeleye Span on bass; and a young session guitar player, Phil Palmer, who was Ray Davies's nephew and would later play second guitar with Eric Clapton. We also had Pete Wingfield on keyboards. Pete had a huge national hit with 'Eighteen with a Bullet'.

The album was a pure pop record and very different to the R&B/jazzy style I had recently been playing. I used some of the songs I'd worked up with Bill Lamb in our aborted duo. I also brought several songs to the table that I'd heard on KZAM in Seattle, including two by Terence Boylan – 'Shake It' and 'Don't Hang Up Your Dancing Shoes' – plus the Robert Palmer song 'Gimme an Inch Girl'. KZAM was a terrific station and every time I heard a song I liked I would call my friend Jon Kertzer, the programme director, and say, 'Hey Jon, it's Ian, what did you just play, who wrote it and what album is it on?' More often than not he'd have no idea what they had been playing and would have to ask one of the jocks. They would tell him what it was and I'd then go out and buy the album. Other songs on *Stealin' Home* came from friends. 'King of the Night' was written by my pal Jeffrey Comanor for the Eagles. They inexplicably turned it down and I snapped it up. 'Yank and Mary' was written by another good friend, Richard Stekol. A part of that song includes a very subtle nod to 'Smile', a tune written in the 1930s by none other than Charlie Chaplin. 'Man in the Station' I knew from my copy of John Martyn's *Solid Air* album. The legendary Duffy Power took the train from London, turning up slightly refreshed to play harmonica on the song. I remember saying to him, 'Can you play like a steam train Duffy?'

I love John Martyn's music. From *London Conversation* onwards I collected and listened intently to each of his albums as they hit the street. One of my favourites is the album *One World*. I adore it for the sound and its wonderful lyricism. It's quite bare bones, but at the same time as soulful as songwriting gets. John was a rare talent and sorely missed.

While Sandy and I were discussing the album cover design, I was idly flicking through a cheap magazine and noticed a full-page photograph for a Reckitt & Colman shampoo ad. I loved the photograph and instantly recognised it as the work of my old Pyramid bandmate Steve Hiett. I wanted it as my album cover. Sandy phoned Reckitt & Colman and my hunch proved right. They told him that Steve had indeed taken the picture and that I was free to use it. All they asked in return was a company name check, reasoning that it would be as advantageous to them as it was to me.

The album was released and I put together a strong touring band. We retained Jimmy Russell on drums and I was reunited with my old Matthews Southern Comfort guitar player Mark Griffiths. Mark had decided to become a bass player after leaving Southern Comfort and became a very, very good one. He played with David Essex before auditioning for The Shadows. He got the job, realising a childhood dream and even though he's still considered the new boy, has now been with them for more than thirty years. Mark also played on the legendary *The Everly Brothers – Concert Reunion* album, recorded live at the Royal Albert Hall. I had the great fortune to work with Mick Weaver, aka Wynder K Frog, on keyboards. Mick became a marvellous exponent of the Hammond B3 organ and was much in demand in later years by the blues and funk fraternity. He played with Buddy Guy, Joe Cocker and, later, Taj Mahal, creating the opportunity for him to move to Los Angeles and become part of the city's musical fabric. Our utility man Joel Tepp is an LA native who'd driven coast-to-coast with me in my vintage Porsche and later played slide and harmonica for me in the *Go for Broke* band. Now we were back together again. For the next two years, with some minor tweaks, this new band toured Europe, America and Japan.

Back in Seattle, Nils and John at Beaux Arts went in search of a US release. Sandy had put up the money to make the record and needed to license it in America if he was to make something back on his investment. Nils and John were friendly with Shelly Siegel who ran Mushroom Records in Vancouver. Mushroom was funded by a paint company and had built a massive reputation with the Seattle band Heart, fronted by the Wilson sisters, Ann and Nancy. Shelly was curious to hear my album. Nils and John gave him a copy and he phoned back within a week saying, 'I very much like the album and we've done a survey. There's a Top Ten hit on it, but I'm not going to tell you which song it is unless you license the record to Mushroom.'

The record was licensed to Shelly and 'Shake It', a song buried eight-deep in the album, became my first US Top Ten hit. (My version of 'Woodstock' had got to number 13 or 17 in the US, depending on which trade you subscribed to.) Shelly put every resource he had into working the record, particularly after his brash statement about the Top Ten single. I'm quite sure he pulled in more than a few favours as it glided effortlessly up the charts. Whatever he had done, the success of the record put me on a few high-profile tours, something I hadn't been doing much of in recent years. During the album's shelf life I opened for David Gates from Bread, Jo Jo Gunne and The Beach Boys. We played some big venues with Gates, 1,000 to 2,500-seat auditoriums.

With The Beach Boys the venues were even bigger, 5000-seat ice hockey and basketball arenas. All of this live action helped propel both the single and the album even higher.

Just as my career seemed to be on an undeniable upward swing, disaster struck. It was early 1979, I was on a European tour and playing in Bruges. I had just come off stage and Bruce Barrow, my tour manager, took me to one side and said, 'Ian I've got some really bad news for you.' I thought 'Oh really, how bad can it be, the tour bus won't start, or maybe the hotel has given our rooms away?' Bruce said, 'Shelly Siegel has died.' Boom. It was like a heavy kick in the head. I couldn't take it in. It was inconceivable. Shelly had only signed me a year ago. I had seen him just two months ago. We had a Top Ten hit all across North America and he was dead?

I stood in that dressing room with Bruce and Sandy, all of us alternately staring at the floor and at each other saying nothing. No one verbalised it but I could sense we were all thinking, 'Why us? Why now? What now?' The gossip on the street was that Shelly had probably overdosed. The truth was that he had a brain defect from birth and had died from a massive aneurysm. He was just thirty-two years old. A little piece of me died with Shelly that day.

Several days later word came from Vancouver. They were putting on a brave face. 'Don't worry, all will be fine. We're looking for someone to run the company.' The advice was to carry on as per normal, whatever normal was. A second single from the album was released, 'Gimme an Inch Girl'. It did reasonably well, reaching the Top Fifty, but without Shelly creating his magic it quickly faded. The writing was on the wall for Mushroom Records and my future as a Mushroom artist. When auditors finally went through the company books they discovered it had been a fine juggling act and only Shelly had known where the balls were and how many he'd had in the air. It had been a one-man operation and no one could understand how he had been running it. He was borrowing from Peter to pay Paul but left no clues to help solve things. Even Susan Gershon, Shelly's girlfriend and second in command, didn't know what had been going on and what needed to be done. She was in deep shock and left the business shortly after Shelly's death, never to return. All I could do was follow advice and try to carry on as per normal.

Prior to all the turmoil surrounding Shelly's death, Sandy and I had already begun work on the next album, *Siamese Friends*, back at Chipping Norton. Now it served as a good distraction, forcing us to focus on the future and more positive things. By then we'd replaced Joel Tepp with Los Angeles-based guitar player Bob Metzger and saxophonist Craig Buhler. In retrospect, *Siamese Friends* is one of my favourite albums of that period. The production, the song choice and the playing all came together on that album. It features an unrecorded John Martyn composition, 'Anna', and a Stevie Nicks song called 'Crying in the Night' which I'd heard when I bought the duet album she made with Lindsey Buckingham. I covered my first Jules Shear song, a great tune called 'Home Somewhere'. It's one of the few albums I can still listen to and enjoy from beginning to end. Mushroom again licensed the record for the American market but were in such utter chaos it barely got off the ground. Such a pity.

Sometime in the spring of 1979 I received an animated phone call from Sandy. He'd just had a conversation with a booking agent at NEMS. The agent, let's call him Paul, worked in the London office and had picked up on a buzz about a contract clear-out. They needed more file space and had to dispose of thousands of old tour contracts. Word was that some of these files were from The Beatles' 1965 USA tour. The usual procedure with contracting tours is that there are three copies for each show. One stays with the promoter, in this case Sid Bernstein in New York. A second copy goes to the artist management and a third copy goes on the road with the tour manager. NEMS, being Brian Epstein's company, were both management and the responsible European agent.

Paul had surreptitiously gone into the dumpster behind the offices and discovered that the entire Beatles tour had been thrown away. He'd pulled the files out of the dumpster and now had them in a secure place. They were all signed by Brian Epstein and Sid Bernstein. He'd called Sandy to say that he wanted to sell them and asked if he was interested in buying any. Sandy instantly phoned me. The asking price was £200 each. My first thought was that the renowned New York Shea Stadium concert had been part of that tour. But surely that had been the first one sold. In actuality, Paul hadn't begun the selling process, he was still assessing interest. I told Sandy I would die to have the Shea contract.

Several days later we met with Paul and the deal was made. Sandy bought the contract for The Beatles' final concert at Candlestick Park in San Francisco and I bought the infamous Beatles at Shea Stadium, complete with rider. The rider is an addendum to the contract, usually stating artist requirements. More often than not it's non-negotiable. This particular rider contained such things as a riser for Ringo's drums, 10'x 6'x 4'high. A hi-fidelity sound system with an adequate number of speakers and four hi-fi microphones. The artist will not be required to perform before a segregated audience. Oh yes, and there will be a $5,000 donation made to the Police Athletic League of New York. I immediately had all four pages framed and proudly displayed on the wall above my Wurlitzer jukebox in the living room, explaining to guests exactly what it was.

I had been living in Seattle for three years. Judith and I had settled into our relationship and bought a house together in an area of town called Phinney Ridge. It was an ideal location for me. Secluded, it sat in a tight circular driveway, shared by two other houses, surrounded by mature fir trees. The house was less than half a mile away from the Seattle Woodland Park Zoo. On any given day, if the wind was blowing in the wrong direction, it was apparent that we lived near the zoo. The house itself was what you might call a rambler, quite beautiful in its own way but with no real cohesion – you had to pass through the master bedroom to go upstairs. Every time we had guests, they had to walk through the bedroom at night and in the morning. The bathroom, for some inexplicable reason, was downstairs next to the back door. It was charming without being functional. Its saving grace was the basement which had been completely finished and had its own entrance, making it accessible from the street. It was a wonderful space to rehearse in and had two custom-built closets, perfect for equipment storage and my growing collections of thrift-store purchases.

One of my passions in Seattle had been 'thrifting' as they called it there. This entailed visiting second-hand and charity stores. In Washington State they had some very good department store-sized ones. The Salvation Army was always good and one called Value Village. This became my favourite. I would laughingly tell friends I'd been shopping at my favourite French store, Valoo Veeage. I began collecting 1950s and 60s children's lunchboxes, with matching thermos flasks. I was fascinated by them and built a very nice collection of around a hundred pieces. You could buy them in excellent condition for pennies and the hunt was fun. They all featured scenes from popular kids' TV shows and movies. I later learned that some of them – Roy Rogers, Hopalong Cassidy, some of the Barbie ones and a Flintstones – were quite valuable. I also collected salt and pepper shakers from the same era. They were made in fun combinations, like a pineapple and a palm tree, a ten pin and a bowling bowl, or a Martian and a flying saucer. You get the picture.

Darcy and I became closer again. She visited me in Seattle twice during her summer holidays. These are some of my favourite memories of her childhood, having her with me for those two precious weeks of summer. She came first as a nine-year-old and again when she was eleven. She wanted to visit so much that she agreed to fly the 10,000-mile round trip all by herself. I try to imagine myself agreeing to that at her age and cannot. It was the first time she'd ever been so far away from her mom and she sobbed in her room that first night.

Compared to Los Angeles there weren't a lot of glamorous things to do in Seattle. We had fun doing the simple things like visiting the islands or feeding the ducks at the lake. We would go up to the Seattle Zoo for a day, go shopping and sometimes a movie. I had a friend who owned a second-hand clothes shop in Ballard called Fritzi Ritz. Darcy loved rummaging through all of the fifties American girly things. They were so different to anything she had ever known. But it wasn't as much about the doing, as the being together. I believe these visits helped bridge the gap towards mending our cracked and fragile relationship.

Sandy was hungry for yet another album. This time he wasn't quite sure what, but he believed we needed to contemplate a change of direction. He wasn't interested in another record like *Siamese Friends*. As good as it was, it had been a commercial failure and he'd decided that anything in a similar style would be a complete waste of everyone's time. By the early 1980s, new wave music had taken hold and everyone seemed to be playing eighth notes. Sandy thought we might give it a go and prompted me to step outside myself and my self-imposed comfort zone. His plan was to make the album and then send out press copies with no clues as to who it might be. Then wait for a response. At which point, with great fanfare, he would reveal the true identity of the artist. We recorded an album called *Spot of Interference* and sent out press copies in plain white sleeves with nothing but song titles printed on them. Initially the music press embraced it, but on learning who it was, they almost all uniformly changed their minds. I don't think they necessarily disliked the music, but they disliked the fact that they had been duped, that it was me and not some new hotshot act they were about to discover. It's a fickle business.

The album went nowhere and I didn't particularly care for it either. Although it had some great material on it, it wasn't me nor a style I should ever have attempted. In retrospect I wish I had stuck to my artistic guns and followed my musical heart. I tried my best to promote it and toured Europe incessantly. There's footage from a German television show called *Rockpalast* that has recently been released on DVD. Try as I may to like it, I cannot, and stylistically it remains a regret. At year's end, I threw up my arms and went home.

I didn't know what to do. I felt I'd lost my way. Even that I'd been a little misled. I was back in Seattle a disillusioned man. But fate has a way of closing one door whilst opening another.

I first met David Surkamp at the Beaux Arts office. David had relocated from St Louis when his band Pavlov's Dog had split up. He travelled west with his co-writer, keyboardist Douglas Rayburn, and set up residence in South Seattle. Their initial idea was to form a new Pavlov's Dog, away from all expectations, and they signed with Beaux Arts Management.

I liked David instantly. He had a deep knowledge of pop music and a seemingly unstoppable need to create. He was a charming and engaging character with intense, piercing blue eyes and a skittish, insatiable energy. We clicked. He explained to me where he wanted to take his music and I was sympathetic. We spoke about the possibility of me producing something for him. I hadn't really considered myself a producer. I'd done some years earlier when I'd worked with Longdancer, plus my own *Tigers Will Survive* and *Some Days You Eat the Bear*. Maybe now was the right time to test those skills again. I was keen to give it a try. Rather than simply reform Pavlov's Dog in a different location, David wanted to give his band a brand-new identity. At its core it would essentially still be Pavlov's Dog, but with new local players and under a pseudonym. I agreed and along with guitarist Bruce Hazen and drummer Bob Briley, David, Douglas and I went into Kaye-Smith with our engineer pal Reed Ruddy to make an album that David called *Mad Shadows*.

Steve Miller had also recently become a Seattle resident and was next door in the big room at Kaye-Smith recording a new solo album. Occasionally we'd bump into each other in the coffee room. I was a fan of his earlier albums and we'd chat. On a whim, I invited him in for a listen. We played him a mix.

'Let me hear another,' he said.

We played him a second track. At song's end he shook his head.

'Jesus, you guys really like high end, don't you?'

'Do we?' I replied.

He took us next door to hear what he was doing and the sonic difference was staggering. His mixes sounded smooth and cohesive. The highs were crisp and the lows were a subtle balance of bass and kick drum, creating a nice chest thump.

'Now, go back and listen to yours again,' he said pushing us towards the door.

He was right, our mixes had far too much high end. I learned a valuable lesson that day. If you ever think you might be using a little too much treble in the mix, put on some Steve Miller and hear how the pros do it.

For various reasons, David's album was never released and he found himself at a loose end. We began hanging out together, kicking around a few ideas until it dawned on us that despite our stylistic differences, perhaps we ought to consider playing together. We debated what we hoped to achieve from our band and what form it should take. David already had a fine set of musicians in place, so why not simply add me to the mix and see what shakes? We talked about direction and goals and discovered we both had an urge to create music that people could dance to. Neither of us had ever really paid our dues, in that we'd never had to struggle to get where we were musically. We had both more or less started in bands that had clicked right out of the gate and we wondered how it might feel to begin at the bottom rather than having that instant success. What would it be like to play cover tunes in smoky, sweaty clubs, playing maybe three to four sets a night? I was intrigued and more than a little curious as to where this unlikely combination could take us. The only way to experience it was to just do it and explore the local club circuit.

Seattle had several downtown rock clubs and plenty more in the surrounding area. You couldn't play the kind of music we were envisioning in theatres. Besides, we didn't want people listening; we wanted them up and participating. I know it sounds crazy, but the more we discussed it, the better it sounded to us. We called the band Hi-Fi and despite the miserable time I'd had with *Spot of Interference*, Hi-Fi was a hard-driving rock band, begging for eighth notes. We found ourselves an agent.

I'm sure these rooms are long gone now, but we acquired a residency at Astor Park downtown, run by a shady character named Jean Baptiste. We played Broncos, The Lynnwood Tavern and Michael J's in Pioneer Square. We developed three- to four-night residencies, often getting home stinking of cigarette smoke some time in the early morning hours. Yep, this union we called Hi-Fi was just the ticket.

We played constantly around the Seattle area and made a live-in-the-studio recording we called *The Hi-Fi Demonstration Record*. We started working further afield and did a short Californian tour, playing a few shows with The Beach Boys along the way. They didn't know what to make of us. We invited national A&R people to come and check us out, but none of them seemed to understand what it was we were doing, so we recorded a studio album for First American Records, a local label, and called it *Moods for Mallards*. The cover was duck footprints set out as dance steps. We were loving it. We were a hard-gigging band and a good one at that. Judith could not make head nor tail of it. She was completely baffled as to my motivation, direction, or goal. I tried to explain that there was no goal. I was having fun. But it was like trying to shout to someone from a moving train with the windows closed.

Our drummer Bob Briley was known within the band as 'Gumby' after the bendy children's toy. When he played he was all energy, flailing away, all bendy arms and legs. He had the kind of personality you could play practical jokes on and he'd never get angry. He was a good sport who took it all in his stride. We'd heard of a rock'n'roll gag and thought we'd try it on Bob. You take a shit in a paper bag, leave it outside someone's hotel room door and set fire to it. You then knock on the door and run and hide, waiting to see what happens. We wanted to see if it was true. Would he really stamp on the bag to put the fire out? He wasn't too happy about that one, but it worked. It really worked.

Most of our shows started with the Buffalo Springfield tune 'Mr Soul'. It's a similar riff to the one Keith Richard plays on 'Satisfaction': Da dahhh, da da dahhhh, da da da da. We made up a silly rule that we'd only start singing when there were at least two couples on the dance floor. It was fun. One night in Astor Park the riff went on for more than twenty minutes before anyone got up to dance. All the while we were nervously glancing at each other, 'What if nobody gets up to dance? What then?'

The fun lasted for a couple of years. It all began to unravel when David decided he needed to move on. The rest of us struggled to hold it together, initially thinking we might be better off without him, but quickly realising that we weren't. We lost direction without David and missed the unpredictability. I had loved the stage dynamics of him so frantic, skittering around the stage in his wooden clogs and me, almost static, staring daggers at him for being such a wild man. That was gone and I slowly realised that was a big part of what had made it hang together. All of the consistent inconsistencies.

In desperation we made a four-song demo to try and attract a label. There was a dispute over one of the songs on the demo – a Pete Townsend/Ronnie Lane co-write called 'Heart to Hang Onto' – and we ended up at loggerheads over it. The rest of the band loved it, but I didn't like the way I had interpreted it. I thought it blighted an otherwise good demo tape. It wasn't worthy. We scrapped like cats and dogs over it. At a meeting one day, I arrived at the designated time to find the others already deep in conversation, scheming. It smacked of my Fairport experience all over again. I walked in and the room fell silent. I asked what was going on, even though I already knew.

'Oh, nothing,' they chorused, 'we're just talking.'

'I don't think so,' I said, 'I think you're planning something and I don't want to be in this kind of band any longer. I'm gone and don't call me.'

They did call, several times. But I was done. I never went back and that was the end of Hi-Fi. Bruce Hazen and I patched things up later and played together a couple of times but I never saw the others again. Some years later David went back to St. Louis and remains a dear friend to this day.

I found myself at a loose end and cash poor. I was looking round for things to do to raise some money. I decided to sell my prized Beatles Shea Stadium contract. I asked around my immediate circle of musical cohorts and word came back that Ann Wilson of Heart was a collector of Beatles memorabilia and wanted it. I sold it to her, framed, for $1,000. Much-needed cash for me and the bargain of a lifetime for her. It's now believed to be worth in excess of $25,000. C'est la vie.

I took on a few innocuous jobs that under normal circumstances I wouldn't have bothered with. I had developed a nodding acquaintance with Howard Leese, the guitar player from Heart. We'd met one day at Kaye-Smith and chatted. He asked me if I had any interest in doing background vocals for radio advertising jingles. I asked him what that entailed. He said it was easy and the money was good, adding that it would help if I could read music. I told him I didn't, but I was a good listener and could pick things up quickly. He said he would speak to his contractor about using me. Most of the work was done at Kaye-Smith in an atmosphere I already knew and liked. I ended up doing a few of these sessions with Howard and a select group of local singers. It paid some bills and I encountered new people.

At a particular jingle session a smiley-faced keyboard player told me that he had been asked to take up residency at a hotel lounge in a remote community in Alberta, Canada. He wanted to form a duo, playing covers of 1960s hits, and wondered if I might be interested. I wasn't sure. I had never done anything like that before. He reassured me it would be fine.

'I'll show you the ropes,' he said, 'It's simple and the money's great.'

Against my better judgement, I agreed. We called ourselves Flashback. We rehearsed a couple of hour's worth of material; him smiling and playing keyboard and me on acoustic guitar. We interpreted songs like 'You Can't Hurry Love', 'I Can't Explain' and 'I Can't Stop Loving You'. For a while it was fun, but I only knew him from our jingle sessions and it transpired that we were incompatible. He was very low on self-esteem and quite envious of my past. He would verbalise that. We played three sets a night for loggers and truckers and might as well have been a radio. We were the background music while they drank, cursed and hooted. Things got worse with the keyboard player. He took great joy in telling me I was a shit guitar player and should be ashamed of myself. But there we were, stuck in a northern outpost working out a contract. It was an experience I'll never forget and one I will never try again.

More seriously at this time something life-changing was happening. Judith and I had reached an impasse in our relationship. Things were not going well for me and I became dour and moody. I'd had bouts of this throughout my entire adult life. I wasn't yet equipped to handle the downside of life and Judith had difficulties with that part of my personality. One day she simply told me she'd had enough.

She had started taking ceramic classes, wanting to carve out a new career for herself in sculpting and design. She was in a happy place. Things were looking up for her as they were turning sour for me. She told me that my misery and complaining was affecting her day-to-day and holding her back. I tried to dissuade her, telling her I'd change, but she wouldn't be swayed. I slipped further down. This was a low I'd never experienced before. In previous relationships I'd been the one doing the leaving and now I was being left. It was time to pay the piper and I wasn't sure how best to do that.

Early in our relationship, Judith had introduced me to two of her best friends, Sherwin Strull and Lois Listopad. They were transplanted New Yorkers who'd moved out west in the 1970s to Los Angeles to escape the East Coast weather. When we met, Lois was an airline stewardess with Pan Am and Sherwin made beautiful, ornate leather bags which he sold to record-company people. Later on, after trips to Tokyo with Lois, he took up framing old Japanese woodblock prints and selling them on. He had an entrepreneurial spirit. Together they owned a house in Studio City. We made an instant connection and to this day they are still my longest-running and dearest friends. They are very generous and loving and two of the most grounded people I know, with nothing to prove to anyone and very peaceful to be around. When Judith despaired of me, Lois and Sherwin were the first people I called. They said to come down to Los Angeles and stay with them until I found my way.

I put my share of the furnishings into storage, to be rescued later. I had to decide which of my thrift store collections to keep and which to let go of. I chose to keep the salt and pepper shakers as they were far more portable and nice to display. I still have them, bubble-wrapped and stored in a box in my attic. I advertised my lunchbox collection. A Japanese collector came round to the house to look at them and said he wanted to buy the lot. From his offer I realised how valuable they were. Still, they had to go. I took his money and he drove away with my entire collection piled high across the back seat of his car. I resigned myself to Los Angeles again, and struck out to stay with Lois and Sherwin. I was miserable once more, but at least I was with friends.

Three months later I went back to Seattle to collect my things: a 1960s dinette set with a Formica-top table and four chairs, some oriental rugs, a book case, an armoire, a couple of standing lamps, all of my LPs and a stereo system. Judith had already sold the house and we'd split the proceeds.

I suspected there was more to Judith's reason for leaving than met the eye. Sometimes you sense things that are never said. From my point of view it happened so fast and she'd been so inflexible about trying again that it made little sense to me. When I arrived to clear out my storage, she'd already begun a relationship with a guy called Billy. He and I had been softball team mates. Judith had met him at one of our games. She was adamant that nothing had happened. I suspected something had.

I loaded all my things into a removal van and rented a trailer. Securing the front wheels of my little Triumph onto it, I towed it behind the van. Slipping onto Interstate 5 south, watching Seattle disappear in my rear view mirror, I sang a Jimmy Webb song to myself, 'If You See Me Getting Smaller, I'm Leaving'. It takes a little over seventeen hours to drive non-stop from Seattle to LA. I'd brought two talking books on cassette with me for company: Richard Bach's *The Bridge Across Forever*, a spiritual story about true love; and a four-cassette version of Alistair Cooke's *America*. In one broadcast, Cooke talks about being in the Ambassador Hotel kitchen with Bobby Kennedy the night he was shot by Sirhan Sirhan. I listened to both books in their entirety.

MONEY

M.O.N.E.Y. Let me hear you shout
M.O.N.E.Y. It's money that it's all about
God knows, it's money that it's all about

I've got a friend, wrote the perfect song
Beyond a shadow of a doubt
The words dig in and the hooks are strong
But it's money that it's all about
He knows it's money that it's all about

Why don't you twist that dial round a couple of jolts
Come on and let the music out
Stand up, stand up and reveal yourselves
It's money that you're all about
We know it's money that you're all about

It's all that
M.O.N.E.Y. Let me hear you shout
M.O.N.E.Y. It's money that it's all about
God knows, it's money that it's all about

You can take my house and burn my car
You can make me shut my mouth
When all else fails the truth prevails
It's money that it's all about
We know it's money that it's all about

I've seen boys made kings and dreams grow wings
Now they're tearing down the house
It was cups and caps and victory laps
Now it's money that it's all about
Oh yeah, it's money that it's all about

M.O.N.E.Y. Let me hear you shout
M.O.N.E.Y. It's money that it's all about
God knows, it's money that it's all about
It's M.O.N.E.Y.
It's M.O.N.E.Y.
It's M.O.N.E.Y.

11. JOY MINING. THE A&R YEARS

I spent my first few weeks back in LA partly in a depression and partly in deep reflection, as the reality of being single again wormed its way through my system. I was determined to emerge from it a happier and wiser man. I liked to drive down to Santa Monica and walk along the beach, or sometimes just sit quietly on a bench at Paramahansa Yogananda's Lake Shrine down near the Pacific Coast Highway feeling my sadness and reflecting on things. I read books on self-help that in time led to more spiritual understandings. I had no clear picture as to what I wanted to do. I was single, approaching forty and feeling that I'd taken a musical path less travelled and lost my way.

I met Melissa Ward at a mutual friend's birthday party. We found ourselves at opposite ends of a line of cocaine just a few short months after I'd moved down from Seattle. She was an attractive brunette in a Sarah Jessica Parker sort of way, and single. A native Californian, she was an ex-hippie and ex-fruitarian who had been an avid LADET crusader (Love Animals Don't Eat Them). She'd quit marching but was still a hardcore believer and a vegan chef for hire. She could be abrasive, argumentative, insensitive and unerringly unaware of any of these attributes. We were total opposites and had very little in common. None of my close friends liked her, but tolerated her on my behalf. I persevered.

What I didn't know when we met was that Melissa had just given up on a long-term relationship with a movie industry credits designer named Pablo. The problem was she hadn't actually fallen out of love with him, they'd just split up. After we became an item she would spend ages in the next room on the phone with him. I felt I was doomed to be constantly compared to Pablo in every way possible. I tolerated it because at that time I felt that being in a relationship was better than being alone.

It was a relationship doomed from the offset but I was numb and determined to make it work. Before long we found a little two-bedroom rent-controlled house on 23rd Street in Santa Monica and moved in together. Melissa loved the concept of rent control, she could be annoyingly thrifty at times, usually with her own money. Within a couple months, living together became fraught and tense. I barely knew the woman and I wasn't sure if I even liked her, yet here we were. We reached an impasse and I moved out, fleeing back to the more peaceful existence of the San Fernando Valley, back to the sanity of Sherman Oaks. I was far happier living alone and my friends Sherwin and Lois were happier to have me within visiting distance.

Sandy Roberton unwittingly came to my rescue. He called to ask if I was interested in picking up the pieces and making another album with him. Of course I was. It was exactly the kind of pick-me-up I needed. My focus and joyfulness kicks in when the process of creating music comes calling. It makes me whole and gives me something to hang my spiritual hat on.

Sandy and I made an album together called *Shook*, as in having recently been shaken. I took my Hi-Fi experience and the sound the band had developed into the studio with me, along with Hi-Fi guitarist Bruce Hazen and a handful of songs I'd written with David and Douglas. We recorded on a farm in North Wales, using the Hot Wax mobile studio. Sandy wanted to try a state-of-the-art sound. We employed some of my past bandmates, including drummer Bob Henrit, who later joined The Kinks. Bob played a mix of drum kit and programmed drums. It was my first experience in using synthetic drums. In retrospect I didn't care for the sound too much. At Sandy's suggestion we recorded all of the basic tracks on the mobile and took them back to Livingstone Studios in London where I did my vocals and he mixed the album.

After the vocals were finished, I took a few days off while Sandy brought in a young synthesiser player.

'Leave me alone with him for two or three days,' Sandy said, 'I'll let him loose to do what he wants and when we're done, come back and sit with me and tell me what you like and what you don't like.'

The synth player was Adrian Lee, who later worked with 10cc and Mike + The Mechanics. Sandy played me what he had done and I liked every single note.

MTV was reaching its peak popularity in the mid-eighties and Sandy persuaded Polygram, his European distributor, to invest in a concept video. We chose a Duncan Browne song from the album called 'The Wild Places'. The video was filmed in an abandoned hotel in downtown Los Angeles with a full-sized swimming pool in the basement. It was quite spooky in the basement, with water reflections from the pool rippling across the walls and ceiling. The director, Bud somebody, wanted a naked girl to dive in and swim the length of the pool. She was nervous about being naked with so many men around so the director cleared the room, allowing only one cameraman to stay. I was asked to leave too. It was all done very tastefully and discreet, never explicit. They filmed extra shots of me in the upstairs ballroom miming the lyrics behind a modesty screen. It was beautifully directed and cost Polygram upwards of $50,000, but the album was never released in America and the film remains unseen to this day. I have a VHS of it somewhere in my archives. A still from it was used on the cover of the album.

I did some press and touring but Polydor didn't promote the album very well and my heart wasn't in it. I had for the longest time considered the USA to be my domestic market and when Polydor decided not to release it there I decided it might finally be time to hang up my dancing shoes. It crept up and blindsided me. I thought, 'Is this what all that work has come down to?' When Jac Holzman brought me to LA in 1973, the plan was to take my career to the next level. A decade down the line, I'd consciously given up on the existence of that next level and let it be known to the music world that I was retiring.

After I made my decision to quit being an artist, I needed to take my energy somewhere else. Where that somewhere else was, I had no idea. One evening I was playing backgammon with Lionel Conway. He told me that Island were looking to expand and wanted someone with artistic experience to seek out new talent.

He offered me a position working for him as a West Coast A&R man. I felt I was in the right place at the right time. It would keep me at the cutting edge of the music I so loved. I accepted his offer.

I worked for and with Lionel for roughly eighteen months. I suggested acts I thought might be suitable for the label, learning the job as I worked. Things ran smoothly until we fell out over a band from Sacramento called Bourgeois Tagg. All things considered, I'm quite satisfied with the work I did for Island. There had been warning signs and I conveniently ignored them, telling myself that I was doing good work and because of this my job would be safe.

I decorated my office with memorabilia from my days as an artist. Out of the blue one day Lionel walked in and told me to take it all down. In his words, I was A&R now, my artist days were over. He thought my souvenirs might intimidate prospective acts. I didn't see it that way at all. Another time, a group of us were sitting around a dinner table at a music convention. Island's owner Chris Blackwell was talking about a new album by an Irish band he'd signed called In Tua Nua. He was very enthusiastic and said it was a great album but needed remixing. He turned to me and asked if it was something I could do. I said, 'Yes, I can do that.' At which point Lionel leaned over and whispered in my ear, 'Think carefully about this, Chris is a stickler for perfection. Fuck it up and you're gone.'

One day an old friend from Seattle, Kelly Curtis called me. I'd met Kelly during his scuffling days when he was a roadie for Heart. He said he had something he'd like to play me. We set up a meeting and Kelly came in and made his pitch. He played me a style of music I'd never heard before. It was a young Seattle band he and his partner were managing. I wasn't quite sure what to make of it, the music was loud, raw and aggressive. There were aspects of it that I liked but overall it didn't really move me and I passed on it. The band was called Soundgarden and they went on to have a huge career on the grunge scene, selling millions of albums, and Kelly became a very successful manager. All I had to go on was what I liked and what I thought was appropriate for Island. You can't win them all.

In tandem with Island's UK office I worked closely with the Paisley Underground acts, The Long Ryders and Rain Parade, particularly on the Rain Parade album *Crashing Dream*. I helped the band find a producer, a young up-and-comer from North Carolina called Steve Gronback. Matt Piucci, the leader of Rain Parade, didn't care for Steve's authoritative front and would refer to him as Greenback.

At my prompting, Island signed a Southern Californian, high-energy pop band called The Prime Movers. They were stylistically not unlike U2 and a terrific live act. When I found them they were a tight and exciting three-piece. They had all gone through school together. The band felt like three brothers, but Island messed with their formula and insisted on adding a Bono-type lead singer, in my mind destroying the delicate chemistry. They were never the same and I let it be known. Unfortunately their album didn't sell too well. Possibly their lack of success was a nail in my coffin, but then I've never met an A&R man with a 100% record.

I also offered Island, early in her career, a fine young Canadian singer-songwriter called Jane Siberry. Lionel listened to Jane's music and his response was, 'We've already got one.' What he meant was that he was busy making demos with Jamie Bernstein, the daughter of the great Leonard Bernstein. When Lionel turned down Jane, I was flabbergasted. I thought she was ten Jamie Bernsteins. I went straight back to my office, picked up the phone and called a friend, Jeff Heiman. I knew Jeff from when he'd worked at KZAM in Seattle. He was now at Windham Hill Records in Los Angeles. I told him about Jane and suggested that he should listen to the recordings I had. We met for lunch and he took the cassettes with him. The next time I heard from him he was inviting me to a party at Windham Hill. They were announcing the signing of Jane Siberry. She had a glorious career, gaining a huge following, winning multiple Juno's, the Canadian equivalent of a Grammy. Jamie Bernstein never progressed beyond the demo stage with Island.

Bourgeois Tagg came Island's way through an old acquaintance, songwriter Ian Samwell. Ian had written 'Move It' for Cliff

Richard and was now managing the band. Ian called me from Sacramento and sent me some very classy recordings. I played these for Lionel, who loved what he heard and a couple of months later a deal was struck. Together we found a suitable producer. We booked studio time and the songs were chosen, arranged and recorded. Bourgeois Tagg delivered a wonderful debut album. It was cutting-edge rock, full of hooks and musical twists and turns. A release date was set, at which point things became a little sticky.

The traditional guidelines for an A&R man's job are to oversee an artist's recording from beginning to fruition. Lionel saw it a different way. He became friends with the band and saw me as some kind of threat or stumbling block to that friendship. This in turn made my access to the band and my job difficult. When Lionel told me that I wouldn't be going to the album release party, I was angry and frustrated and kicked back, voicing my displeasure by pointing out his unfair behaviour. A short time later, my employment at Island records was terminated.

My fortieth birthday was a depressing affair. I was broke and out of work. My head felt completely scrambled. I had decided that I needed to find out who I was and what I might be doing wrong. With whatever cash I could scrape together – most of it came from selling the bulk of my treasured vinyl – I began undergoing some intense therapy sessions. Despite my relative poverty, these sessions turned out to be the best money I ever spent.

I returned to an incident that happened when I was a young boy. I was at my gran's house. As I was leaving to go home she took a clean, folded, light-blue handkerchief out of a drawer and said, 'I want you to give this to your mother.' When I got home I gave the handkerchief to Mom. Mac was there too. There was an eerie silence as she took it, first glancing sideways at him, before looking back at me without a word passing between us. I couldn't quite put my finger on the way she accepted the handkerchief, or the look on both of their faces. It had me believe that something was not quite right. My gran had never particularly liked Mac. I had suspected at quite a young age that Mac might not be my real father; my two younger brothers were treated significantly better by him. In photographs I didn't look anything like him, or anything like my brothers come to that. Mac had died seven years before in 1979. I'd just finished recording my album *Siamese Friends* in Chipping Norton when Sandy Roberton broke the news to me. 'Ian, your dad has died.'

It was during these therapy sessions that I wrote to Mom, demanding to know the truth about my birth father. After what seemed like an eternity, but was in fact only two months, her distressed, guilt-ridden response dropped through my mailbox. My mother had been married before, to a man named Eric Thomas Pratt. They'd met in the army, fallen deeply in love and after their wedding in October 1943 had lived with the in-laws; first at my gran's in Barton-upon-Humber and then at his parents in Palmers Green, North London. I suspect that the handkerchief my gran gave me to pass on to Mom was the 'something blue' from the bride's wedding day requirements: something old, something new, something borrowed, something blue.

Eric's family were middle class and apparently had high aspirations for their son. Mom, being a simple, working-class northern girl, didn't quite match up to their lofty expectations. She loved Eric, but the daily grind of outright rejection and disdain for her roots got to her. She came undone and retraced her steps back home to safety sometime in the autumn of 1945. It was then, for reasons unknown, that she began an affair with Mac. I have the divorce papers in my personal archive and they state that they met at a place called The Mayfair Hotel in Hull and also in a flat at Exchange Street off the Beverley Road in the same city. Just before her affair, Eric visited my mom in Barton to try to reconcile. The reconciliation did not work and Eric went back to London alone. Not long after this, my mother discovered that she had become pregnant with Eric's child during that brief reconciliation. I was that child.

I can't imagine how she coped with her predicament. I can only think that after deciding to leave Eric, then discovering she was pregnant by him, Mom realised that she needed a father for her unborn child. Although they were officially separated in early 1946, immediately after her affair came to light, Eric and my mom weren't divorced until September 1947, a year and three months after I was born. By this time Eric had left the army and was working as a trainee film printer back in North London. When he served the divorce papers, he cited my mother's adultery with Mac. The truth was that Mom had already decided to leave him. There's a heart-wrenching letter I inherited in which Eric talks about 'never realising his dream' – presumably that he would be there to raise the child that Mom was carrying.

Recently I rediscovered a second letter Mom had written to me at the time. I'd kept the letter and found it buried deep in my archives. I have never shared the contents of this letter with anyone beyond my closest family. Maybe now it's time.

> Son, I know what you're wanting to hear.
> I can tell you so little about your father. How I wish I could, but forty years is a lifetime away. Please don't set your heart on him still being alive, because whilst he was in the army he contracted black water fever, a disease that most white people never survived at the time, but he must have been quite tough. No, he wasn't a doctor. [I had asked her in an earlier letter if he was a doctor]. He served with the RAMC [Royal Army Medical Corp]. He was a sergeant radiographer and was very good at his work. I cannot remember his army number, but it must be amongst the RAMC records. They would also know his address when he was discharged, but I feel sure that would be the one on the North Circular Road. The one I already gave you. He mentioned a few times that he'd been offered a job after the war at the Mill Hill hospital in North London, but I don't know if he ever accepted. It would almost certainly have been this type of work, as he was fully qualified.
> One of the reasons why I've taken some time to answer your last letter was because you had asked for a photograph and I knew I had one somewhere, but just cannot find it, though I've searched everywhere. Recently I went to stay at Barton for a few days and eventually told your Aunt Carrie what was happening. It's the first time I've ever confided this in anyone. Fortunately she had a very small photo tucked away, which I've sent. It was actually one taken on our wedding day and I don't know why she only

kept his piece unless I was in her bad books too. You'll notice, I'm sure, how very much you resemble him.

You asked me why I wanted to find your father after Mac died. I suppose I had never forgotten him and often wondered over the years how he fared. It's impossible to banish anyone you've ever loved from your mind and I always hoped that he was happy. One day I switched on the television and was watching a football match. Spurs were playing and a young player on their team looked so much like your father as I'd known him years ago. It could be a coincidence I know, but his name was also Pratt and every time the team were on TV I watched out for him. His name was John. I was convinced he must have been some relation, as strangely enough White Hart Lane was the only ground I ever went to with your father. I may be wrong, but it could give you a slight lead if I'm not.

I then had the vague idea that it could do no harm to contact him (your father I mean) but I only got as far as trying to find an address in the phone book. When I couldn't trace anyone by that name I came home and thought it was maybe for the best. He could be alive, happily married again and have a family who may resent my interference, so I let it rest. Now you have more incentive to find him and I hope you succeed. I just wish I could help more and had told the truth years ago, but I was too cowardly. I loved and needed all my family, especially you, as I always will.

I hope you find what you want.

All my love

Mom x

I looked at the photograph Mom sent me and there was an uncanny resemblance between him and me. It had been crudely scissored in two. The very tip of Mom's elbow was still visible, curled around my father's. Understanding precisely what that photo implied was a huge moment for me, as though the universe was giving me a present, a sending-off gift for the rest of my life journey. I stared at that picture, sobbing uncontrollably. It was an intensely emotional moment, a pivotal moment in my life and difficult to describe, but it served to lift me from my pit of despair, replacing it with an incredibly serene sense of belonging. Many years later I can see and verbalise the significance of that photo. In the moment I could not. It was the writer Karen Joy Fowler who said, 'An oft-told story is like a photograph in a family album; eventually, it replaces the moment it was meant to capture.'

Towards the end of my tenure at Island I had been contacted by Dave Pegg, Fairport's bass player. He wanted to know if I was interested in participating in their annual Fairport Convention Cropredy Festival. Apparently I was the only original member to have not played it and they thought it was time. I told Dave that I hadn't played live for quite some time and that I was not sure I had the confidence to pull it off. He said I'd be fine. They would give me a tight forty-five minute set and Fairport would back me. There would be plenty of rehearsal time beforehand to get things ship shape. The festival was during the second weekend in August and I agreed to be there.

After Island had let me go, Jeff Heiman suggested to Windham Hill that maybe they should hire me to do A&R for a new vocal label they were launching, reminding them that I had tipped him off to Jane Siberry. I went up to Palo Alto for an interview and was grilled by the label's founder Will Ackerman and his second in command, Dawn Atkinson. They told me they knew and liked my music and that they saw my experience with acoustic music as a bonus. I was relaxed throughout the interview and felt that it had gone quite well. Will said they would pow-wow and get back to me. A couple of weeks later Dawn called to offer me the position. I made it clear that I could only begin working for them after my Cropredy commitment, to which they agreed.

I turned up a week before the festival to rehearse my ten-song set with Fairport. While I was in the UK I spent a little time in London and decided to try and find my father before it was too late. In my hotel room I was thumbing through the Greater London area phone book when, lo and behold, there he was: E.T. Pratt. 55 North Circular Road. Palmers Green. N13. Damn, I thought, Chris was from Palmers Green. I'd been in the area so many times in the late sixties, never realising that he was there too.

There was a telephone number.

I got up and made myself a cup of tea. Pacing and thinking. What should I say? Okay, just stay calm, be polite, verify the name and then tell him who you are and let it flow from there. I dialled the number. It rang three times before a man's voice answered. 'Hello.'

'Hello,' I said, 'is this Mr Eric Thomas Pratt?'

'Yes, it is,' said the voice. 'May I ask who is this?'

'You don't know me,' I said. 'Can I ask you, were you ever married to a Dorothy May Matthews?'

'Well, yes I was,' he replied, 'But that was a very long time ago.'

'Yes, it was, more than forty years ago,' I said, 'but I believe you may be my father.'

CLICK. The line went dead

Shit. What did I do wrong?

I dialled the number again. It just rang and rang. I knew in my heart he wasn't going to pick up a second time, but I tried anyway. No one answered.

I was very nervous the day of my festival appearance. Fairport had put me in a nice hotel in Banbury, the nearest big town. I awoke bright-eyed and alert around 6am. I showered and dressed before making the short walk into the centre. It was still only half past seven and the streets where all but deserted. My mind raced with what-ifs as I fretted uncontrollably about my first stage time in more than two years. I knew in my heart it would be fine and that worrying wouldn't change a damned thing, but that's who I was.

I thought I'd dress for the occasion and before leaving LA had bought myself a white terrycloth suit. I'd phoned my friend Joe Patrick, who had arranged with Washburn for me to borrow a guitar, which I'd picked up while I was in London. It was an eye-popping black with a bright-red binding. As if I didn't have enough to think about. A simple spruce top would have sufficed.

I needn't have worried about my performance. I was welcomed and embraced by some 20,000 adoring fans. Fairport were great as my band, hitting all the cues and endings. Simon Nicol smiling at me from one end of the stage and Dave Pegg from the other. I felt surprisingly comfortable up there, even sparring good-naturedly with the crowd. The highlight for me though was an a cappella version of 'Woodstock'. I'd thought to do it with the band and at the last minute had an idea to invite Richard Thompson, Christine Collister and Clive Gregson on stage with me to sing it in four-part harmony. We quickly found our parts backstage and ran through it a couple of times, arranging as we flew. It sent the crowd into hysterics.

In the backstage area after the show, I bumped into Robert Plant, who was also performing that day. We stopped to chat and he congratulated me on my performance. Back in 1970, *Melody Maker* had asked famous singers to name their own favourite singers. Robert named Peter Lewis of Moby Grape, Roy Harper and me. I was gobsmacked and had followed his exploits ever since. Robert asked me what I was working on. I told him that I had officially retired from the creative side of music and was about to take on my new role as an A&R man for Windham Hill. He asked me why and I told him that I didn't think I had anything left to say. His reaction was unexpected.

'Well for what it's worth, and judging by what I've just witnessed out there and the way the crowd reacted, I think you still have plenty to say.'

He said if he was me, he'd think about getting back on the horse that threw me and start writing and performing again. I took what he said very much to heart and re-ran the conversation over and over in my head.

When I got back to California I wrote my father a letter. I told him that I wasn't looking for anything, I just wanted to meet him. I'd had a copy made of the photo of him that Mom had sent me and slipped it into the envelope, along with one of me. The facial similarities were startling. His lopsided grin was so much a part of me too. I sealed the envelope, mailed it off and waited two months, but there was no response.

One more time, I thought. I'll give it one more try and wrote a second letter, saying more or less the same things, but adding that I had a daughter who I thought looked a lot like him. I placed a picture of Darcy inside the folded letter. He didn't respond. I hadn't expected him to. I had hoped and prayed that he would, but in my heart I felt he wouldn't.

I told Darcy the story. 'Oh Dad,' she said and tears ran down her pretty face.

Years later she called me. By that time she had taken matters into her own hands and hatched a plan. She was still in London and had been to find him herself. She had knocked on the door of 55 North Circular Road. An older lady had answered. Darcy told her she was doing a survey, recording how long people stayed in the same place. Pretending to check a list, she asked the lady if this was the home of Mr Eric T. Pratt.

'Well, yes, it was,' the lady said, 'but I'm afraid he died several years ago.'

'Are you living here alone now?' Darcy asked.

'Yes, I am,' she replied.

'Thank you,' said Darcy.

'Thank you dear,' said the lady and closed the door.

I never met my father and Darcy never knew her grandad.

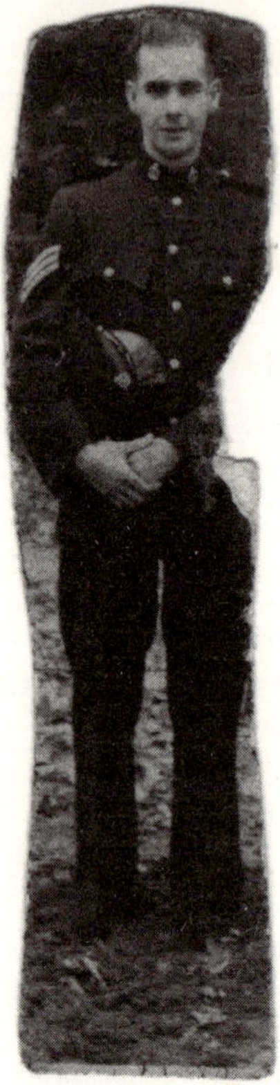

GOD'S EYE VIEW

I just stumbled on that picture Mama gave me
Where someone separated her from you
And I cannot for the life of me explain it
Won't you help me from your God's eye view?

I just wanted her to tell me all about you
Sharing every little detail that she knew
But I didn't learn the half of it
Till she was on her own
And you'd found yourself a God's eye view

Now I'm staring at the picture contemplating
Why someone truly hated it and who
Why it's been covered up for years
Through all the pain and guilt and fear
And you've known it all along now, haven't you?
From your God's eye view

Some days I'll be the image of my mama
I'll be defeated, overwhelmed without a clue
And I just can't figure out what might have happened
Can't you help me from your God's eye view?

Lately I've been dwelling on that question
What could have made that picture so taboo?
Why Mama thought her bridges might come tumbling down
I know you saw it from your God's eye view

12. THE BIG IDEA

I went to work for Windham Hill. My first signing for the label was a fine jazz pianist/composer from Chicago called Fred Simon. He'd made a recording called *Time and the River* which had become one of my favourite relaxation albums. I thought that Fred was perfect for Windham Hill. I played his album for Dawn and she loved it. She played it for Will who liked it too. My idea was for Windham Hill to license the album and reissue it. It had originally been released on a small Chicago label called Quaver and was difficult to find. Windham Hill could put their new age muscle behind it to give it a bigger profile and a far wider distribution.

I called Fred and left a message on his answerphone. 'Hi Fred, this is Ian Matthews at Windham Hill. We are interested in speaking with you about being on our label.' Later that day a very excited Fred Simon called me back and talks began. I introduced him to Dawn and left the two of them to get on with the negotiations. The resulting decision was to not reissue *Time and the River* but to make a brand-new album with the title *Usually/Always*. That's where my job resumed. Fred said he wanted to make a jazzier album with some of Pat Metheny's musicians. I was a tad sceptical of this, Metheny was jazz and Windham Hill's reputation was that of a new age label. I asked Fred to run this by the powers that be, meaning Will and Dawn. They said they were fine with it and gave him the go-ahead. *Usually/Always* is a gorgeously heartfelt piano-based recording, packed with skilfully crafted, incisive compositions, backed up by terrific musicianship. Fred also features on a best selling Windham Hill sampler, *Soul of the Machine*. He and I have stayed in touch and he is still a good friend to this day.

After six months of living on my own I moved back in with Melissa again and struggled for a while juggling this loosely-tied relationship and my new job at Windham Hill. A relative peace of mind came when the company transferred me from the Hollywood office up to Mill Valley, 400 miles north. I loved my life by the bay. Things felt almost European there. I spent my weekdays in the office and would try to make it back to LA at weekends, but quickly tired of the commute. My dear friends, David and Kate Hayes, lived slightly north-west of me in Fort Bragg just off Highway 1 and I loved to visit them and their young family. It gave me a sense of belonging which I sorely missed in LA. Instead of making that gruelling commute I started spending my weekends with them in their large rambler in the woods.

David was the bass player and bandleader with Van Morrison at the time and Kate was an FM radio personality in the city. David was making preparations for a European tour with Van and they were looking for backup singers. I told David I was interested and would he recommend me for the job.

'Really?' he said.

'Yeah,' I replied, 'I can picture myself doing that. Would you speak to Van for me?'

'Sure,' said David and we left it at that. The tour came and went and I'd heard nothing, so I called David to ask why.

'Do you really want to know what happened?' he asked.

'I don't know, do I?'

'Well,' he said, 'I gave Van your message and he looked at me quizzically over his glasses and said, "Tell Ian Matthews to get on with his own fucking career and stay out of mine."'

'That was it?' I asked.

'That was it,' said David.

Windham had hired me because they were starting a new vocal label. That label didn't materialise and I was put to work scouting instrumental acts. Quite honestly, it wasn't my niche. I got lucky with Fred Simon, but mostly I was unfamiliar with the genre and quite ineffective. I didn't know where to look or who to ask and all the time Robert Plant's words were ping-ponging around in my head.

The dilemma solved itself. I had an idea for a concept album.

It involved recording an album's worth of songs by a relatively unknown songwriter. The album would be acoustically driven with a guest keyboard player on each track. Through Windham Hill, the idea was offered to an artist already on the label, Barbara Higbee. She turned it down, but I couldn't let go of it. I believed that it was a strong concept and someone should do it. It suddenly dawned on me, maybe that someone could be me.

Let my reason for consistently getting back on this horse that threw me go on record. It stems from an early love for recorded music and, eventually, the creative process. When I was young, I became captivated by the music my mom played at home, even though it wasn't music I particularly cared for – Scottish pipe bands and Frank Ifield are at best an acquired taste. My mom was passionate about a vocal quartet called the Deep River Boys, a black gospel group from Virginia. She owned one of their albums, which I still have. This album influenced me towards nurturing an early love of soul and gospel music. Whenever she would play something for me, this was the music I'd usually request.

In the beginning I wasn't allowed to touch the hi-fi system myself. If I wanted to hear something it was always by request. As time went by I became trusted with the stereo. By the time I was fifteen, the bulky wooden-cased dinosaur was long gone, replaced by a sleek blue and white portable Dansette player. When I bought my first single, The Hollies' 'Searchin'', I learned from reading the label that it was written by an American duo called Jerry Leiber and Mike Stoller and was originally released in America by The Coasters. This knowledge led me to The Impressions. I bought my first LP, The Impressions' *Big Sixteen*, a compilation album made specifically for the European market. Then when UK pop music kicked in with a vengeance I became a consumer and the world was my oyster.

What I'm dodging around the houses attempting to say is that I didn't begin this tenuous journey to become famous, or to attract girls, or to amass a fortune. It began with a fascination I've never completely let go of. For me it was the fact that someone had created the music I was hearing and then found a way to archive it. And now, despite knowing practically everything there is to know about the music business and the people who run it, despite being alternately damned and blessed by it, the right music will still move me to tears. From the outset, I promised myself that if I ever became complacent about it, or found myself bored by it, or take it for granted, then I would stop. I have quit a couple of times, but fortunately the muse has always returned to rescue me. It might sound as strange to hear as it does to say, but the further I journey on this tentative musical quest, the more often I re-state my vow. To this day, I can truthfully say that I walk this chosen path because of a lifelong passion for music and because of how much music in return has given back to me and enriched my life.

I left Windham Hill to look for help to develop my project. I found myself a new manager, Bill Trout. Bill had been around the proverbial block several times and had a son, Ross, who was already a professional musician. Bill's real passion was jazz. He was on the board of directors at the Recording Academy, commonly known as the Grammys, and knew many people in the business. He told me about a young studio owner he knew in Austin, Texas. His name was Mark Hallman. He felt that Mark and I could make a good team. 'I think the two of you will really hit it off,' is what he said. I flew to Austin to meet Mark and discovered that Bill was right. Mark was in the early stages of his studio build and wide open to new musical challenges.

I explained my concept to Mark. It was still rough around the edges but he embraced it enthusiastically. All I had to do now was decide on my writer. I considered Van Morrison, someone I admired greatly as a songwriter, but maybe he was too well known for this purpose. I thought about Richard Thompson, but he seemed a little too obvious and close to home. I then came back to my original idea of finding someone relatively unknown. What about Jules Shear? He'd already written two big hits, one for The Bangles and one for Cyndi Lauper, but still no one really knew who he was. I had recorded his song 'Home Somewhere' on the *Siamese Friends* album and I was currently enjoying his latest Jules and the Polar Bears band record. I played a selection of his writing for Mark who gave it a mighty thumbs up.

I had first become aware of the music of Jules Shear in 1976 when he was in a band called The Funky Kings. A friend drove me down to Laguna Beach to see them play an outdoor show and I became an instant fan, but not just of Jules. There were other great writers in the band, Jack Tempchin and Richard Stekol. Jack's song 'Slow Dancing' from their 1976 Arista album would crack the American Top Ten a year later with a version by Johnny Rivers.

Jules is a Pittsburgh boy, another one who had drifted west in search of the Holy Grail. I tracked him down in Hollywood and explained my idea. He said he was honoured that I had chosen him and wanted to help. I told him that the first thing he could do was to send me as many of his songs that he thought might interest me. I was overwhelmed by the amount of music I got from him. During a two-month period he sent me upwards of a hundred songs. They were mostly on cassette and came complete with handwritten lyrics and lead sheets. There was always a note enclosed saying if I needed more to just ask. I told him I was looking for a song to sing a cappella and he instantly wrote one for me. The way he had arranged and sung it made it sound almost Eastern European. It's called 'On Squirrel Hill'. He'd written it as an homage to the area of Pittsburgh he had grown up in.

It was an embarrassment of riches. I went over and over a process of elimination, agonising over which songs to keep and which to discard, eventually rooting out the ones Mark and I felt didn't quite work for us. We ended up choosing around twenty-five of them. We carefully listened to those twenty-five, dissecting them, considering tempos and subject matter and then reduced the number to seventeen. We then committed to recording seventeen acoustic demo versions with vocals, acoustic guitar and drum machine at Mark's Congress House Studio.

In the meantime, Bill Trout was searching out a record deal. From all the numerous labels he contacted, the one that surprisingly showed the most interest was Windham Hill. Now they could hear it! I was bemused but committed to making the album for them. Dawn Atkinson and I had a standing joke that I was the only person to have been welcomed into the Windham Hill family twice.

During my A&R residency at Windham Hill I had been forced to listen to an awful lot of bad new age keyboard players, but I'd also been introduced to some very good ones and wanted to try them out. I decided that a mix of genres might be the best approach for the album and drew up a list of roughly fifteen players I wanted to participate. I already sensed that Joe Zawinul might turn down such a request and I was right. I wasn't jazz enough for him. Mark Isham, who I desperately wanted to participate, was understandably far too busy with his film composing to find the time. For varying reasons, more than half of my list were unable to, or didn't want to participate and we finally reached commitments from an exotic mix of eight keyboardists. I cheated a little by adding Japanese koto player Osamu Kitajima, who technically is also a keyboard player, but I opted for his koto expertise. Osamu played a breathtakingly beautiful koto solo on a track called 'Except for a Tear'. My friend Fred Simon digitised his two contributions and mailed them in from Chicago. Van Dyke Parks added to 'Only a Motion' what he playfully described as 'a sashay across the veranda on a grand piano'.

We decided to improvise and make the bulk of the record in California rather than Texas. The majority of the guest players lived there and it created room in the budget for a more state-of-the-art mixing facility. We recorded the basic guitar and percussion tracks in Texas before I flew home and Mark drove the 1,400 miles to Venice Beach with his mobile studio components in the back of his old red Renault.

All of the overdubs and vocals were done in the tiny apartment I rented above a four-car garage, half a block east of a bustling Venice boardwalk. The keyboard players had to lug their equipment up the aging, wooden staircase into my cramped quarters. The final recordings we did there were the vocals on a stifling summer weekend with the windows closed in 100-degree heat.

Windham Hill arranged for me to do a publicity photo shoot with the legendary Jim Marshall. Although his star was fading by the eighties, Jim was still the pre-eminent photographer in San Francisco and had been for many years. He famously shot Jimi

Hendrix setting fire to his guitar at the Monterey Pop Festival. Jim and I spent an entire day walking and shooting around the streets of Haight-Ashbury in San Francisco. When we were done he took me back to his studio to show me his archives. He had photographed absolutely everyone and asked me if there was a particular photograph I might like to have. I told him I was a huge fan of Tim Hardin. He slid open his 'H' drawer and pulled out a candid shot he'd taken in Greenwich Village back in the late sixties. It was of Tim emerging from the subway with a startled look on his face. He graciously gave me a print of the photo and signed it for me. I treasured it for many years before gifting it to a friend and fellow Hardin fan in Germany.

The album *Walking a Changing Line* remains a unique addition to my catalogue. I suppose you might call it part of my tribute series. It was an important record to make in that it served to get me back in the public eye and performing again.

Amazingly, my on-again, off-again romance with Melissa lasted well into the autumn of 1988, when I finally despaired of both her and Los Angeles for good. I sold my little MGB that I'd found when I'd moved to LA and had kept through my time as an A&R man, as it was no longer practical with barely enough space for an acoustic guitar and suitcase. In its place I bought a hulking, bright-blue Volvo station wagon.

When a situation turns sour, I tend to put as much distance between myself and the situation as I possibly can. It's almost like going cold turkey but without the drugs. I need a change of scenery, with time to collect my thoughts and reflect. It's not always to my benefit but almost part of my DNA and one of the reasons there are people all around the globe I care for and call my friends. My daughter Darcy lives in Devon and we speak maybe a half-dozen times a year, yet she knows that I love her dearly, think about her constantly and would do anything for her at the drop of a hat. She also knows that I'm not a very communicative person and she will see me when she sees me. All of my friends know and accept this as being part of who I am. You'd think being a songwriter and a performer that I'd be outgoing and have hundreds of friends, but I don't. I have my family and a few friends and that's all I need. Time is just numbers. Family and close friends are forever.

I called my friend Joe Patrick. He lived on Whidbey Island, just off the Washington coast near Seattle. When I met Joe he was the Pacific Northwest rep for Washburn guitars. We found each other through David Surkamp, who would on occasion borrow guitars from him. Washburn also had a nice acoustic line in the early eighties and Joe signed me up as an endorsee. He and I became friends through guitars and that carried over into other areas. We had a common love of baseball so began going to Seattle Mariner games together and slowly the friendship blossomed. In later years, Joe moved from the mainland and opened his own guitar shop 'Joe's Island Music' on Whidbey Island and that's where I sent out my SOS. He invited me to visit him up there and told me about a holiday let that was vacant for the winter months. It was hard to leave my California friends again, but I'm a mover. I faced up to that fact long ago.

PART FOUR
WALKING A CHANGING LINE

GHOST CHANGES

Something's shifting in my life
I'm not feeling quite the same
A murmuring way deep inside
A shift impossible to name
I marvel in that moment
When life's fabric rearranges
Ghost changes

Hearing without knowing
What it is I'm listening to
Watching without judgement
From a different point of view
Knowing how it ends
Without turning all the pages
Feels like ghost changes

Philosophers and sorcerers
All wrestle with the notion
That mankind is so miniscule
In God's beautific ocean
That we are only castaways
Upon the rock of ages

Somewhere in the universe
A million miles from here
The echo of some long-lost soul
Might suddenly appear
Aching for a reason to be welcome among strangers
It's just ghost changes

Something's shifted in my life
I'm not feeling quite the same

13. REPAIR AND RESTORATION

Whidbey Island is in the Puget Sound, an inlet of the Pacific Ocean. It has a population of around 58,000 people and is said to be one of the largest American offshore islands. The north end of the island is a naval base and at the south end an eccentric Bohemian community have settled. I was looking for repair and restoration and, thanks to the generosity of my old friend Joe Patrick, I had a place to regroup and think about the future.

The house I rented was near the community of Greenbank and a holiday let during the summer months. There were maybe eight to ten houses along the beach, most of them empty for the winter by the time I arrived. The approach was a steep, spiralling road down from the main two-lane highway. It was called Hidden Beach for good reason and the perfect seclusion to meditate on my future. The house was really just a single room, wood-framed structure with a backwards sloping roof to allow maximum sunlight, and a small loft bedroom area made accessible by a hastily-constructed ladder. The downstairs had a 180-degree view of the Saratoga Passage through a ceiling-to-floor glass sliding window. Outside was a large, wooden deck area. Upon arrival I activated the house telephone line and opened a bank account in Coupeville, the nearest reasonably-sized town.

During the day I would wander lazily along the shoreline, stopping to crouch and meditate on the pebble beach, or pick up unusually marked stones and the occasional shed golden eagle feathers. On other days I would just sit on my veranda at low tide and watch those beauties feed on the sandbar. I played a little bit of guitar, which I hadn't done in a while, and worked on some new ideas for songs. In the evenings I'd visit Joe or stay in and watch a movie. I lived a low-key existence, kept a simple journal and pondered on what I might do next.

As late summer turned to autumn I began to wonder what

winter at the water's edge might be like. I spoke to Joe and his partner Gail about it. They told me that soon it would begin to turn chilly and before Christmas there could be snow. They said it may be a wise move to buy some chains for the car and a shovel as the access road could get tricky. They also advised me to stockpile logs because it can get pretty cold down by the water. I felt a slight fretfulness coming on. I hadn't prepared myself mentally for winter. What if it snows and I'm stuck down here alone? What if the phone goes down? What if? What if?

One night in early October I was feeling a little nervous and isolated. I called Mark Hallman. He could tell from the tone of my voice that all was not well. I spewed out my fears to him and he said that perhaps I ought to consider moving to Austin, Texas. It would be a good place to work from.

'It's a songwriter's town,' he said 'You'll love it here. You'll be amongst friends and it's not going to snow.'

He told me there was a spare bedroom in his studio and I could have it until I found a place of my own. I began to feel calmer as he talked and thanked him profusely as we said goodnight. I put the phone down, brushed my teeth and climbed the ladder up to the futon in my loft. I read a little Stephen Levine, listened to Willis Alan Ramsey crooning on about Spider John and Old Missoula before falling into a deep, dreamless slumber.

The next morning, my talk with Mark still fresh in my mind, I drove over to Joe's store and explained to him that I had all but made the decision to head south. He completely understood and said that in my shoes he would probably do the same. He said it was good to see me smiling again and that he could tell that I had achieved whatever needed doing here on the island. I called on my landlord, apologised for the abrupt notice, told him I was leaving and handed back the keys to my short-term paradise. I closed the dwindling bank account and cancelled the phone. Less than a week later I packed the Volvo – Old Blue – to the gills one more time. I coaxed her up onto the main road, checked in at the Clinton ferry terminal for one last time and began my trip south. I heard recently that Joe himself moved on again and these days he is one of the top guitar repair and restoration men in eastern Washington. I haven't seen Joe for almost thirty years, but I know when I eventually do we'll pick up right where we left off in 1988.

The drive from the island to Austin took me three long days. I covered slightly more than 2,200 miles and drove through seven states, including Washington, the northern tip of Oregon, Idaho, Utah, a tiny piece of Colorado, across New Mexico and down through North Texas into Austin. The first night I stopped in a campsite full of vacationing motor homes near the south-eastern border of Idaho and slept in the back of the Volvo, all the while acutely aware of my belongings piled high in the rear and my bike strapped tightly to the roof. Staying in a motel would have meant unloading everything into the room and vice versa the following morning and I wasn't really up for that. The second night, somewhere in New Mexico, I again slept in Old Blue, this time at a brightly-lit freeway rest stop, parked directly outside the main entrance; the upside being that I could tumble out of the car in the morning, use the café bathroom to brush my teeth and eat breakfast with my belongings in clear view. Ahh, this rock star life.

Around 4pm on the third day, in 80-degree heat, I eased the Volvo into the gravel driveway of the Congress House Studio in South Austin, ready to pick up the pieces and start over yet again. I walked in expecting to see Mark but he wasn't there. I was greeted by a skinny, dark-blond, bright-eyed young fellow.

'Haah,' he exclaimed in his Texan drawl. 'Ahhm Brad. You must be Eean.'

I figured out that he meant, 'Hi, I'm Brad.' He told me that Mark was delivering emergency equipment to a friend down at *Austin City Limits Soundstage*.

'Hill be raaaht back,' said my new friend. 'Coffee?'

This was how I first met Bradley Kopp. He and I would soon become what they call in Texas 'bosom buddies', eventually touring and recording together. Today he's like a blood brother. Little did I realise on that first balmy October evening I was about to enter the most rewarding and prolific ten years of my professional life.

I tell people who have never been to Austin that it's like a tiny oasis dropped unceremoniously into the middle of a cultural wasteland known as Central Texas. There is no other town in Texas remotely like Austin. It's as though God thought to himself, 'Okay, what can I do to really piss off the natives? I think I'll create an alternative community right here in Central Texas and see what happens. Then I'll stir the pot a little and make it the state capital.'

During the time I lived in Austin I developed a love-hate relationship with the area. I loved the creative force field that appeared to tug on any songwriter moving there. The spring weather was wonderful, a breezy 65 degrees, but as May approached so did the oppressive heat and by the end of the month it could already be a brutal 90 plus, slowly creeping into the 100s. The heat and oppressive humidity came hand-in-hand and there would be no relief until late October.

Central Texas has several varieties of wildlife that could do one harm. There are coyotes with their childlike yipping and whining, beginning at sundown and lasting long into darkness. Snapping turtles are common to the area. They have incredibly long necks and a jaw that I'm told can bite a baseball bat in half. It's rumoured that one can spot a snapping turtle by a red dot on the top of its head, the problem being that by the time that dot is clear of the shell it may already be too late. Brown recluse spiders are just that: very small and love to hide in dust-ridden areas. They have a bite so lethal it can rot the flesh a quarter-inch deep and an inch around the bite. The dreaded rattlesnake and its chilling high-pitched maraca-like shake scared me to death. Unless you can actually see the snake, it could be anywhere within 360 degrees.

In 1988 the music scene in Austin had not reached the oversaturated state it's now in, it was still fresh and vital and writers were pouring in. They hit town in all forms of musical evolution, beginners to intermediates and professionals. The law of averages dictates there has to be more than a reasonable percentage of good ones, but the majority of new arrivals have to play month after month for next to nothing hoping to be spotted.

Some never break through. I got lucky. I had a history and a reputation so established writers were more than willing to give me the time of day. Through Mark and Brad I met and interacted with the cream of the Texas songwriters: Jimmie Dale Gilmore, Butch Hancock, Jimmy LaFave, David Halley, Tish Hinojosa, Charlie Sexton, Lucinda Williams. The list goes on. I also first encountered my über talented friend Michael Fracasso in those first few months. Songwriting seemed almost infectious and soon I found myself on a writing spree. Songs literally poured from me. The rest had done me good and Robert Plant was right, I still had plenty to say.

But first of all I had an album to promote, *Walking a Changing Line*. In the spring of 1989 I put a simple trio together with me and Mark Hallman on acoustic guitars and a local keyboard player, Craig Negoescu. We called him Biff Nabisco because of his steady diet of boxed breakfast products. Craig was a technological whiz and could program drum parts and appropriate sounds into his state-of-the-art machine, leaving him free to improvise over them. That was until the final night in Seattle when the entire rig broke down and began throwing out random sounds and tempos to practically every song in the set, causing much consternation from the audience, greatly perturbing Craig and throwing me and Mark into uncontrollable hysterics.

All things considered, the tour signalled that I was back again and meant business. Mark and I took the album to Europe as an acoustic duo later that year and enjoyed it so much that we decided to dispense with the keys altogether. Unbeknownst to me at the time, by eliminating a band member at the age of forty-two, I'd begun slowly edging towards being a solo performer. When Mark became unavailable to tour because of production commitments, I began taking Bradley Kopp with me instead and I embraced the duo life. It was a new and extremely simple way of touring for me. I was making more or less the same fees that I had with a full band but with a far more practical overhead. There were no bus rentals to begin with. We could fly to a central location, hire a car and share the driving, moving around in a huge three- to four-week long circle before returning the car to the original point of departure and flying home again. I became my own tour manager and bookkeeper. All these years later I have it down to more or less a fine art and would not dream of having someone else do it on my behalf. The preparation has become almost as enjoyable as the trip itself.

With a year of steady touring under my belt and suitably re-established as an acoustic recording artist, I was consciously writing again and subconsciously planning my next record.

Anneke Speller was a songwriter I met while she was making demos at the Congress House Studio. She was easy-going and an engaging conversationalist. We were talking one day about relationships when she made a proposition.

'I have a friend Veronique who I'd like you to meet. She's emerging from a tough divorce but she's open to meeting someone. I think the two of you might really hit it off. Are you interested?'

I was curious. We set up a blind date at a party at Anneke's house and I got there early – I'm habitually early. Veronique arrived from her job, tired and cranky and, to my surprise, quite loud and brash. I remember thinking, 'Who the hell is this woman? Not my type at all.' I was not impressed. She spoke in terms of things belonging to her, about her this and her that and her kids and her ex and all the time I was thinking, 'How could Anneke have possibly thought that we might have anything in common?'

I told Anneke the following day that on first impressions I was very underwhelmed by Veronique. She reassured me saying that Veronique was really very nice, had been quite nervous about meeting me and that I shouldn't give up too easily. She said that Veronique was probably trying too hard because she had known our meeting was a set-up too. I agreed to give it another shot. We went to a movie, then dinner, and somehow we began seeing each other. In time I drove out to her house in North Austin and met her two kids and she would visit me in South Austin until slowly the relationship grew legs.

Veronique Gay worked as a receptionist for an insurance company in a multi-storey building in the north-west part of

Austin. Born and bred in Houston of a French mother and a Texan father, she was fluent in French. She'd unwillingly spent almost all of her childhood summers in Brittany at the family seat attending school alongside the area's youngsters. Veronique had been married to – and recently divorced from – a travelling salesman, a devout catholic of Italian descent. By the time I entered the picture he was still to be seen from time to time picking up the kids and taking them to his place for the weekend. I tried to be friendly towards him but he seemed to have an irrational phobia towards musicians, as though he thought if you made music you had to be deranged and into drugs. To him it seemed musicians were the scum of the earth. He had a strange, convenient morality and constantly judged people, yet he was extremely uncomfortable in his own skin and his morals were questionable at best. Note to self: avoid at all costs. I considered him what I like to refer to as a real piece of work.

A few months into our relationship I found out that when they were together, a relative on Veronique's side had died and left the kids some money while they were still babies. He'd set up a bank account for each of them. After their divorce Veronique told him that she needed access to those accounts. He made a thousand excuses as to why he had to be responsible for the accounts before eventually admitting that there was nothing left in them. He had been out of work and when the going got tough he'd simply helped himself and cleaned them out.

While he was on the road, one of his friends had broken into the house and raped Veronique at knifepoint, intentionally cutting her in the process. The salesman (I still, to this day, cannot summon up the courtesy of using his name) returned home and in complete denial that one of his friends would do such a thing, he refused to let her report the rape to the authorities on the grounds that it could throw shame on the family name. She reported it herself, divorced him and enrolled in self-defence school. After she filed for divorce he cut off her credit, leaving her and their two children to sleep in her car for a couple of months while she hunted for a job. Veronique was enterprising and devised a rotation for visiting friends to make sure the kids were washed and cared for. She'd sometimes let them spend the night in a friend's spare bed while she slept in her car in the driveway. Twice a week they visited Happy Hour bars to let the kids fill up on snacks in lieu of dinner. She never let it visibly get her down and made the pair of them believe they were on a big adventure. I entered the picture almost a year later.

When we began seeing each other regularly, the salesman told her that he did not want his children to be subjected to a strange man around the house and threatened to sue her for custody. His constant interference in our lives was like having a Peeping Tom looking over our shoulder, letting us know in no uncertain terms that we were going about things completely wrong. She was being humiliated by this beast of a man and I was tired of his heavy-handed concerns. He would repeatedly ask the kids if they had ever seen me naked. At which point we decided to hell with him. In February 1990 we tied the knot. I see now that I did it because I wanted to save her from him and from her life as a struggling single mother. There was also a part of me that will never be told what I must and must not do. I had grown to like Veronique. I realised that she was more than just bravado and a stoic front. She had a pioneering spirit and a zest for life. I believed I could rescue her and she was willing to be rescued. I was lonely and looking for someone I could take care of. And I suppose I was hoping that someone might take care of me.

We set up home in a house in North Austin. Veronique and I would take turns in running the children, Genevieve and Dominic, to school. They had to be driven into the city, a forty-five minute drive away. One morning after dropping them off I was pulling into traffic when from the corner of my eye I caught vague movement in the bushes by the roadside. I thought maybe it was a homeless person and stopped to investigate. Deep inside a thick cluster of hedgerow I found a large, black Labrador puppy. He was beautiful and possibly a pure breed. He was wearing a collar but without a tag. He tried to stand and couldn't, every time he tried his back legs would collapse under him. He was frightened but let me touch him. I stroked his rear right leg and he yelped in pain. Slowly I guided him into a clearing assuring him I was his friend and lifted him gently into the passenger seat of the car. The veterinary said he'd most likely jumped from a moving pickup truck and dislocated his hip, it might heal but probably not and the chances of him living longer than two more years were slim. The damage could be surgically repaired but it would be very expensive. The alternative was to work with him myself and see what happened. I took my new friend home and named him Trio.

He was lucky. The house backed onto an extensive lake and jogging track complex and every morning I would put on my shorts, sneakers and T-shirt, and exit the back gate with Trio. We would then cautiously work our way around the track. It was extremely laborious at first, taking an hour to an hour and a half. But each day became a little easier and a little quicker as we slowly added more weight onto the damaged joint. Within two months he was walking tentatively on all four legs, at which point I put him on a very long leash and forced him to swim across the lake while I walked around it. Within six months his limp was barely recognizable and by year's end he was galloping again. Trio became my best friend.

Grandparents.
Tom and Carrie Matthews.

Mom, 1944.

Mother and child. Nice hats, 1946.

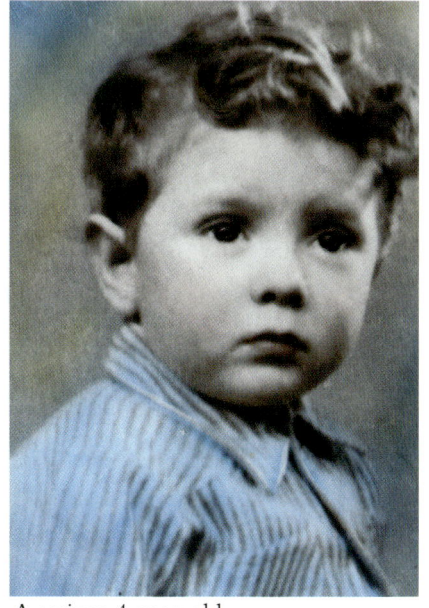

A serious 4-year-old.

Family portrait, 1957. Mac, IM, Andy, Neil, Mom.

IM and Derek Cottam astride his Vincent Black Shadow. Outside the paint shop, Kirton Lindsey.

The fabulous Classics with pop star quiffs.

Ready for work at Ravel's in my Lord John suit.

Pyramid. The Dougie Millings suits. IM, Albert Jackson, Steve Hiett.

The artsy press shot. Pyramid, 1966.

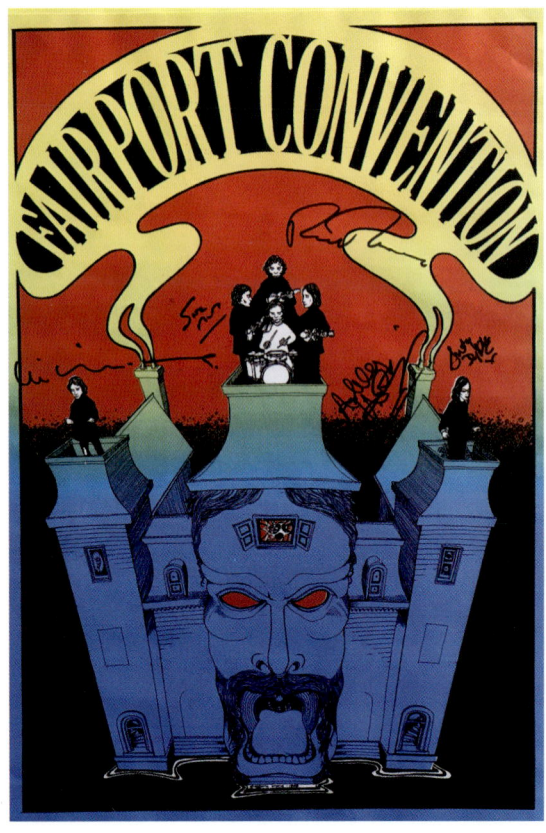

1967. Psychedelia rules.

The conga man.

Fairport Convention, 1968. Simon Nicol, Martin Lamble, Sandy Denny, IM, Ashley Hutchings, Richard Thompson.

Signing day with Uni execs, 1970.

Joni and Matthews Southern Comfort at the London Palladium. Gordon Huntley, Ray Duffy, Joni Mitchell, Andy Leigh, Mark Griffiths, Carl Barnwell, IM.

Plainsong, Sound Techniques Studio, Chelsea, 1972.

Plainsong in full flight. Andy Roberts, IM, Bob Ronga, David Richards.

Darcy and Dad by the pool, Van Nuys, California, 1973.

Valley Hi recording session at Countryside Ranch Studio. IM with Jay Lacy, Bob Warford, Danny Lane, Terry Dunavan and Michael Nesmith.

Hit and Run band with IM, Ken Collier and Steven 'Captain' Hooks.

Mushroom Records office, Vancouver, Canada, 1978.
Sandy Roberton, Susie Gershon, IM, Shelly Siegel.

Hi-Fi Mk.1, 1980. David Surkamp,
Bruce Hazen, Bob Briley,
IM, Gary Shelton.

A man and his Jazzmaster.

'Woodstock' a cappella, Cropredy, 1986.
Richard Thompson, IM, Christine Collister, Clive Gregson.

Trio, North Austin, 1990.

The money pit. Swine Lake, Texas.

Darcy and Dad, Doncaster railway station, early 1990s.

Hamilton Pool, 1995. Mark Hallman, Michael Fracasso, IM.

The Swinelakers, Paradiso, Amsterdam. Mark Andes, IM, Bradley Kopp. Drummer Larry Thompson is out of shot.

Backstage at Quasimodo, Berlin. IM, Steve Young, Bob Neuwirth.

Darcy's drawing for *A Tiniest Wham* cover.

Solo show, Philadelphia, mid-1990s.

More Than a Song cover shoot, Amsterdam, 2001. Ad Vanderveen, Eliza Gilkyson, IM.

IM and Egbert Derix. *In the Now*. Music Star, Norderstedt, Germany, 2012.

With Andy Roberts, Plainsong farewell tour.
Union Chapel, Islington, 2012.

Matthews Southern Comfort, 2018.
Bart-Jan Baartmans, Bart de Win, Eric Devries, IM.

Best day of my life. 5th February 2004.

Family selfie, 2018. IM, Marly, Madelief, Luca.

SIGHT UNSEEN

Whose are these hands, they are not mine
They have not stood the test of time
They have no right being on display
Whose are these hands
Take them away

Whose are these eyes that glare and squint
And see as far as my intent
They magnify my vanity
Whose are these eyes that will not see

Whose are these feet that limp and groan
No longer choose the swift way home
No longer fly down carefree street
They are not mine, come claim these feet

Whose are these candles burning bright
A celebration of the night
When I appeared all twist and scream
To be accepted sight unseen

Whose is this mind of cheap distrust
This sad defensive cut and thrust
It's not the way I meant to be
Whose is this mind, Lord set it free

Whose is this face, it's all my fault
Too many drams of single malt
Too many lines of free cocaine
Whose is this sea of broken veins

Whose are these candles burning bright
A celebration of the night
When I appeared all twist and scream
To be accepted sight unseen

Whose are these ties I never see
That temper my ability
That feed upon my urge to run
Whose are these ties that came undone

Whose is that voice I strain to hear
So distant, yet so crystal clear
I wish that I could let it be
And just accept things sight unseen

14. PRACTISE MAKES PERFECT

Walking a Changing Line had been a fanfare album for me. It announced that I was back and intended to stay around a while longer. The next album was another stellar Mark Hallman production. We called it *Pure and Crooked*. During the recording of the album, Veronique's young daughter Genevieve made a painting in school of me performing. It had my name written above it in childlike letters but she'd spelled my name wrong. It said 'Iain Matthews'. I liked her creation so much that I kept the painting as it was. I then had her write the album title at the bottom in the same unsure hand. Afterwards I made it my album cover and never went back to the old spelling of my name.

Pure and Crooked was released on a Los Angeles-based label, Gold Castle Records. It had eight of my new compositions on it, letting it be known that I was writing again. It was ecstatically reviewed and created a solid enough platform for me to establish myself on the singer-songwriter circuit. I took full advantage of it and toured extensively, promoting the record while building a valuable grassroots following. I felt it might be too little too late but hoped not. To this day, two of my most requested live songs – my own 'Rains of '62' and Peter Gabriel's 'Mercy Street' – are on the record. The album was licensed to an important Japanese independent label. This opened a door for me to also begin touring in Asia.

At the same time as a major door cracked opened for me, another slammed deafeningly shut behind me. My agent called to say there was an opening slot going begging on a major US tour with the South African group Johnny Clegg & Juluka. Was I interested? Yes indeed, I was very interested. Johnny Clegg's music was close to my heart. However, the offer came with the stipulation that I had to play solo. I declined, causing the agent, who was well respected and influential in singer-songwriter circles, to drop me from her roster. It was a tremendous body blow for me. It had been difficult enough for her to find me work and now I had turned it down because of my insecurities.

I was disappointed in myself and determined that it would never happen to me again. There and then I set the wheels in motion towards being a solo performer. I cornered Mark at the studio one day and drilled him as to what I needed to do.

'Well,' he said, 'the good thing is that you already have a voice everyone wants to hear. Now you need to put together a collection of songs that you can alternately fingerpick and flatpick, or sing a cappella. Maybe fifteen to twenty tunes!'

The heat was on. I could strum and pick out bass notes just fine but I'd never learned to fingerpick and if I was to conquer this beast I had to figure it out. I was forty-four years old and the time had arrived. Mark showed me a simple Travis pick (named after the country guitar player Merle Travis) to practise and I sat for days, maybe even weeks working on it. Once I had reached a self-appointed level of proficiency we chose the song 'Mercy Street' from *Pure and Crooked* and Mark showed me how it was done. I cannot pretend it was easy but I kept reminding myself how important it was to be independent and how good I would feel reaching that moment. It took me a solid two to three months, but with Mark's encouragement I put together two hours of competent singing and playing. Now it needed a test run.

Veronique and I invited a half-dozen friends over for dinner, including Mark. After dinner I was to play a short solo concert. I was mind-numbingly nervous about it and less than half a song into my performance my fingers cramped so badly they wouldn't move no matter how hard I tried to coax them into doing so. I felt embarrassed and defeated.

'Okay,' Mark said taking me to one side, 'we're all your friends here and no one is judging you. No one cares how well you play we just want to hear that voice. Now relax, take some deep breaths and pretend it's just you and I working things out. It doesn't matter if you stumble. We all stumble, all the time.'

I picked up the pieces and began playing again, moving from being self-conscious and tentative to feeling a whisper of confidence, to absolute enjoyment and confidence. Soon I was flowing from song to song, chatting with my guests and before realising it I'd played for almost two hours. The moral was, don't be afraid to learn. It's never too late to learn something and thanks to a good friend having absolute confidence in me I had conquered the beast that had stalked me for all those years.

Once I'd finally learned how to play solo there was no stopping me and for the next several years I would drive the length and breadth of the country touring. I still vividly remember my first paid solo concert as if it was yesterday. An English friend, Len Holton, a nurse and part-time radio DJ in Little Rock, Arkansas was running a songwriter series called 'Folk Fairport'. He made me a sensible offer and I drove the 500-odd miles from Austin to Little Rock, before showering, soundchecking and performing that same night. The room held 150 people and I arrived to discover that it was sold out. I played for a solid two hours, recalling everything Mark had taught me. It wasn't until I reached my encore that I let my audience in on the secret. I had done it. I'd played solo for the very first time and there was no going back.

I bought a large cab Nissan pickup with a metal toolbox bolted into the bed. On a dull day my truck looked black, but in the sunlight it was a metallic, almost sparkly dark-green. I would stash my guitar and suitcase behind the seats and everything else would go into the locked toolbox. I'd lay an open box of my favourite CDs on the passenger-side floor before hitting the highways and byways for a couple of weeks, criss-crossing the USA alone in search of the wily dollar.

I played in places that I had never visited before. With each trip it seemed that I was slowly getting further and further away from home. A lot of the time I stayed in what they called 'host housing', with promoters and managers and sometimes even audience members. That can have its downside. Sometimes after a show you just want to kick back and relax but can't always do that in someone's house. I remember one time I drove from Austin to Boston. It was one of the longest drives I ever made on tour without playing along the way. Then I looked at my tour sheet. The next night I was scheduled further north just outside Portland, Maine and the night after yet further north in a town called Blue Hill. It's in moments like that you just want to turn around and head west just to get back to your friends, but instead I was going north and further north. There is a kind of despair in those moments that is hard to explain. You want to tour and perform songs you have worked so hard to write. You want to play them to people in places that you have never visited, but at the same time you need familiar faces around you for comfort and reassurance. I would talk to myself while I was driving, 'Here I am flitting around the USA experiencing the joy of making music, but there has to be something more to it than the hour on stage that it gives back. I will find that something.' In Colorado, I drove through incredible red-rock canyons. I saw rock formations sculpted by millions of years of adverse weather. I saw crystal clear rivers running through ancient fir lines with snow-capped mountains in the distance. But so what? If you are on your own and have no one with you to share the experience, there's the dichotomy. In the evening you can feel the warmth of an audience who appreciate what you do and in the morning you have to slide out of somewhere like Northampton, Massachusetts in the snow and ice on to the next commitment.

Songwriting became my daily focus. It forced me to concentrate, to dig deep and hone my guitar playing skills at the same time. It was infectious and cyclical. The more I played, the more likely I was to stumble on a song. The more I wrote, the better my playing became. I recorded everything and in time I graduated from a chunky cassette machine to those mini voice-recorders known as Dictaphones. They were easier to transport and simple to use. I bought three and had one within reach at all times: one at home, one in the car and one in my guitar case. I all too easily forget ideas, so this was a wonderful tool for me. I would still jot new songs down on paper of course but I was never without a means to document new ideas. Just like the pros.

Songwriting is a process. The more one writes, the better the flow of ideas. I grab my inspiration from the air around me, wherever I am and whatever I'm doing. Watching television can inspire me. Reading a book or having a conversation can trigger songs. I've even taken lyrical ideas from listening to someone else's album. For instance, I think I've heard a great line and go back to hear it again to discover that what I thought I'd heard didn't exist, making what I thought I'd heard an original creative thought.

Pure and Crooked was almost a pop album. After that, I wanted to regress and make more of an acoustic roots record, leaning back towards my first solo effort *If You Saw Thro' My Eyes*. I went into Mark's Congress House Studio to record my next album. My friend David Hayes came down from his home in northern California, bringing his Earthwood acoustic bass, the kind the Mexican mariachi bands use. This tied in with the sound I was hearing in my head. We used drums, but they were laidback and played with brushes. Fresh from George Strait's Ace in the Hole Band, Gene Elders brought his fiddle to the party. We added a mandolin and an accordion, giving my new songs an almost Tex-Mex feel. *Skeleton Keys* is perhaps my most organic album. It is also the first album I fully participated on as a musician as well as a singer. I flatpicked and fingerpicked on every track. More importantly, it is my very first complete album of original compositions; twelve songs and not a single cover or filler among them. It was a landmark for me. I could also take those twelve songs on the road and play every single one of them solo. The *Skeleton Keys* tour took me into more rooms I'd never played before: the Iron Horse, a famous venue in Massachusetts; the Tin Angel in Philadelphia; I even got up as far north-east as Vermont.

The first four years of my marriage to Veronique were a whirlwind of touring for me. I criss-crossed America and made it back home when I could. We bought a ten-acre field with a small lake on it to the south-east of the city near Lockhart, Texas. Veronique paid for the land from money she had been left in a will. We built a house there, an unfinished monstrosity we named 'Swine Lake'.

We sited the house on the highest ground we could find on the property. The build was done by basically just three people: Veronique, myself, and a friend called Mike Miller. Mike was a self-proclaimed jack of all trades and had built his own house just up the hill. The land was bought from a local farmer and cost us just short of $10,000. We loaded most of our belongings into a storage unit and after moving into a caravan in Mike's backyard, we began the build. When the foundation needed shovelling out, we invited friends along for a trench digging party. When the framing needed doing, we had another gathering and so on. You get the idea.

Between Veronique and Mike, the design for the house was drawn up and a blueprint made. Various types of construction were considered including a reinforced straw bale adobe-style build. In retrospect I'm so glad we didn't go down that route as I'm not sure it would have stood up to the unpredictable Texas weather. I voiced my opinion from the very beginning that the plans were too grandiose and the house far too cavernous for my liking. But it was what Veronique wanted and I went along with the programme. I stayed away from most of the decision making. I just wanted a place in the country that I could call my own.

Excluding Mark Hallman, Veronique was one of the most accident-prone people I ever knew. While we were building the foundations for Swine Lake, she had a belief that if we put a special holy water into the cement mixer it would bless the house. I don't know where she got the idea or the water from but she had a bottle of it that she sprinkled directly into the cement drum while it was turning. Distractedly chatting, explaining her reasons, she left her arm dangling inside as the blades closed around it. At the last second I had to pull her away otherwise she could have lost her arm. Another time when Brad Kopp and I were on a playing trip to California I got a phone call in the night. 'I've had an accident,' she said. I asked her what had happened. She told me that the neighbour's dog had pups and she'd gone over to see them. She was naive enough to try to stroke the puppies and the mama dog bit her while protecting them. The dog's teeth raked down her cheek and left side of her nose, opening her up down to the bone, just missing her eye. She needed a lot of stitching up. I was on the road again when she drove into Lockhart to buy fence posts in her Nissan with a trailer hooked on the back. She loaded on too many posts and coming home she took a bend too fast and the car got into a wiggle. She couldn't control it and the weight of the fence posts flipped the Nissan, dumping it and the load into a ditch by the side of the road. The car was a write-off. Veronique was lucky. In retrospect I don't think she had any real sense of danger. She owned a muscular ex-military stallion called Hurricane, a real brute of a horse. The two times I saw her try to ride him she ended up on the ground. Thankfully it was only minor aches and bruises. It could have been far worse, but it never slowed her down.

The eventual build of Swine Lake was an industrial process called tilt-wall, normally reserved for supermarkets and warehouses. The basic procedure is to bring in a cement truck to pour a concrete slab, leaving huge bolts sticking up around the perimeter. The walls are then attached to these. When it's dry, the entire slab is polished to a shine giving the appearance of a marble floor. It's then covered with a protective industrial-strength plastic wrap until the roof goes on. The walls are framed out in wood while laid flat on the slab, leaving space for windows and door frames and the all-important stabilizing bolts. Concrete is then poured into the frames and left for a couple of weeks to dry. Once the walls are dry, a crane is brought in and the walls are 'tilted' upright and hoisted into position before being bolted down and braced. The house is then ready to be stabilized with framing. Once the build was sturdy enough to work in, the window and door frames and room dividers could be made and installed.

We added six-foot-wide wooden balconies, stretching the length of the house on the west and east sides. These protected us from the violent thunderstorms indigenous to the area. Once the balconies were up I could sit there facing east to watch and listen to the storm approaching from as far as ten miles away. They could on occasion be an ominous sight. First the dark and foreboding, low-hanging clouds would form. Followed by the distant thunder and the heaven-to-earth forked lightning. Then the heavy winds would hit like a truncheon to the chest to be capped by an eerie silence as the eye of the storm passed over and finally the cacophonous storm itself. The lashing, driving, squalling rain would be accented by snaking, blinding lightning followed by the ear-splitting thunder. Many are the times I sat on the west side balcony recording a passing storm on my cassette machine as it clattered by overhead.

The funding for the build came from an advance payment on a German publishing contract I had recently signed. Both Mike and Veronique believed it would be enough to finish the job. But it wasn't. Not even close. Over a period of four to five years we poured more than sixty thousand dollars into it in an attempt to complete it. But the house refused to be completed. Every time I went out on the road, I would return with enough hard cash to pour into the next phase of construction.

GOD LOOKED DOWN

God looked down, said Holy Moses what is this
It does not do a thing for my own Godliness
I gave them all they needed
They took my only son
God looked down, said Holy Christ
What on earth have I done?

God looked down, said cancel all my interviews
Thomas said, old man, who are you talking to
I know they pick on one and other
But I doubt they'll turn on you
God looked down, said Holy Christ
What in my name shall I do?

When God looked on Los Angeles what did he see?
He saw a city built on artifice and energy
He said, I cannot blame them
The fault must lie with me
God looked down, said Holy Christ
What must be must be

There's cracks in the mirror now
Cracks in the mirror now
It came without warning
Not even a clue
Déjà vu

God looked down said, Holy Mother, what a mess
The world has torn apart through my creativeness
Now they fight on every grievance
And they'll fight for evermore
God looked down said, Holy Christ
What do they need me for?

Who said John F Kennedy will never do
Who looked on while Mama popped a pill or two
Who gave Jackie Robinson that follow through
And who said, Brother Judas, I know it was you?

God looked down, said Holy Moses what is this
It does not do a thing for my own Godliness
I gave them all they needed
They took my only son
God looked down, said Holy Christ
What on earth have I done?

15. THE ROAD GOES ON FOREVER

In March 1990, Mark Hallman and I toured the UK. We played a balanced mix of songs from *Pure and Crooked* with a half-dozen Jules Shear tunes and a couple of standards. By standards I mean Iain Matthews standards: 'Meet on the Ledge' and 'Woodstock'. Upon arriving in the UK, we both came down with a heavy, soul-destroying flu. For the first week all we could do was lie in bed in the north of Scotland and recuperate. Our host would bring us daily soup and hot medicinal drinks.

The entire tour had to be rescheduled. We eventually began at a venue called The Lemon Tree in Aberdeen in the north of Scotland. We played The Winning Post in York as well as the Fleece and Firkin in Bristol, The Spread Eagle in Leicester and the Half Moon in Putney. We ended up in London, by way of Brighton. The Brighton show was very special for me. Not because of the venue, on the contrary, it was a simple back room in a pub. Nor was it the performance, although Mark and I had reached a high level of competence that we rarely fell below. It was because of who came to see me that night.

Mark and I took the stage and powered through our opening song and as I thanked the crowd at song's end, there standing directly in front of me was my old pal and Plainsong partner Andy Roberts. I hadn't seen Andy for a long time, and there he was like a friendly ghost from the past flashing that inimitable Andy 'hiya' in my direction. It felt so damned good to see him again. We met him and his girlfriend Sally for a drink after the show and did some brief catching up. I felt elated, rejuvenated and more than a little relieved as the angst of our musical break-up all those years earlier seemed to melt away. I nervously invited him to come join us in London the following night and to bring his guitar, which he joyfully accepted.

The London show was at an intimate acoustic venue at the

Oval cricket ground in Kennington, just south of the river. It was perfect for a low-profile reunion. We loosely rehearsed two or three songs with Andy backstage between soundcheck and dinner and then introduced him near the end of our set. It proved to be a remarkable combination with the three of us, and an emotional reunion for me and Andy. We were three voices and three acoustic guitars in perfect harmony on 'Louise' and a total surprise for the unsuspecting audience. It seemed to me that Andy and I had some unfinished musical business to take care of.

That summer I was supposed to tour Europe again with Mark Hallman. All the publicity was printed up but at the eleventh hour Mark had an offer from his old friend Dan Fogelberg to tour America. With my blessing, he pulled out of our tour. I called Bradley Kopp and asked him to come with me, but he had a production to finish. I then had a brainwave, I called Andy and he was available. The tour was based around a good paying country festival in Mayrhofen, Austria, a ski resort in the Zillertal Valley near Innsbruck. Andy and I played the festival and then did further dates together in Innsbruck, Chur in Switzerland, the Quasimodo club in Berlin, plus a couple of others in Hamburg and Bremerhaven.

My friendship with Andy was truly renewed on that tour and during our trip we began discussing the possibility of reforming Plainsong after a hiatus of nigh on eighteen years. We were still very fond of each other and highly motivated to work together again. We agreed that because it had all ended so badly the first time around we needed to mend the break and give the band another shot. I also felt that I needed to make amends for leaving so abruptly and fleeing to America the way I did. It was very much about unfinished business and finding a way to put things right.

We both wanted it to be a quartet again, but better than the original band. We called Mark Griffiths and invited him to work with us. Mark and I had played together on and off ever since Matthews Southern Comfort. I had always admired his superlative fretless bass playing and he had a great, high-harmony singing voice. Mark agreed to be part of the new unit. Now we were three and began to think in earnest about a fourth member. I thought of Simon Nicol. I knew he was no longer working with Fairport and thought he might be looking for something, but I was too shy to ask. I asked Andy if he would mind giving him a call. When Andy rang him the first thing he asked was, 'What's Iain like to work with?' Andy was taken aback and replied, 'Well you should know, you were in Fairport Convention together!' Simon then said, 'Well that was a long time ago. How is he now?' The upshot was that Simon was about to re-join Fairport. He was also finishing work on his solo album, *Consonant Please Carol*.

I found myself playing a small indoor festival called The Road Goes on Forever. There were multiple stages and someone said that I should go downstairs to the basement to check out a man called Julian Dawson. He was by all accounts a fine songwriter and could put on an impressive display playing acoustic guitar and blues harmonica. I was very taken by what I saw and heard. Julian is one of the best white blues harp players I've ever experienced. I invited him to meet up with Andy and me and a short time later we made the decision to ask him to be our fourth Plainsong member.

We made plans to record a new Plainsong album and I flew over to the UK from Texas. I had a few new songs, as did Julian and Andy. We also wanted to try writing together. Griff told us about a studio he knew of called Outrider, close to where he lived in his home town of Northampton. He said it was state-of-the-art with a good young engineer in Mark Thompson. More importantly it was inexpensive. The studio also had a guard dog, an Alsatian called Max. He was a good guard dog but we quickly learned that Max came with a nasty habit. During the night he would take a shit on the studio floor. Every morning the door was unlocked to the gag-inducing stench of Max's previous night's dinner. Each day's recording session was pre-empted by a severe fumigation. At the end of our final mixing session our engineer Mark gave us a nice Max deduction.

We recorded the album during July and August of 1991. Mark and his wife Mary were most gracious in offering us sleeping space in their little terraced house and we all crammed into Chateau Griffiths for the duration. The money for the recording was funded by Uwe Tessnow of Line Records in Hamburg. I knew Uwe through Sandy Roberton; Sandy had licensed several of my earlier Rockburgh recordings to him. The majority of the songs on the Plainsong album were new and, in a nod to our heroine Amelia Earhart, we featured an Andy and Iain co-write called 'Sweet Amelia' about the continuing gossip surrounding her last flight. I also re-worked the tune 'And Me' that I'd written and recorded years earlier with Matthews Southern Comfort. It took on a new persona as 'Say a Prayer'. We playfully called the album *Dark Side of the Room*.

Julian Dawson and I began touring together, not as a duo, but as a package. We did a short Irish tour booked by a prominent promoter in Dublin named Derek Nally. The trip was to end with a showcase at the prestigious Whelan's in Dublin, but we began the tour in Belfast. Julian and I took the ferry over from England and drove blindly around Belfast trying to find our hotel. When I think about it now, it's hard to believe how oblivious we were to the Northern Ireland situation. There were soldiers patrolling the streets, tanks even, and there we were, two English guys driving down the Ormeau Road with an English licence plate on our car. It's fortunate in a way that we were so naive, because like a drunk weaving through traffic, we sailed on through to our appointed lodgings.

We checked into our hotel and waited for the local promoter to meet us and take us to the venue. He eventually arrived and took us to a pizza parlour. It wasn't even a nice pizza parlour, it was a scruffy takeaway with a hastily put together PA system. He turned to us and saw the look on our faces.

'Don't worry lads,' he said, 'it gets better after tonight. This is the worst place you'll play on the tour.'

I looked him straight in the eye.

'This is already the worst place I've ever played in my entire career and I won't do it. I don't play pizza parlours.'

Our promoter weighed up the situation.

'Okay, boys, wait here' he said, 'I'm going to make a phone call.'

He came back fifteen minutes later and announced, 'Right, I've fixed it. We're going to a place by the docks called The Rotterdam Bar, you'll be playing for a private party and the band that were booked there are coming here.'

The Rotterdam Bar was a cellar-like maze of a venue in the famous Sailortown district, a working-class, dockland part of town, with a bright mural painted on its gable end. We soon discovered that The Rotterdam had a proper PA and a fine reputation for music.

Since leaving Southern Comfort I've developed a liking for changing my touring profile whenever possible. I'm easily bored by the predictability of touring and try to experience it in as many ways as possible. Becoming a solo artist afforded me that opportunity and I've never really looked back. Around the time of *Pure and Crooked* I teamed up with an old friend, Steve Chapman, who I had known all those years ago when I met Chris at his birthday party in North London. When I first met Steve he was a drummer in a promising young band called Junior's Eyes. Much later he moved to the West Coast of the USA where he was a long-time member of Poco. After leaving Poco, Steve became Al Stewart's drummer, then his tour manager and eventually his manager. When I found Steve again I asked him if he might also consider managing me. He listened to the Gold Castle album and told me he thought he could be effective.

The first thing Steve did was to put me on a countrywide UK stint with Al Stewart. One of the venues we played at was The Municipal Hall in Colne, Lancashire. I asked my mom if she'd like me to pick her up and take her along to the show. I knew Mom was familiar with the music of Al and thought she'd like to meet him. Mom asked if she might bring her sister along, my Auntie Eileen, as she and Uncle Ray lived close to the venue. I set it up so that they both had tickets for the show and passes for the green room. After the show, Al and I were backstage, standing around chatting. Mom walked in full of pride and joined us. We were in mid-conversation when Auntie Eileen sashayed through the door and marched right up to us, already talking as she approached.

'Ooooh! I right enjoyed that Iain love, you were great, but I didn't reckon much to that Stewart fellow.'

Mom and I didn't know where to put ourselves but fortunately Al saw the funny side of it.

Thanks to Al, I played before some big crowds on that tour and his fans loved to see us come out together to sing 'Meet on the Ledge' as an encore. I was a good opener for Al and later that same year he took me on his German tour. One of the shows was in Munich. By then they had built a brand-spanking-new airport and the venue for the night was the old abandoned airport. After the soundcheck, one of the promoters walked up beside me.

'I've been looking for you,' he said and took me by the arm. 'Come with me, I want to show you something.'

He walked me away from the terminal, out into the darkness, until we were away from all the commotion going on inside. Looking back, I could see large chunks of stonework missing from the walls of the old building.

'Okay, stop here', he said, 'this is it. This is the spot. This is where it happened.'

As if I'd been hit in the back of the head with a brick it dawned on me what he was talking about. I was standing on the very spot I'd seen so vividly in those old black and white television images. This is where my heroes died. For a moment I was that distraught eleven-year-old kid again. I re-experienced the sheer hopelessness I'd felt all those years before, the absolute irreplaceable sense of loss. I turned and walked back towards the terminal, forcing myself into a workable reality. I had once thought I was over it, but now I don't know if it will ever leave me.

On my album *Pure and Crooked* I wrote eight of the songs. One of them, 'The Rains of '62', was about leaving home for the bright lights of London. Another was a tribute to my boyhood heroes and called 'Busby's Babes'. This was the song my German guide had heard.

> I'll see you again my Red Devil friends
> I'll hear you around my door
> Touching my life, like so many memories before

> I was a child and so easily led
> And you were the leaders of men
> I doubt in my life if this ever happens again
>
> Oh how I cried when my mama said
> Busby's Babes son, they're dead
>
> How well I remember that miserable day
> When something was taken from me
> Out on a snow-covered runway in West Germany

I always visited Mom whenever I was in England and she loved to have me pick her up and take her to watch me play. In her late sixties she'd moved herself into a retirement home called Dorchester Lodge on Scotter Bottom in Scunthorpe, quite near to where I had lived as a teenager on Enderby Road. She had her own apartment with a living room, bedroom, kitchen and bathroom. It came equipped with red pull cords in the bathroom to summon the warden in emergencies. They had all kinds of arranged activities like bingo and tombola nights, things that Mom didn't much care for but joined in with just for the company. After Mac died I think she resigned herself to a more sedate and quiet private life. She loved reading and did so avidly. I'd bring her books and we'd have long discussions about the good ones we'd both read. She liked to listen to music on her boom box, accompanied by the occasional glass of Grant's whisky. Mom enjoyed a good laugh too. Some of my favourite photos of her are where she's laughing, completely unaware of the camera pointing in her direction. Without Mac looking over her shoulder she was far happier and much more forthcoming about her past. She told me that she felt much freer and more her own person by then too.

Before she moved to the retirement facility, she'd had a small upstairs flat and when I'd visit I'd stay and sleep on the sofa for a few days. I took her out for drives and she liked to go back to Barton to see how it had changed and visit the Humber Bridge. It was on one of those visits that I asked her to tell me more about my father, Eric Pratt. She tried, but would always end up in tears.

She found it painful to talk about their time together and I so wanted her to.

Mom died in 1994. My brother Andy phoned me in Texas to say that Mom had been admitted to hospital because she wasn't very well. 'No need to panic,' he said. I asked him what was wrong with her. He said he wasn't sure. It transpired she had lung cancer; she had been a keen smoker when she was a younger woman. I asked Andy to please keep me posted and to tell me if he thought I should fly over. He called back less than a week later and said, 'I think you should come now.' I booked a flight right away.

Two days later, Andy met me at Heathrow Airport and drove us straight to the hospital in Scunthorpe. Andy's wife Rita met us there. When we got to Mom's room, she wasn't there. A nurse told us that she had passed away just a few hours earlier. They let us visit her in another room. She looked at peace. I asked Andy if he minded me having Mom's rings. He said 'of course not' and I eased them off her cold fingers.

I stayed over for a week, moving around in a daze, like a headless chicken. My recollection is that Andy did most of the funeral arrangements. Mom was cremated at Scunthorpe Crematorium and her ashes were scattered in the grounds there. At Andy's and my other brother Neil's urging, I chose the music for the funeral, selecting an instrumental track I'd written with Griff called 'Towie' from the first reunion Plainsong album, *Dark Side of the Room*. Mom had told me many times how much she loved it, how the sound of it always transported her into a quiet and reflective place. It felt like an obvious choice. The second piece I chose was also an instrumental called 'Grand Tour' by the baritone sax player Gerry Mulligan from his album *The Age of Steam*. Mom had been a big jazz fan and loved Mulligan. I'd brought her a copy of the album on one of my trips home. Mom was hip when it came to music and had wonderful taste. She once wrote to me to ask if I could find her a tape of Ry Cooder's soundtrack music. She had sat down one night in her retirement flat to watch the Wim Wenders film *Paris, Texas* and had been entranced by the music. She was very much like me in that respect. Many people don't even hear the background music when watching a movie. For me and Mom it was almost paramount to the film itself. Her letters were full of surprising moments. She wrote beautiful letters in a gorgeously sophisticated handwriting.

Both of my brothers had joined the Royal Navy at a very young age. Neil went first. He was sixteen when he signed up. Then a year later, Andy joined. I rarely saw them after I left for London in search of the Holy Grail.

Neil wasn't cut out for the navy and became a heavy drinker. When he was drunk he became aggressive. Stories began to filter back to Mom and Dad about his brawling. During his third year he was dishonourably discharged from the navy after getting into a big fight with an officer, throwing him into the sea from an aircraft carrier. Neil became an engineer by trade and in civilian life took on the role of motor mechanic. That is when he could make it out of bed in the mornings. He spent more and more time at the pub. His few friends only ever saw him there. After a torrid failed marriage he died of alcohol poisoning. He died lonely, in a house next door to where we all grew up on Enderby Road in Scunthorpe.

Andy was far more outgoing, though a bit of a mother's boy. He was the competitive one, quick thinking and literate – a real grammar school lad. Andy had a mantra, 'Whatever our Neil can do, I can do better.' He stayed in the navy for most of his adult life and when they eventually turned him loose, he moved to Fareham in Hampshire to manage a marina. There he fell in love with and married the lovely Rita. They had two sons. While he was still in the navy and I was living in California, he visited me for a weekend. His ship, an aircraft carrier, had docked for repairs on the East Coast and he called me.

'Hey Bro, I've unexpectedly found myself with some downtime and want to see what the life of a pop star looks like. Are you up for some R&R?'

I was. Any excuse to see my little brother. He flew west and we spent three sun-soaked days driving around southern California, catching up as best we could and seeing the sights with the top down on my little, bright-yellow MGB.

He too died young our Andy. They both did. Andy developed bowel cancer in his early fifties and by the time he went to the doctor it was too late. Despite our little differences and the vast distances between us, I miss them both. Very much.

TIGERS WILL SURVIVE. PART II (DARCY'S SONG)

Twenty years later you're still a teenager
Anxiously sifting through life
That guy in New York, he borrowed your heart
Then he returned to his wife
At exactly the moment you pulled down the shade
Determined to shut out the light
I was thanking Chicago from somebody's stage
Calling it quits for the night
Oh I know how you're feeling
I've been there myself once or twice

Sometimes in the morning when London's still sleeping
And Texas is barely alive
I come to my senses but only half conscious
With a vision of you in my mind
Say, who was the father who let you down early
A little girl not even five
And I've wanted to tell you of fears and of freedom
How not only tigers survive
Oh I know how you're feeling
When things get too close to describe

Darcy, oh Darcy you entered my life
You came on the edge of a dream
Darcy, oh Darcy they gave you my eyes
Show me where to begin

So I'm writing to tell you I see it all clearly now
What happened back then wasn't right
I cheated you girl and I cheated myself
But I thank God we've made it in spite

It's a dangerous weapon, a mind overloaded
And not an unusual sight
What I'm trying to tell you is Darcy I love you
In so many ways we're alike
Oh I know how you're feeling
When things get too hard to decide

16. MAKING WATERMELON WHINE

I signed a new record deal for my solo work with a local boutique label run by a German friend of mine, Heinz Geissler. The label was a joint venture between Heinz and John Kunz, who owned Waterloo Records, the biggest independent record store in Central Texas. The label, called Watermelon Records, had an interesting and eclectic roster: Santiago Jiminez, a Mexican accordionist; Omar & the Howlers, a loud rock band; Alejandro Escovedo and Steve Young all made records for Heinz.

Early 1994 was an extremely busy time for me. In January, Julian, Griff, Andy and I reconvened to create a second Plainsong album. We decided to record it in Austin. We rented an apartment in town for the three of them and recorded *Voices Electric* at Congress House Studio with Mark producing. Immediately after we'd recorded the Plainsong album I went back into the same studio to record my solo album, *The Dark Ride*.

That same month, Darcy came to stay with me in Texas. She had just turned 22. I hadn't spent much time with her since she'd visited me in LA as a teenager. There had been visits when I was touring England, but never much more than an afternoon on a day off in the London area, or on the way from one concert to another. Now here she was, a beautiful young woman with opinions and baggage of her own. She had a full six weeks until she needed to return home and came to our house at Swine Lake. She and Genevieve seemed to connect quite well. There was a significant age difference, but they didn't seem to mind. Darcy didn't seem to care much for Veronique and when I asked her why she said she thought Veronique was too pushy and opinionated. What could I say! Darcy was offered the opportunity to house-sit for a songwriter friend of mine, Sara Hickman, who was going on tour. She grabbed the opportunity, packed her bags and moved into town. I was more than a little disappointed to see her go, but understood completely why. She developed a life for herself there and began going out at night and hanging out in the studio during the day. She became friendly with one of the engineers. I watched her flirting with him. In the meantime I tried to not be clingy and got on with my work. If she needed me, she knew where I could be found.

I brought in a couple of female singer friends to put harmony vocals on the album. Once Sara Hickman returned from the road she sang on the Tim Buckley song 'Morning Glory'. Kris McKay of the Wild Seeds helped out on my song 'The Breath of Life'. Darcy sang harmony on 'Rooted to the Spot'. She loved the experience and wanted more. She has a very good singing voice and because of her ability and the fact that she was my daughter, I suppose in her mind it gave her entitlement and an automatic ticket to be on more tracks. We argued over it and I had to explain how it all worked. There were dues to be paid and the fact that she was on the album at all was a feather in her cap.

I'm not sure if I'd initially led her to believe that she would be singing more songs on the record, but she expressed her bitter disappointment and said that she thought I didn't need the other women. She probably could have sung their parts, but as I explained to her, it was my album and my call and she had to respect the decision. I have to say that she did a terrific job on 'Rooted'. She was quick, soulful and for someone without studio experience, very tuneful. If I had to consider it over again, I may well have used her more. I think she knew that too and that was the reason for her disappointment.

I took a phone call one day from City Hall in Austin. They told me that they wanted to honour me as a European musician living in their city. They said I was someone who had contributed to the fabric of local culture and they wanted to initiate 'Iain Matthews Day'. I was duly invited to City Hall. I took Mark Hallman with me and we played them a couple of songs in the council chambers. There was an accepted amount of back slapping and the mayor shook my hand. He then made a proclamation from behind a lectern. He announced 'Iain Matthews Day' and named me 'Lone

Star Iain Matthews'. I have the document he gave me, officially stamped to prove it.

Back at Swine Lake, on a Saturday morning during the football season I would sit on the west veranda listening to the faint audio vestiges of a Premier League football match, usually fading away completely by half time but lingering long enough to leave me pining for home and wondering what the final score might have been.

One of Veronique's passions was rescuing abandoned dogs. On any given day we housed up to a half-dozen mongrels of all shapes and breeds. Trio was one of the first and after that it was open season. They would come and go but all of them lived outside where they would roll the dice with Mother Nature.

We had built a fence around the property but with enough holes to fill the Albert Hall and easy enough to climb over, or through. I'd sometimes take visitors on long walks with the dogs, past the abandoned farm houses while talking music. I wrote the song 'Funk and Fire' on such a walk, taking the initial inspiration for it from the crunching rhythm of my feet on the gravel road.

We would have two or three gatherings each year at Swine Lake. They could be vaguely described as parties but it was more about old friends coming to town and visiting. Mostly it comprised of musicians and music-related people that I hadn't seen in a long time. The first one of the year was at the end of the South by Southwest Music Conference (SXSW) which is held every March in Austin. The conference was founded by a good friend of mine by the name of Louis Meyers. In its fledgling state, I played it three or four times. These days it draws perhaps 30,000 people from around the world.

On the final Sunday of the conference, before everyone scattered to the four corners, we'd have a farewell gathering at the house. They would be potluck affairs with around fifteen to twenty people. We'd play pool and listen to music and sit outside to talk and drink. We'd even toss horseshoes. I'd dug a simple horseshoe pit for such occasions and it was always fun to watch how ungainly musicians can sometimes be when it came to physical activity. I had a basketball net erected in the driveway and occasionally a group of us would muster up the energy to play a game called 'Horse'. But more often than not it was too hot and we'd just stand around gabbing while pathetically lobbing up balls in the general direction of the hoop.

In 1995, I put on a big show at SXSW with a band I'd formed with Mark Hallman called Hamilton Pool. Mark and I had started the band on the heels of our admiration for the songwriting talents of our friend Michael Fracasso. Michael hails from Steubenville, Ohio, the hometown of Dean Martin and the famous sports punter from American TV, Jimmy the Greek. Michael writes beautiful songs. He's a great lyricist and I say that with a twinge of envy. He'd been living in New York and came to Austin around the same time as I did. I first met him at a room called The Chicago House on Trinity Street. It was a secondary club in that they didn't have the budgets that other places in town had, but it was a true music listening room and I liked that. A mutual friend told me that I needed to go and hear this new guy. I went and was highly impressed by what he was doing. I told Mark about him and the next time he played we introduced ourselves.

Michael and I did a couple of solo shows together and became good friends. Whenever I played at The Ice House, next door to Waterloo Records, I would extend an invitation to Michael to join me. It was a great package. We made each other look better. My idea was to get more people to hear him, but there was a selfish reason too, I adored his music and wanted to be associated with him.

Mark Hallman is also a good songwriter, and together we contrived to form a trio with Michael. The three of us got together and talked. Michael said he would like to do it but his solo career would still be his main focus. We recorded a few songs and it sounded great to all involved. We discussed concept. We wanted to be a local act that could have international appeal and based on that we came up with a name that meant something in the Austin area and sounded cool to everyone else. We took the name Hamilton Pool after a swimming hole in a place called Dripping Springs, just west of Austin. We piqued Watermelon Records interest in the project.

Over a period of about two years, sandwiched in-between Michael's and my solo work and Mark's producing, we'd meet up to choose songs, find a sound, rehearse and record. Ultimately we stockpiled quite a lot of material. We were searching for an identity, it was important that we didn't just sound like three writers playing together, we needed it to be a cohesive whole. Eventually Watermelon became impatient, pushing us to make a record. We made the album *Return to Zero*. It was well received by people in the know but didn't sell very well on a national level. Outside the USA it meant nothing, a lot of my hardcore fans still don't even know of the band's existence. Let's face it, we may have also undersold it. We perhaps ought to have put our individual names on the cover, as well as the band name. It was a lesson learned. If you are going to collaborate, make sure that the people know who it is that is collaborating.

We showcased the album at SXSW, putting together a big band of about ten players in order to make a fatter, more impressive sound. We brought in all of the session players from the album recording: we had accordion, double bass, fiddles, and yes, pedal steel. It was a great showcase, but hardly the sort of unit one could take on the road. The three of us later did do a short tour, from the Midwest to the East Coast, about ten dates in all, but it wasn't going to be something that could hold water. The band, good as it was, had a short shelf life. Mark had his producing career, Michael wanted to plough his own furrow and of course I had all sorts of solo commitments of my own. The upside is that I can still put the CD on and feel great about what we did as a trio and for me that's success.

In the spring of 1995, my musical cohort and label boss Heinz Geissler drove me 170 miles south one evening to see Eric Taylor play at a club in Houston called Anderson Fair. Throughout the three-hour trip, Heinz played me cassette after cassette of Eric's songs. I liked what I heard very much and couldn't wait to hear and experience the live version. By the time we arrived at the club on Grant Street there was already a hastily-written sign in Sharpie taped to the door: 'SOLD OUT' it said in bold capitals. Eric had to be located to vouch us both inside. The performance was spellbinding. I've never seen anyone stop and start songs as many times as Eric did and still have the audience howling for more. It was just Eric, his mighty tenor and a delicately fingerpicked acoustic, with his friend James Gilmer slapping away beside him on the conga drum. The set comprised of some remarkable storytelling and tunes that appeared to have been dragged kicking and screaming from the backwoods of Texas, sung by a man who had obviously lived them.

Afterwards, in a cramped backstage area, Heinz introduced me to Eric. He was a giant of a man who liked to lean in to make a point. He towered over me and addressed me as 'Fifi'. I wasn't sure what to make of that, whether it was an insult or endearment, but let him get away with it. I learned later it was a friendly gesture. I sat and listened into the early hours, occasionally adding support as Heinz convinced Eric that it was time for him to make a new album. His first one had been a simple voice and guitar affair, self-released four years earlier. Now he needed to be heard nationally, perhaps even internationally.

On the way home, Heinz sensed that I had really enjoyed Eric's show and asked me if I would like to produce the album he was planning. I would have been a fool to turn that offer down. I co-produced Eric's eponymous album for Watermelon with Mark Hallman and had a great time with the experience. Eric and I became solid friends. One day, the phone rang at Swine Lake. I picked it up and it was Eric on the other end.

'Hey Fifi,' he bellowed. 'Nanci wants to know if you'd be interested in going to Ireland to sing on a couple of tracks. She's making a new album with some Fairport Convention songs on it, so I suggested you. Do you wanna go?'

The Nanci in question was none other than Nanci Griffith, who had been Eric's wife back in the seventies. Nanci wanted me to sing with her on Sandy Denny's 'Who Knows Where the Time Goes?' and sing lead on Richard Thompson's song 'Wall of Death'. I was both flattered and honoured. The sessions took place at Windmill Lane Studios in Dublin. My friend Clive Gregson was there too playing guitar. Nanci was taken by my contribution and asked me if I would like to join her entourage on the road when she took the project on tour. *Other Voices, Too* was a big collaborative project and she had already secured the services of folk music royalty: Dave Van Ronk, Odetta, Tom Russell, Dolores Keane, Carolyn Hester, Eric himself and Clive Gregson were all booked for the tour. How could I reject the offer to tread the same boards as the Mayor of MacDougal Street and the legendary Odetta, the woman who Martin Luther King Jr. had called 'The Queen'?

We played sold-out shows in Dublin, London and Glasgow. The Glasgow show was filmed for posterity and eventually released commercially. To say it was one of the highlights of my touring career would be an understatement. It was the best of times with no pressure and because it wasn't my tour, I simply had to show up and be myself. Donovan turned up unexpectedly in Dublin and shared a microphone with me to sing the choruses on 'Who Knows Where the Time Goes?'. I was in folk heaven. I wished that my mom could have seen those shows.

Odetta had the presence one associates with royalty. She entered the room in flowing African robes and headscarf and telepathically commanded attention. All heads swivelled and respect oozed from those assembled. She was a beautiful lady inside and out and I will never forget her. Carolyn Hester I knew already. I had played with her years before at The Bottom Line in New York. She had broken a string and seeing her predicament, I rushed on stage to change it for her. She and I became fleeting friends. Before we met I only knew of Carolyn as Richard Fariña's first wife. Tom Russell I'd met once briefly in Texas, but he was the one on the tour who I really bonded with. Tom let me use his precious black Collings guitar for my segment of the show. We spent a lot of downtime together playing and talking about our lives in music. Dave Van Ronk was in pretty bad physical shape. Every night he was guided slowly on stage by his wife Andrea and played sitting down with a prompt sheet, after having his guitar placed in his hands. He was, however, still possessed of that high and eerie growled tenor that was unmistakable Van Ronk, but personally he gave off a distinct 'Do Not Disturb' vibe.

I enjoyed the trip and the company so much that I didn't want it to end. It was over far too quickly and before I knew it we were saying our goodbyes as everyone scattered back to their respective homelands. I pinch myself sometimes when I watch the DVD of the performance at Glasgow's Armadillo and think, 'Did I really do that?' Odetta and Van Ronk are gone now. Carolyn Hester still tours and my pal Eric Taylor never seems to tire of the troubadour life. Tom's out there too, singing his song about 'Who's Gonna Build Your Wall?'. No one I speak to seems to know where Nanci is, or what she's doing.

Watermelon began having financial problems. I heard through the grapevine that they were being investigated by the IRS. Despite this, Heinz gave me the green-light to make a new record for them. I had some great new songs burning a hole in my book. Mark and I rehearsed a group of musicians and went into Congress House to record all the basic tracks. When it became time to pay the band and make a down payment to Mark, as per usual I called Heinz. He was distinctly uncomfortable on the phone. Out of the blue he said that he had talked to his business partner John Kunz and they'd decided not to pick up my option for another record. At first I thought he was talking about an album beyond the one I had been making, which would have been understandable as I hadn't been setting the woods on fire with sales recently. Then it dawned on me that he was talking about the current one.

'How do you mean Heinz? You told me to start recording. I've already got half the album done and I owe the musicians for their work and Mark for studio time.'

'Well we're not picking up the option,' said Heinz.

'It's a little late for that. You already gave me the go-ahead to start making it.'

'Well we're not picking it up,' he reiterated.

Heinz wasn't budging from his position and at that point things got quite tense.

'So you are telling me that you are not going to give me the money you owe me for an album that you have already green-lighted?'

There was a long pause.

'Yes, that's correct.'

I couldn't believe what he was saying, knowing he was in the wrong. It was such a ridiculous and cowardly thing to say and do. He all but admitted he was about to renege on a contractual agreement he had made with me, knowing that I was powerless to do anything about it short of hiring a lawyer, which would have meant spending even more money that I didn't have. It wasn't the first time I had seen this in the music business. I just believed that when you make deals with friends you're on solid ground. But once again, people you think are your friends can turn around when the programme doesn't suit them and screw you over. Now it was happening to me and I was about to be roughly $10,000 out of pocket.

I was furious with Heinz. I tried to speak to John Kunz, but of course as Heinz's business partner, he took his side. I spoke to Mark at the studio, who took a more pragmatic approach.

'Speak to them again, and ask them for the money we have spent so far and I'll finish the album for you for free.'

The album was in its infant stage with a lot of work still to do. All we had were backing tracks. We still had to do vocals, solos, mixing and editing. This meant that Mark was willing to bite the bullet and do the rest of the album for free on my behalf. I guess it's in situations like this when you find out exactly who your real friends are. Mark was coming through with flying colours and I was indebted.

I phoned Heinz back. I knew that he had me over a barrel and that I was calling cap in hand. I didn't want to compromise and ask for half the money, but given the circumstances I didn't have much choice. Even then I had to bargain. Heinz was reluctant to agree to anything concerning finances, but eventually gave way and agreed to pay me the money I had already spent. He still wanted the finished album for his label of course.

Watermelon were in deep financial trouble. They stumbled along for a couple more years before finally going out of business. It transpired that I wasn't the only artist on their roster who had been treated in this way.

In retrospect I regard *God Looked Down* as one of my better artistic efforts. It's also one of my worst selling albums from that period. Watermelon were a shambles when it came out and consequently it received practically no promotion at all. There is irony in this tale. Heinz got his record done for half price, but he also got his comeuppance on the sales return.

Despite all of the problems associated with the *God Looked Down* album, I was very happy with it as a collection of songs. There are four tunes on the album that I still include in my live set to this day. There's also a song on it I wrote for my mom. It's called 'This Train' and of all the personal songs I've written, that's the one that comes the closest to explaining our journey as mother and son.

BACK OF THE BUS

You talk about disease like its part of the plan
Another God-sent plague on the common man
You talk about love the way you think about lust
Like it's something obscene you don't want to discuss
Like it doesn't exist in your neck of the woods
You think it's overrated and misunderstood
You'd rather ship them like cattle to the Hindu Kush
I'm gonna write it all down in the back of this bus

Oh I feel the heat
Oh I feel the rush
Oh I feel the heat
I'm gonna move on down to back of the bus
Oh I feel the heat
Oh I feel the crush
Oh I feel the heat
I'm gonna write it all down in the back of this bus

They got eighty-six thousand less today
In the name of freedom in the USA
We got to stick it to them before they get to us
They've got enough heat stashed to blow us all to dust
You've got control, greed, conformity
Just three little words that don't apply to me
In a couple of summers when you all adjust
You'll be riding with your buddies in the back of this bus

Chorus

Man look at that monkey over there
I bet you think you're tough, well I'm not scared
You've got a face like that damned Sun Myung Moon

I saw you praying to the east this afternoon
Now you've taken our women and you've got our jobs
With your Chinese writing and your foreign gods
We don't want you sitting down here next to us
Why don't you take that seat in the back of the bus

Chorus

Now TV's flashing the subliminal lie
They're gonna bend you, shape you and crucify you
If you know your wines then it's understood
You don't need a good reference you can join the club
Then before you even know it there's a couple of kids
It's a fine line you're walking and God forbid
You want to talk to him, you've got to give to us
Man I think I'm gonna throw up in the back of this bus

Chorus

Well this aint no time to celebrate
We've got too much sorrow and too much hate
There's too much them and not enough us
There's too much heat in the back of this bus

17. THOUGHTS OF LEAVING

In the mid-1990s a surge of interest occurred in Germany and the Netherlands for American-based singer-songwriters. I began travelling to Europe twice a year, touring the arts centres, theatres and clubs. The Netherlands had traditionally been a good market for me and now my Dutch booking agent was not only getting me decent concerts but also plenty of exposure on radio and TV. Once that kicked in, the promotion people also became enthusiastic and involved. It was on one of these promotional sorties that I met my saviour. I was performing on a TV show in Hilversum when a bright-eyed, motorcycle-jacketed female introduced herself as Yvonne Elenbaas, my Dutch publishing contact. The first thing she told me on meeting her was, 'Hi, I'm Yvonne. I work for Rondor and they are not poor. Whatever you need while you are here, just let me know and I'll make it happen.' I told her that I was on a tight budget and maybe a little help just getting around would make a huge difference. 'No problem,' she said, 'just send me your petrol receipts and Rondor will take care of them.'

Yvonne is the sort of person to walk the walk and get things done with the least amount of fuss. She explained to me that Rondor, my German publisher, had developed a strong presence in the Netherlands and she was running their Dutch office out of her Amsterdam home. Yvonne was easy to talk to, quick to laugh, amusing to be around and made sure that all the t's were crossed and the i's dotted. We developed a warm rapport based on mutual respect and the ability to have a good time with our respective jobs. Occasionally you meet people who do what they do because it's fun and Yvonne is one of those. It's a business that can stomp you into the ground if you allow it to, but I could tell that she wasn't about to let it. Although Yvonne is now semi-retired from that war zone we laughingly call the music business, she's still a dear friend.

In 1997 I acquired the services of a very good German booking agent. He always flew over for South by Southwest to scout potential clients and that March he came to see me perform. Afterwards we spoke about future work and when he discovered that I didn't have a current record deal, he said he'd like to introduce me to some friends of his who were running a small independent label based near Heilbronn in Germany. They were called Blue Rose Records and the company was run by a man named Edgar Heckmann. I went to dinner with Edgar and his partner Karsten one night where they made me a very fair offer to record for them. They apparently knew and liked my music a lot and saw me as a flagship artist for the label. They didn't have big budgets but they were forthright in admitting it and I liked and respected their honesty. We decided to give it a shot with a single 'getting to know you' album deal. I asked them for a budget of $10,000 and they countered with $7,500. It felt right and we shook hands on it. I then had to work out how I could make an album for that amount of money. It was a challenge, but one I felt ready to take on. I called Mark Hallman.

'Here's the situation Mark. I've just made a deal with a small German record company. They have given me $7,500. I need a bit of that for myself, can I make a record with you for the remainder?'

Mark knew me well enough to be able to say no and I respected his honesty. By then Mark's Congress House Studio was booming, but so were the overheads. He had taken on a couple of extra engineers and was constantly updating his equipment. He wanted to see me make the album and suggested that I call Bradley Kopp who had recently moved back to Boulder, Colorado to be with his love Lori. I called Brad and relayed the story.

'I think I can make it work if you can come and do the record in Colorado.'

I made the album that became known as *Excerpts from Swine Lake* in Colorado, on favours and downtime. I stayed at Brad's father's house and we completed the whole thing in three weeks, recording and mixing at different locations. My abiding memory of the album has nothing to do with the recording or the songs. It was an incident. We'd had a long tracking session and I got back to my lodgings late. I was tired but not sleepy and turned on the television for company. That's when I learned that Princess Diana had been killed in an underpass in Paris. It was a very sombre moment that has stuck in my memory ever since. Whenever that album comes up in conversation, Diana's death springs to mind before any song titles. There's a particular song on the record called 'Horse Left in the Rain', it's a song about being misunderstood. I wrote it in aftermath of the Watermelon debacle. It was the last track we had recorded that day and hearing it always triggers the Princess Diana incident for me.

    I could probably make an entire album of songs I've written about the indiscretions of the music business and my experiences on the other end of those indiscretions. This goes all the way back to the seventies and the album *If You Saw Thro' My Eyes*. The opening track is called 'Desert Inn'. It's a gentle song really. I was still learning the game, but as time went by the lyrics grew a little more muscular.

By 1998, Veronique and I were no longer romantically attached. The four of us, Veronique, Genevieve, Dominic and myself, lived there together in sickness and in health and ultimately in declining harmony. I spent most of my time at home in my own room. I became depressed by my circumstances and simply could not take living a lie. I was lying to myself that it could be fixed and lying to my friends that all was well. There's a familiar saying about it taking two to tango. It does and I was a shitty dancer. I've never thought of myself as being easy to live with. My entire adult life has been a search for whatever vestige of perfection there may be inside of me and I've beaten everything and everyone from my path in a quest to find it. Nietzsche said that one must have chaos in oneself to be able to give birth to a dancing star and I understand that.

    There were plenty of good times too, I know there were, but the sour and bitter taste at the end of a relationship tends to overshadow them. We wanted to build a relationship together but, like the house, it was never complete. I never felt that I was truly in the relationship as a family. Veronique wouldn't let me discipline the children; they were her kids and hers alone. At first there was a lot of affection but this didn't translate into deeper caring. I look back now and realise what we had was a practical relationship and I had wanted a loving one.

Being a touring musician is a 'special' life and sometimes partners are able to adapt to it and embrace it. Sometimes it becomes a cross to bear for the one left at home and that's what happened with us. It quickly became a delicate partnership ripped apart at the seams by music and my quest for a musical life. It can create an unbridgeable distance when love is not part of the equation. Fights about priorities begin that can never be resolved and when music is the mistress, as it was for me, it wins out every time. Home life can become fraught and strained to breaking point. For Veronique and me it stretched to the limit and eventually broke due to a lack of a solid foundation, love and understanding. We married for convenience rather than love. She didn't want anybody to get too close but I chose to ignore that. It was a relationship built on need.

I broached the subject of going back to Europe. I think I knew she would say no, but I asked her if she would like to come with me. She did say no. Her kids wouldn't want to go and she was staying with them. She said she was a Texan and needed to stay in Texas. I was thinking just the opposite. I was English and had to get back to England. I had no idea where I would land, but I knew I wanted to learn to be European again. After twenty-five years America had beaten a lot of the spirit out of me and Texas had simply worn me down. I couldn't take those brutal summers anymore.

Things had changed. Austin had always been a cultural oasis for free spirits, writers, musicians and the like, all congregated there to taste the waters. Now the town marched to a different drum. Dell computers had imported a lot of their people. New high-tech companies were realising that Austin might be the new land of opportunity and that was attracting Yuppie/techno types who were used to high wages and grand living. This influx dramatically increased house prices and drove a lot of the locals to the outskirts of town. The changes were dramatic and the whole feel of Austin shifted, as did the politics. Ann Richards, a Democrat, had been our governor. She had worked her way up into politics from being a school teacher and was known as a no-nonsense but compassionate woman. She was a music lover too and came to lots of shows, sitting in the front row, whooping and a hollering along with the rest of the crowd. Then in 1995 came George Bush Junior. He blew down from North Texas like a rogue tornado and after that everything changed.

The house at Swine Lake wasn't a happy place. After ten years of constant construction it was still nowhere near finished. We had a front and a back door, but none yet on the interior. All of the doorways had curtains and blankets hanging over them. We had big problems with the weather on the east side. Every time it rained we had to mop up. This sometimes meant getting up in the middle of the night to put towels down to soak up the water. We fixed that problem after a while by building the balconies and the sloping roofs, but beyond that the work was slow in getting done. It was a big project, too big to be finished with such a small workforce and a meagre budget. There was an underlying bitterness floating around the place that was hard to take. I can't say there was anger, more like passive aggression, but you could sense it constantly. We all but gave up on the relationship. I tried to be there when Veronique wasn't and vice versa. We both put on our brave faces, but the proverbial writing was on the wall for our relationship as we ground it out in order to work and function.

Blue Rose seemed to be pleased with their investment in me, even though we were having limited success. They said they wanted more. I told them that I thought it might be time to make another Plainsong album. The band hadn't worked together on a record since 1996 when we made an album called *Sister Flute*, after which Julian Dawson decided he would leave us to focus on his solo career. Griff, Andy and I brainstormed about who we might get to replace Julian. My immediate thought was Clive Gregson. I liked Clive and his music a lot. In fact we had recorded his song 'I

Love This Town' on our previous album. I first met Clive when he and Christine Collister were in Richard Thompson's band, and of course he sang with me that time at Cropredy and we'd played together on the Nanci Griffith *Other Voices, Too* tour. I loved his songwriting and particularly his guitar playing and thought his entire musical package could give Plainsong the boost we felt it sorely needed. The moment I mentioned Clive to the others they thought it was a great idea. Clive liked it too and agreed instantly. I think he had reached a point in his own career where he felt he was beating his head against a wall and was ready for a change of pace.

We decided to make the album in Austin. Clive was living in Nashville at the time and could drive there, leaving us with just enough cash in the budget to bring Griff and Andy over from England. I arranged for Griff and Andy to lodge over in a guesthouse at the Hobby Ranch. Clive stayed with us at Swine Lake. I don't know what I must have been thinking to have anyone stay with us during that time. You could cut the atmosphere at Swine Lake with a kitchen knife. I was in a deep funk for most of the recording. Clive was confused and thought maybe I was in that state because I wasn't enjoying the recording and he consequently had a miserable time. I didn't want to mix what was happening in my relationship with the music we were making, so I didn't verbalise anything. I'd get up very early each morning to go run and then sit in my room on a couch trying to get my head on straight enough to make it through another day of work. But I was fooling no one. Clive would sit with me and try to vibe me up for the session. Then he'd go downstairs and ask Veronique what she thought the matter was. Of course she wouldn't volunteer anything. Eventually it became too much for Clive and he moved out to stay with the others in the guest house. Some years later when the dust had settled and I was happier than I could ever have imagined being, I bumped into Clive. We talked about the time we'd spent together at Swine Lake and I filled in some details for him. He said, 'So that's what it was. I thought you were just a right moody bastard and I wasn't sure I ever wanted to work with you again.' Mind you, so far he hasn't.

In retrospect, that line-up of Plainsong, particularly live, was the best one we ever put together, including the original band. The album we made, *New Place Now*, for me is on a par with the *Amelia* album. We took it on tour the year after recording it and slayed audiences with our power and enthusiasm. The verve and joy of playing together is captured for posterity on a simple four-song self-released recording we made in Austria.

When we got to England I was looking around to find my new home. We played perhaps two-dozen dates the length and breadth of Britain in arts centres and small theatres to enthusiastic audiences. It felt like a coming home. For me it was a new beginning and everywhere we played I found myself consciously wondering, 'Is this the sort of town I could settle down in? Is this where I'm meant to be?' I was searching for a feeling, a vibe, a sign of some kind, but sadly we reached the end of the tour and that vibe, that sign, never appeared. At tour's end I flew to Amsterdam and upon walking out of the airport terminal the strangest feeling came over me. I suddenly felt as though I had come home. I was at peace with my demons and all was good in my world.

Frank van der Meijden was my Dutch manager. When Andy and I first formed Plainsong back in 1972, Frank had worked in London for our booking agency Gemini and had booked Plainsong on several Dutch tours. Frank is the same age as me, give or take a month, and when it came to career, we thought along similar lines. He's a great creative thinker. After working with Gemini he returned to his native Netherlands to become a highly-successful manager. These days he's retired and has become an established artist in his own right. He creates elaborate installations from doll parts and has exhibitions all over the world. His art is highly sought after.

When Frank and I renewed our friendship in the late nineties, he had just taken on a young Dutch rock band called BLØF. They were about to be dropped by their record label due to lack of sales and were floundering as to how they might continue. They wrote and sang their songs in Dutch, which was unusual. Most Dutch acts I'd seen were intent on being as international as possible, but BLØF were different. They wanted to appeal to an audience on their own terms and I admired that. It meant they were limited in what they could achieve, but it also endeared them to a vast army of young Dutch rock fans who followed them around avidly.

Frank took them on and gave them direction. They consequently took off like a sky rocket. Frank saw this as a piggyback opportunity to give my career a boost and sent me out with them as a support act. I agreed with Frank that it was good for me to perform in front of vast audiences of teenage rock fans and try to sway them with gentle acoustic music, but I wasn't sure they would listen. In retrospect, it didn't work out and one June night in Leiden, in an incredibly sweaty room full of raging, barracking BLØF fans, I'd had enough. I remember the night clearly. It was 16th June 1999. I played my heart out but nobody was listening, they were impatient and only wanted to hear their heroes BLØF. I tried but I couldn't reach them. At one point, one of the band members came on stage to try and calm them down. He said, 'This man is a friend of ours, he plays great music, you need to listen.' Still nobody paid attention. I stayed up there for perhaps twenty-five minutes, working my way through my set. I did what I do and in the end threw my hands in the air and said to them, 'You know what? Fuck it! Today is my birthday and I don't need this. Good night!'

I retreated back to the dressing room, expecting Frank and the band to be upset and disappointed in me, but they weren't. They'd admired my stance and cheered as I entered the backstage area forming a circle around me, chanting 'Happy birthday. Good on you!'

Yvonne had driven me to the show. I packed away my guitar, we said our goodbyes, jumped into her car and drove straight back to Amsterdam. In the hour it took to get there we talked about what had just happened. I said that if I was going to play for these bigger audiences in these kinds of situations I needed more than just my voice and an acoustic guitar. 'What I really need is somebody who can accompany me and sing harmony vocal.' Yvonne, eyes straight ahead, spontaneously said, 'I think I might know just the person. I have a friend. His name is Ad

Vanderveen. He's a fine songwriter and a very good player. His voice is not unlike yours and he's playing in Amsterdam tonight, shall we go and see him?'

She took me to an Irish bar called Mulligans down by one of the canals. Mulligans was on Amstel, practically next door to De Kleine Komedie, the famous Amsterdam theatre. Ad was already on stage when we got there. As we walked in, Ad glanced in our direction and gave a casual nod and a smile to Yvonne. I was quickly taken by the style in which he played and the authority with which he played it. The quality of his songs was first-rate and his onstage presence was very appealing. Even though he spoke to his audience in Dutch, I could tell he was a man comfortable in his skin and at ease with his abilities.

After the show, the three of us sat in a corner of the bar and talked. It transpired that Ad had been in a successful Dutch duo called Personnel, but had decided that it wasn't for him musically and left to pursue a solo career. I asked him if he might be up for collaboration. He said he might be and invited me to sing on a couple of new songs he'd just recorded for his next album.

Ad was holding down a part-time job to help make ends meet as nightwatchman at a prominent Dutch recording studio called Wisseloord and they had given him carte blanche on late-night studio time. A week later we convened at the studio at around 11pm and I put my vocals on some of his new recordings. We had a unique and ear-pleasing blend; quite rare at first meeting, but for us it was no big surprise. It was obvious to me that we could work together simply by speaking to Ad.

Several days later we met at Yvonne's flat to play a few of my songs together. It was again apparent from the start that this was a match made in heaven. Yvonne had recognised that too, sight unseen. Yvonne was full of enthusiasm and while Ad and I were coming from the creative angle, she seemed to have great practical nous and a second sense about what we ought to be doing. Together we put forward an idea to form a songwriting collective. For all intents and purposes it would have the appearance of a band, but what we envisioned was for four singer-songwriters to come together as a musical democracy.

Ad and I threw some names around and came up with a shortlist of those we might invite to join us. I thought the New Mexico-based singer-songwriter Tom Russell would be perfect. I contacted him and he was interested enough in our proposal to say he would give it some thought, but then came back to us with a no. Tom was having success as a solo troubadour at the time and his schedule was full to overflowing. Ad told me that he very much liked a songwriter called Eliza Gilkyson. I told him that I knew her well and that I too was an admirer of her work. We spoke to Eliza. She liked the idea enough to discuss it some more, but was focused on her solo career and made it clear that would always be her priority. She wasn't against a collaboration though if the time could be found for it. Eliza was careful to say that although she knew me, she didn't know Ad and she wanted to take it a step at a time before committing. We started an email rapport between us and decided to move forward as a trio.

In the meantime, Yvonne had taken an extended leave from her work because of a physical disability and had been made redundant by Rondor. She'd received a decent severance package from them and volunteered to invest some of her money into getting our project off the ground. We devised a plan to record some songs at Swine Lake. Eliza was based in Austin and had some downtime, so it made sense to fly Ad and Yvonne over to us. Ad brought with him a Roland digital recorder. We borrowed some microphones from Mark at the Congress House Studio and rented the rest of the outboard equipment we needed. In a period of seven days we recorded eight songs, ostensibly as demos. Ad, I quickly discovered, is a brilliant sound recordist and what we had originally perceived as demos turned out to be of master quality. We used the huge living space at Swine Lake as a sound studio. Due to its unfinished condition it had wonderful acoustics with its highly reflective surfaces and extremely high ceiling.

Yvonne took the resulting recordings back to the Netherlands and shopped them around to her many contacts. A Dutch label called Coast to Coast loved what they heard and said if there was more music forthcoming, they would like to invest in the completion of an album. It was just a matter of sorting out our conflicting schedules. We would reconvene at another time and in another place to complete the project.

I became involved with a hastily arranged and very under-publicised quartet called No Grey Faith, an anagrammatical tip of the hat to one of Sandy Denny's finest artistic moments, her band Fotheringay. Together we recorded *Secrets All Told*, my long overdue tribute to Sandy the songwriter.

I'd first met my co-collaborators Jim Fogarty and Lindsay Gilmour in the early nineties when I had been booked for a house concert in Philadelphia. I wasn't quite sure what house concerts were at the time and arrived at my destination to find a rambling ten-roomed communal affair on Ridge Avenue in the Wissahickon area of Northwest Philadelphia. There were six people living there at the time, the majority of them musicians. Jim, it transpired, was my host. He and his wife Lindsay performed locally as a duo called The SoulMates. Jim played a mean acoustic guitar and Lindsay sang like a nightingale. I soon discovered they were both enthusiastic early Fairport and Sandy Denny fans. We developed a long, deep and satisfying friendship, both musical and personal, that soon developed into a means for the three of us to play together whenever I was in the immediate area.

Flash forward and I'm a guest in the home of Jim and Lindsay one evening. We were having dinner, talking music as usual, when Sandy's name came up yet again and Lindsay brought up the idea of recording an album of Sandy's tunes. It was one of those 'yeah, why the hell not' moments. We all three agreed that the idea had infinite possibilities and at Jim's suggestion we invited his producer-friend Walt Rich into the mix, mainly because Walt is a hell of a nice guy to be around, with a great ear for the right sounds and a talented fretless bass player to boot. He also coincidentally happened to have a very nice digital studio in his home.

Lindsay and I chose a half-dozen each of Sandy's compositions that we'd like to sing and together with Jim we set about reimagining them. The finished album boasts fourteen tracks. We split Sandy's signature tune 'Who Knows Where the Time Goes?'

into three sections – intro, interlude and reprise – as a vehicle to showcase Lindsay's voice, Jim's guitar and Walt's fretless playing. Lindsay sang as well as I've ever heard her, before or since. Jim's acoustic guitar and mandolin work is as good as it gets. And it's all tied together with a delicate multi-coloured bow of Walt's searing, growling, vibrating bass work. It's an album with oodles of spirit and soul and one I'm quietly proud of, but my days as a US resident were coming to an end and I simply did not have the time to coordinate the record and they unfortunately didn't have the connections. It would be another album that would have to wait a while until it saw the light of day.

Jim, Lindsay and I have developed a strong connection over the years and Jim remains my go-to guy whenever I play the East Coast. He transformed me into a diehard Philadelphia Eagles fan and where I had hoped that he might reciprocate, to this day he remains dubious as to whether it's really worth his effort to root for Manchester United. Lindsay sits neutral and bemused on the sidelines.

People ask me about Sandy all the time. I usually decline to offer quotes because the truth is, although I worked night after night with her and in the studio, I didn't get to know much about her. Amongst those who are aware of Fairport Convention's history, many consider the line-up that featured me and Sandy to have been the best. I see how that line-up was an emotional experience for a lot of people, and I know that there is an almost romantic attachment to it. I felt the same way when I saw Grace Slick and Paul Kantner front Jefferson Airplane when we shared the bill with them at the inaugural Isle of Wight festival in the summer of 1968. They were a band I had long admired and I was thrilled to see the interplay between the male and female vocals. Of course, Grace and Paul were a couple in real life. With Sandy and me it was different. I only ever knew her really as a songwriter and the singer I stood next to on a stage. We didn't socialise outside of band activity. I did however connect with her lyrics and her voice and had a deep admiration for her as a songwriter.

Once I'd left Fairport I hardly saw Sandy at all, except for the odd occasion when we shared a bill. The last time we had been in the same room was when everyone who had played on *If You Saw Thro' My Eyes* assembled at Elstree Studios to make a promotional film for the American market. We mimed to four songs. I was in Seattle when she died. The phone rang and a voice said, 'Hi Ian, this is Spencer Davis. I've got some sad news for you. Sandy Denny died last night.' I think Spencer was working for Island at the time and he was the one who'd taken on the task of letting people know. Of course my first question was 'How?' Spencer told me that things were hazy, but said it had involved a fall down the stairs. I'd heard all the stories about Sandy being drunk all the time. In my mind's eye, she was seldom that.

In the summer of 1999 I recorded a solo album with Bradley Kopp, who by then had left the Colorado weather behind and moved back to his home state. I called the album *A Tiniest Wham*. It's an anagram of my name, but more than that it's an appropriate phrase for that time. I dedicated the album to Manchester United who had recently completed the treble, a feat so difficult they were only the fourth team in the history of the sport to achieve it. They won the Premier League title, the FA Cup and were the Champions of Europe. I'd watched the European final just over the hill from Swine Lake at The Hobby Farm, owned and run by my friend Andrew Hobby. Andrew had bought one of those new big-screen televisions and told me I was free to use it any time I wished. Dominic, Veronique's son, was almost a teenager and had never seen a European football game before so I took him with me to see the Champion's League final: Manchester United versus Bayern Munich.

Anybody who saw that game will know that it was unspectacular for the most part. Dominic had been asking questions all through the game and near the end he kept saying, 'They're going to lose, they're going to lose!' I kept telling him, 'No they're not, just watch.' When it got to the ninetieth minute I thought, 'Fuck, they are going to lose.' Then it happened, with only injury time left and Manchester trailing 0-1, Sheringham and Solskjær scored a quick one-two and The Red Devils won the cup.

Manchester United winning like they did was one of the few

truly joyful moments in my life that year. Even making the album felt like a futile gesture and the recording of it proved difficult. At a friend's urging, Brad and I rented time in a home studio. A successful Texas businessman called Jack Rock had built a state-of-the-art recording studio in his mansion up in the hill country at a place called Two Coves. It was basically an expensive toy, built for his amusement. I see these types all the time. He probably did it to impress his friends. Anyhow, we made a deal with Mr Jack Rock to record there. Brad and I had put a stellar group of players together. I'd flown my guitar playing buddy Jim Fogarty in from Philadelphia, it was the first time he and I had recorded an Iain album together. Some musicians have absolutely no idea what it takes to accompany a songwriter and when you find someone like Jim, you nurture them.

The recording studio was really a control room in a converted office at the back of the house. He had installed a top-of-the-line Pro Tools set-up and the rest of the house had become the recording space. The problem we soon encountered was that Jack Rock had absolutely no idea of studio etiquette. During the first couple of days we were recording acoustic guitars and needed complete silence in the house. Jack was oblivious to this and was in his kitchen clattering about with pots and pans, chopping vegetables on a wooden board and generally making lots of inappropriate noise. We were halfway through recording a track when he turned on his blender. Brad went into the kitchen to reason with him.

'Look Jack, you can't just do this sort of thing while we are in the record mode.'

Rather than apologise or understand our predicament, Jack just laughed if off.

'Well hey man it's my fucking house, I can do whatever I damned well please.'

We soldiered on until an hour later when we had to abandon yet another take because Jack was noisily stacking dishes into the sink. In the evening, before going home we left our settings and EQs on the board ready for the next day's work, only to arrive and find that Jack had been playing in his studio after we left and had changed everything. Again Brad confronted him. He simply shrugged and said, 'It's my studio.' After four days we had to tell Jack that it just wasn't working for us and surprise, surprise, he was offended. He seemed to think that by renting us his studio he was doing us a favour, which I suppose he was, but we'd already lost a precious amount of time and money and he was making it impossible for us to stay. After much debate Jack seemed to understand our predicament and had the decency to refund us the entire amount we'd paid him up front. This gesture enabled us to buy enough time in another 'professional' studio to finish the record.

It was somewhat of a melancholy affair making the rest of that album. Brad and Jim, my best friends, both knew my heart wasn't completely in the US anymore and that I was about to move on. *A Tiniest Wham* was my Texas swansong.

The dawn of the new millennium signalled the beginning of my new life back as a European. It had become all but impossible for me to continue my life at Swine Lake. I just couldn't function. Veronique and I were barely communicating by now. I was spending more and more time on the road and most of that in Europe. It made no sense to stay in America any longer. I had been uneasy for too long and it wasn't about to get better by clinging on.

In March of 2000, Edgar Heckmann and the Blue Rose crew came over again for the South by Southwest conference. While Edgar was there I packed two very large suitcases with clothes and personal effects and I asked him if he would take them back to Germany with him and I'd pick them up next time I saw him. That was the beginning of my move back. I had moved to California in 1973 to pursue a dream. That dream became a life and then ultimately that life became something unmanageable.

In the late afternoon of 20th March 2000, Veronique drove me to Bergstrom International Airport in Austin. She parked the Nissan and walked into the departure area with me. I checked my bags in and we made our way to the gate in silence and without lifting our heads to look at one another. At the gate I turned to

Veronique. She barely acknowledged me. Then she looked up and said, 'I need to go now.' With that she spun around and began to walk away. I watched her go. Almost as an afterthought she half turned and said over her left shoulder, 'Have a good life.' I didn't care for the way she said it and didn't respond.

As I sat waiting to board the flight a female voice came over the intercom. 'This is an announcement for all passengers waiting to board Delta Airways Flight 2245 for Atlanta. Because of mechanical problems, the flight has been cancelled and will be rescheduled for tomorrow. Passengers for the flight are advised to reclaim their baggage from carousel two, where a Delta representative will be waiting to advise you.' I sat for a moment trying to take it in. Then I thought, 'For Christ's sake.'

I called Mark at the studio and said, 'You're not going to believe this!' I asked for a ride back to Swine Lake. Mark said he could do it but was busy and that he would get to me in an hour or so. I waited outside for him in the March breeze. He came and drove me back to the house. Veronique wasn't home. I sat there in the quiet for a good two hours then I heard her Nissan coming up the driveway. She walked into the house with her portable massage table. Her jaw dropped when she saw me. I told her that the flight was cancelled. 'Great,' she said under her breath and went upstairs. When I got up the next morning she was gone. Bradley Kopp picked me up and I retraced my journey to the airport. This time I got away on schedule.

PART FIVE
GOT TO GET BACK HOME

MEANING TO LIFE

I've got to find myself a place where
I can be and truly savour
Somewhere I can buy some peace and quiet
It isn't that I really want tranquillity
But that's the point
You never really do until you try it
I'll write a song or even two
To keep my mind off missing you
I hope in time I'll figure out the meaning
The meaning to life
The meaning to life

I've got to find myself a home
A place completely of my own
No uninvited guests or intervention
A place where inner peace will come
Away from all that city humdrum
Somewhere I can lose this nervous tension
My friends are few and far between
They love to ask me how I've been
But how I've been aint something worth repeating
Without a meaning to life

I'll hide away and not feel guilty
Simple joys again may thrill me
Maybe I can lose this endless sorrow
And make me laugh when it's my birthday
Cause man I hate those in the worst way
Wishing all day long it was tomorrow

I've got to make myself a spot
Where I can see who I am not
Discover what it is I think I'm doing
I've got to make myself a home
Where I can see who I've become
I always thought that life was such a shoo-in
Those friends of mine would always say
If what you see is what you crave
Is what you got worth what you gave to get it

I've got to find my heart a home
Where I can roll away the stone
See the light and even know the meaning
The meaning to life

18. AMSTERDAM

I rented a simple one-room apartment from my friend Yvonne Elenbaas. She lived at the busy end of a main Amsterdam artery called Overtoom. It was within a short walk of both the legendary Paradiso and Melkweg clubs and just across the canal from the American Hotel. I spent a lot of mornings staring aimlessly out of my attic window down into the busy street below wondering, 'What am I going to do now?' I pondered on it endlessly until a song began to form in my head. 'Meaning to Life' was the very first song I wrote after leaving America to make a fresh start in Europe.

Shortly after I arrived in Amsterdam I had a recording commitment in France that had been set up a year previously in Texas. Elliott Murphy and I were both signed to the small German independent label, Blue Rose. Elliott is a New Yorker who first appeared on the scene being hailed as the next big thing, the new Bruce Springsteen. He had first travelled to Europe to appear in Federico Fellini's film *Roma* as far back as 1971. He is a singer, a songwriter, novelist and journalist with around forty albums in his catalogue. I had met Elliott at the South by Southwest music conference in Austin when we played in the same room on the same night. The Blue Rose label owner Edgar Heckmann was there and he had an idea. He called us together.

'I think it could work if you two were to make an album together,' he proposed. 'Stylistically you're not dissimilar. You both sell in reasonable numbers, but if you record an album together I believe we might be able to take it over the top.'

During that time Elliott worked mainly at a studio in Le Havre, France. His French guitar player Olivier Durand lived there with his young family, as did Florent Barbier, his drummer and engineer, so it made absolute sense to record there. We agreed to each write new songs and suggest appropriate covers for the album, a fifty-fifty musical split. In the studio it was a very relaxed process: Elliott would suggest a song he'd want to do, he'd play it and we'd either try it with the band and commit to tape, or veto and move on. I'd then play him one that I liked and so on. We had each arrived with a mixed bag of material. Elliott brought along a great Dylan song called 'Blind Willie McTell' which I instantly gave the thumbs up to. I played him a new song 'One Cold Street' by an unknown East Coast writer, Adam Sherman. He liked it. Part of my live set was the Jesse Colin Young tune 'Darkness, Darkness' and we threw that into the pot too. Elliott is a good friend of Springsteen, so a version of Bruce's song 'Sad Eyes' is on there. We approved, learned, recorded and mixed twelve songs in ten days. After committing the songs to tape we decided we had enough. We finished the album and took it to Heilbronn to play it for Edgar. He thought it was a tad short and that we could add one more song. He was friends with Wolfgang Niedecken, the lead singer of the famous German rock band BAP. Wolfgang had shown interest in guesting on the recording, so later in the year we went into a German studio near his home to record a Bertolt Brecht/Kurt Weill song 'Ballad of the Soldier's Wife' which had been previously recorded by Marianne Faithfull. The three of us swapped vocal duties throughout the song. Songs from the German cabaret tradition are not something I had tackled before and it forced me to alter my vocal delivery. It proved challenging, but I felt good about my contribution.

We called the album *La Terre Commune* after a short series of events I'd run in a coffee shop in Austin several years previous. The idea had been to 'give back' to the community that had given so generously to me over the years with some free events based around performing and explaining the art of songwriting. I called these events 'Common Grounds' and Elliott liked the idea so Olivier translated the phrase into French for the album title.

My first year back as a European was a time of both intense reflection and projection. I had no clear plan, my thoughts seemed muddled and my mind was unfocused and cloudy. I did a little touring, as much as I could find, but not nearly as much as I'd have liked to. In early May, Ad Vanderveen and I played a show at the Café De Amer in the tiny community of Amen in the northern province of Drenthe. The café was held in high esteem for both the international acts they magically drew to the room and the extremely high quality of their in-house recordings. For touring purposes, Ad and I called ourselves 'The Iain Ad Venture' and until then we had nothing of our collaboration on disc. The Amen show was a perfect combination of a great recording, with a full house and an inspired evening of music. We were both extremely happy with our performance and the sound quality and decided to self-release the recording to use as a calling card for future bookings. A small investment to get us further work.

I needed to keep myself occupied but also keep enough free time to think. I vowed to stay positive and visualise a plan. I had to do something creative with my thought process and tried to concentrate on writing but I didn't feel ready. In fact, after my morning constitutional, most of my daylight hours were spent wandering the streets of Amsterdam, observing life while listening to other people's music.

A typical day involved getting up around 7:30am, more often than not after a fretful night's sleep. I'd throw on my jogging kit and come hell or high water I would launch myself down the three flights of stairs out onto the city streets, leaning into the wind and spring rain, forcing my feet to propel me forward. I'd usually turn right at the foot of the stairs and head down Overtoom, away from the centre, before crossing the road and swinging left into Vondelpark, then around and around its twisting and turning perimeter until I felt enough was enough. Vondelpark is often considered the 'green lung' of Amsterdam, where visitors and residents alike picnic during the summer months and attend performances at the outdoor stage, or simply socialise at one of the several cafés dotted around the park. It was the perfect place for a morning jog.

After running I'd head home and shower. I would then throw on my Levi jacket with a MiniDisc Walkman buttoned into a top pocket, put my headphones on and, with a half-dozen of my favourite albums in the back pocket of my jeans, I'd begin walking. Most mornings I'd angle across town, zigzagging across the canal bridges, heading towards the American bookstore. I'd buy a *Herald Tribune* before crossing the street to sit in the H&M coffee shop to check the US sports scores. It took me a while to shrug off American sports and restart my passion for English football. Eventually I realised it didn't have to be one or the other, I could enjoy both. After H&M, I'd then explore the inner city, sometimes stopping to rest, or for a coffee, or to sit and watch people interacting, all the while thinking, thinking, before suddenly realising I had been out there for five or six hours and it was approaching dinner time.

In a way, having that flimsy ritual helped me focus and develop a positive attitude about my future, but performing it each day under what I can clearly see now was a mild depression was an achievement in itself. I was packed full of conflicting emotions; I'd swing wildly from being disoriented, lonely and confused, to being optimistic, full of verve and determined to make the move work.

My friend Yvonne was a rock. She was experiencing severe medical challenges of her own but would always find the time to hear about my doubts and fears. During my brief stay in the capital, Yvonne, her dog Jack and I formed a deep bond that will never be broken. But still I could not quite break through into that happy place I knew existed somewhere inside of me.

The moment of surrender came for me nine months after my flight from Texas. By this time I'd found a little third-floor haven of my own overlooking one of the canals about a fifteen minute walk from Overtoom. Believing this would do the trick, I'd enthusiastically moved in, but it did in fact have quite the opposite effect. Within a week I felt isolated and negative and slumped back into an even deeper depression. On top of that, never having the patience to stretch my muscles before jogging, I'd tweaked a tendon in my calf and could barely walk, let alone force myself to run in the mornings. I realised I needed to do something about it fast, or sink.

I called my good friends Greg and Kim Boone in Ohio. I'd first met them during my early solo sojourns into the Midwest.

Greg Boone, apart from being an avid music and sports lover, was a surgeon with a local Columbus practice, while his wife Kim dedicated her spare time to caring for the apes at the city zoo. They had two young boys needing most of their attention, but had graciously opened up their home to me and welcomed me in as a touring musician. Greg and I had bonded during the twenty-minute car ride from the airport to his home when we discovered we shared the same birthday. I'm twelve years older than him, but we're both June 16th. It had proven once again that tiny insignificant moments can lead to lifetime friendships. Greg, Kim and I became close friends and these days our families holiday together every other year.

I phoned Greg but he was on the emergency room night shift so I left a message. He returned my call within the hour and I told him how I was feeling.

'No matter how you feel, don't do anything silly,' he said, 'I'm going to book you an open-ended flight to Columbus. Pack your bag and get yourself out here. I won't take no for an answer.'

I was with them within ten days and stayed through the New Year, by which time I'd listened to professional advice and soaked up oodles of Midwestern TLC. My mind and I were on friendlier terms about returning to my new European surroundings and I arrived back in Amsterdam in early January with a new and steely determination. I decided to give up on the bachelor pad and moved back into my room above Yvonne. At which point my life took on a new course that would change me forever.

The new year became a period of completion for me. I had tossed several musical balls into the air before I left the USA, now they were all on their way back down and required catching, providing a great opportunity for me to dive in and start the juices flowing again.

First on my list was the project that I'd started with Ad and Eliza Gilkyson at Swine Lake. Yvonne and I had been to see her friend Kees Klop. Kees ran the successful reissue label Coast to Coast and was seriously considering getting into the new release market. We met with Kees and I found him to be a relaxed, passionate, forward-thinking music man with a keen sense for business. Yvonne and I were primarily focused on completing the project with Ad and Eliza and finding it a good home, but as a means of identifying my current musical style I had also taken along the No Grey Faith Sandy Denny tribute album to play for him. On hearing it Kees decided he wanted both projects on his label. The No Grey Faith album, *Secrets All Told*, would be released on Coast to Coast as an Iain Matthews appetiser while we finished working on the main course.

The record might as well have been called *Secrets All Hidden* as it caused but a ripple in that great ocean of new releases, proving to be little more than a guinea pig for the label, a musical probe to determine whether or not they were equipped to release brand-new recordings. It transpired that initially they were not, but quickly learned from their mistakes for when the new album hit the streets.

Things were slowly falling into place and I began to feel more creative and appreciated. Yvonne took on a new role to officially become our project manager as we set about finishing the album we'd started in Texas. Yvonne found a holiday park in a town called Norg. It was closed for the winter, but she persuaded the owners to rent her two of the log cabins. We flew Eliza over from Austin and Ad once again packed his recording equipment into his car and set it up in one of the cabins. We used the second one as a living and sleeping space.

We camped out for ten days in the snow and ice of a wintry Norg, adding a further nine songs to the initial recordings. Yvonne had organised some shows for Eliza to cover her expenses, which meant we could record together through the mornings into early afternoon, at which point Eliza would head out to play while Ad and I buckled down to the all-important tasks of overdubbing and mixing the tracks. I had by then written two more songs about my flight from Texas, adding 'A Beautiful Lie' and 'Rerun Matinee' to 'Meaning to Life'. Now I could send them out into the world and make space in my head for more positive musings.

With mixing finished, the album was sequenced, the cover and press photographs were shot, artwork completed and a release date was set. We called it *More Than a Song*. Everyone involved breathed a deep sigh of relief and contentment. Job well done. The album stands the test of time and I will always be immensely proud of it and of my association with all those involved. It gave me the confidence I so badly needed to get back in the saddle, confirming for me that my decision to come home to Europe had been the correct one.

My album with Elliott Murphy, *La Terre Commune*, was released worldwide in February 2001. It was well received by press and fans alike. The reviews I saw were positive and encouraging, but the record didn't sell in the numbers that Edgar had hoped for. That year we toured the length and breadth of Europe, selling out wherever we went. We played some very good rooms, including the Ancienne Belgique in Brussels, the Paradiso in Amsterdam and the New Morning in Paris. Blue Rose released an 'official bootleg' live recording of the entire show, recorded in Solingen in June 2001, but nothing we did seemed to take it up a notch to that all-important next level and by late summer Elliott and I had gone our separate ways. Back to our respective solo ventures.

But there was no rest. I had my solo album *A Tiniest Wham* in the shops via Blue Rose and they were anxious for me to get out on the road to promote it. There was much to do and little time to reflect, or consider what life might have in store for me. In the immortal words of John Lennon, 'Life is what happens to you while you're busy making other plans,' and it most certainly was.

Ad committed to touring with me. In the aftermath of the *More Than a Song* recording he was at a loose end as to what music might have in store for him and this was an ideal way to create a living whilst mulling it over. We rehearsed for a few days and hit the autobahns. It was the perfect scenario having Ad with me. We enjoyed each other's company, we travelled well and loved playing together. It allowed us to hone our already tight musical partnership while imagining our next career moves. It felt much calmer and far more familiar to me to be back on the road with Ad as a duo. Like a well-oiled machine, we learned a few new songs, turned the key and off we went.

The duo set-up of acoustic and electric guitar and two voices is ideal for me. It's become my preferred way of playing these days. It's a tight, affordable way to work and the best of all worlds musically. I'm a decent rhythm guitar player, I can hold it all down while my partner adds colour, stretches out and embellishes. Ad is also a great singer in his own right. People tend to pigeonhole him, saying he's a Neil Young sound-alike. Sure Neil has been an influence, making it an easy tag to hang around his neck, but he's far more than that. He'd be the first to admit his affection for Neil's music, but from that fascination he's developed a writing style and delivery quite unique unto himself. I have developed a deep admiration and respect for both the man and his muse.

On 11th September 2001, Ad, Yvonne and I drove south from Amsterdam to a small town called Horst in the province of Limburg to play at Café Cambrinus. We set off after lunch and the drive took slightly more than two hours. Yvonne took a phone call along the way and I could hear snatches of her end of the conversation. After she hung up she said, 'There's something big happening in New York.' She said it was unclear but there had been some kind of explosion. We left it at that, the conversation drifted elsewhere and we didn't think any more of it.

We arrived at Café Cambrinus at just after five in the afternoon. We walked in and did what most musicians always do, we scanned the room. Over to our right were a man and two women watching a small TV mounted on a stool by the stage. They were Jan Duijf, the café owner, his partner Henny, and an attractive young woman they introduced as Marly who had been called in as extra help for the evening after another member of staff had fallen ill.

Jan asked us if we had seen what was happening in New York. We hadn't. Ad, Yvonne and I sat down by the TV with the three of them and watched as the footage of the two aeroplanes crashing into the Twin Towers was constantly replayed on the screen. The news was in Dutch so they were translating the commentary for me. At some point I asked Jan if I might use the phone to call Texas to see if everything was alright there. All the lines were down and I couldn't get through.

Out of the blue, Jan turned to me and asked, 'Will you still play tonight?' I looked at him surprised and said, 'Of course, it's my job.' In retrospect, I suppose it was a strange response, but it never occurred to me that I should do otherwise. We then went back to watching the news, but I was vaguely distracted by this young woman Marly. I kept glancing over at her, sometimes we made eye contact and there was, I felt, a faint buzz between us.

Despite the events of the day, people came out in droves to the concert and we had a packed house. The room was crackling with electricity from what had happened. We played well, but the day's events hung over us like a dark shroud and music seemed somewhat inconsequential. For me, there was an added distraction. I could not stop glancing at Marly, watching her float around the room, picking up empty glasses from the tables and bringing fresh drinks for her customers. I almost always sing with my eyes tight shut, but not that night. I felt vaguely guilty about being distracted by this beautiful young thing and the feelings I was experiencing, while on the other side of the Atlantic there was chaos and carnage. At the end of the night, Ad and I packed our equipment, loaded it into the car, said our goodnights and drove over to our lodgings.

The following day, Ad and I had an in-store performance at a big independent record store in Venlo called Sounds; it's one of the largest in the country and my favourite place to shop for music. It is a long, narrow space, packed to the gills with CDs. At the far end is a staircase to a second floor jammed with vinyl, old and new. They quite frequently host in-store performances and have built a permanent stage opposite the stairs, complete with a compact sound system. There were around forty to fifty people there to see us. We played a short set that afternoon, maybe five or six songs. As we eased our way through the songs, I noticed that Marly was sitting on the staircase watching. After the performance, the owner said I could choose a couple of CDs as a thank you and as I was browsing the racks Marly sidled up next to me to say hello. As beguiling as I found her, I was far too shy to respond with much more than a simple 'hello' back. Marly told me that Jan had been very excited and proud to have me playing in his café, as he had been a fan since back in the day. He'd bought my album *If You Saw Thro' My Eyes* when it came out and I'd become one of his musical heroes. Sentiments like this never fail to catch me off guard as I find it difficult to think of myself as anyone's hero, but coming from Marly it had a sincerity and warmth I found easy to accept. I smiled.

That night we had a second show at Cambrinus. After we had set up I went over to Jan.

'Is Marly working tonight?'

'No, she is at home,' Jan told me. 'She has an eighteen-month-old daughter to care for.'

I took this to mean that Marly must be in a relationship. I was quite crestfallen. Jan smiled at my expression.

'Is she married?' I blurted out.

Jan kept grinning and said, 'No, she's free.'

My spirits rose and I hoped then that I would see Marly again. After the show, Jan told me that Marly really liked my music and that she wanted to buy the *More Than a Song* album. I said that she didn't have to buy it and gave him a signed copy to pass on to her.

ONE DOOR OPENS

Before my eyes an angel stood
Laughing breathing flesh and blood
Sounding only like an angel can
I felt my senses come alive
My future flashed before my eyes
There was no angel in my master plan
Before I knew what I was saying
Words escaped, I lost my way
And all that filled my mind was
She's the one

Before my time another man
Stood while her mascara ran
Then slipped a goodbye note beneath her door
She said tell me all you feel
I said only love is real
She said I know that, now tell me more
But there are things too dark to mention
Little things that crave attention
Little things that tell me
She's the one

God leaned over, spoke to Moses
Simple truths and one of those is
For each door opening another door closes

Before my eyes a vision danced
All around my circumstance
Humming every note of who I am
I asked her name, I told her mine
Then slowly lost all track of time

*Drifting like a jack-knife caravan
Even though I hardly knew her
There was something strong and pure
And clouding up my mind was
She's the one*

19. IN THE DUTCH MOUNTAINS

More Than a Song was released by Coast to Coast in 2001 to rave reviews by the Dutch music press. We were so enthused by all of the positive attention that we decided to take it on the road. Yvonne helped us find a top music impresario to take the ensemble into the Dutch theatres.

We invited Eliza's son Cisco Ryder to join us on stage to play a scaled-down drum kit. It was a percussion box called a Cajon, a type of Mexican drum box played with the hands while sitting on it. Cisco had ingeniously rigged up a kick-pedal to add some extra punch to the sound and as a foursome the entire thing sounded fatter, with more drive. The tour was a joyful adventure and an unprecedented success. We played to full, enthusiastic houses almost everywhere we went.

Eliza had been born in Hollywood. Her father was Terry Gilkyson, a songwriter with Walt Disney Studios. It was Terry who wrote 'The Bare Necessities', the song popular from *The Jungle Book*. That song became a big encore number for us on that tour. Of course everyone in the audience knew it and we encouraged their participation. Because this was the Netherlands, the people had seen the film as children in a dubbed Dutch language version. We'd sing the verses in English and they sang the chorus back to us in Dutch. It was all very entertaining and highly motivating.

> Als je van beren leren kan, van slimme beren leren kan
> is dat iets wat je echt proberen moet.

On the 5th February 2002, we arrived back at Café Cambrinus in Horst. Coincidentally, my daughter Darcy's 30th birthday. As soon as we arrived I asked Jan if Marly was coming to the show. He said that she wasn't working, it was possible she would be there, but as far as he knew she wouldn't. I was disappointed.

We did our soundcheck and ate a light dinner in the back as the doors opened and the café filled up. For the purpose of concerts, Jan and Henny's dining room becomes a dressing room and after the show it reverts back to a dining room for the band to have a late meal. Ad, Eliza, Cisco and I were sitting together discussing the set list and tuning up while waiting to go on when Marly walked in. I jumped up and said, 'Hey, it's good to see you again.' Marly hurriedly said, 'Oh! Excuse me, I came this way because I need to use the bathroom and the other one is occupied.'

At show time Marly sat in the front row. I sang most of my songs directly at her, eyes open. We even had a moment of chat during the set. I have a song called 'The Ballad of Gruene Hall' which is about a dancehall in the township of Gruene, twenty or so miles south of where I lived in Texas. Gruene was originally settled by German immigrants, as was much of Central Texas, and I was constantly pronouncing the title wrong. Marly, who speaks fluent German, corrected me.

When I first saw her sitting in that front row seat, I sensed that she had possibly come because she had the same feelings as I did. It later transpired that this was exactly why she was there and why she'd sat in the front row, which is something she normally never does. After the concert, when all the equipment was packed away and Yvonne was in the back sorting out the fee with Jan, I waited with my hands in my coat pockets wondering what to do. Marly was sitting on the edge of the stage, smoking cigarettes with a few friends and I desperately wanted to speak to her. She saw me looking, stood up and walked over and for the first time we had a real conversation. I asked for her phone number. She excused herself and went in the back, behind the bar and into the dining room. Later she told me that she'd gone to nervously ask Jan and Henny, 'Shall I give him my number?' Henny told her, 'Give it to him Marly. What's the worst that can happen? It doesn't mean you have to speak with him.' She came back with her number written on a beer mat.

I got into the car that night on cloud nine, with a warm, fuzzy, excited feeling racing around my senses. Marly was all I could think of. Before we reached the highway I said to Yvonne and Eliza, 'I think I've met someone.'

When I left Texas, I was fifty-four years old. I knew I would be starting a new life, but I was preparing myself for a bachelor existence. I'd been through the traumas of several relationships that had crashed and burned and I didn't feel mentally prepared for another one. Yet here I was, finding myself strongly attracted to a beautiful young Dutch woman. I waited a full, excruciating forty-eight hours before purposely calling Marly when I knew she would still be working. I was nervous about speaking to her and unsure where all of this would lead. I left a message. Marly called me back the next day and we embarked upon a series of late-night phone conversations. I told her I was working almost every evening and asked if I could call after I got home from my shows. She agreed and I would sometimes wake her at two in the morning and we'd talk in hushed voices for two hours as her baby daughter Madelief was sleeping in her crib next to the bed.

The *More Than a Song* show rolled on for another month. The collective was never talked about as anything permanent. Ad and I had optimistic hopes of it lasting another twelve months or so but Eliza proved difficult to pin down. She became flighty and quite anxious about continuing her solo career. She didn't commit to any further touring and before too long the entire thing collapsed around us like a house of cards. Ad, Yvonne and I understood her concerns and had anticipated the possibility of it happening, but nevertheless it was a great shame it had to end. I firmly believe that had we given it a little more time we could have created a touring foundation to build on for years to come.

It was a wonderful live experience, highly musical with great sound and visuals. Ask anyone who saw us. We played seated and every night we'd build a tight, cosy living-room set around us. Everything we had was old, bought at second-hand stores. We each had either a standing or a table lamp with a pull chord, small colourful rugs and dining chairs, with a little coffee table beside each of us to put our drinks and capos and set lists on. We would walk on stage, sit down and switch our lamps on. Audiences ate it up.

There was a terrific sense of comradeship on stage. We'd verbally joust with each other in a good-natured way. Eliza in particular was sharp, quick and funny as hell. She would tease the Dutch audiences by calling their future king and first lady Bill and Maxie. It comes across brilliantly on a live disc and a DVD we made from our final concert together on 3rd March. Ad tried to record every concert and finally, on the last night of the tour, he got the recorded sound just right and the concert was edited and released in Europe the following year. Ironically it was at De Kleine Komedie theatre in Amsterdam, right next door to where Ad and I had first encountered each other.

Eventually Marly and I made our first date. I arranged to borrow Yvonne's car to drive the two and a half hours down from Amsterdam to Horst. Then I panicked. I called Marly to say that Yvonne now needed her car and I'd have to cancel. A mature man in his mid-fifties, acting like an insecure teenager. What the hell was going on? 'Grow up,' I told myself and called her back a couple of hours later to say that Yvonne's plans had changed again and I could come after all. Marly said, 'Well I've made other plans now.' She hadn't, she too had panicked. A week later, we both got it together and managed to have our first date. I drove to Horst and had dinner at Marly's home.

Marly was born and raised in Horst, a village near the River Meuse, which the Dutch now call the Maas. The village lies not far from the German border, a mere forty minutes from the industrial city of Düsseldorf. Her father spent his whole working life in the local lace factory, from the age of fifteen to sixty-five. Even after retirement he was called in to lend a hand. Her mother was a traditional Dutch housewife who had come into her father's house initially as a housemaid in service. When he was widowed, he married Marly's mother. He already had seven children and together they had four more. Marly was the youngest, born in 1970, the same year 'Woodstock' got to number one in the pop charts. She studied at a college in Eindhoven and gained a bachelor's degree in speech and language therapy. She then worked near Mönchengladbach for several years as a speech therapist, hence her grasp of the German language. She courted a local lad for some eight years and they were married in the town hall. She thought that she would be happy ever after, but the reality was very different. The marriage collapsed within eighteen months, at which point Marly discovered she was pregnant with Madelief.

I met Madelief for the first time on the evening I had dinner with Marly. She's eighteen now and loves to relate the story of how that evening I tried to woo and charm her with my best baby talk. She was having none of it and cried inconsolably every time I opened my mouth. Marly is convinced that it is no coincidence that my daughter Darcy disappeared from my life when she was a year-and-a-half old and Madelief was exactly the same age when she appeared in my life twenty-eight years later. After the histrionics of that first evening, I managed slowly but surely to engage with Madelief. As she grew she would refer to me as her 'Extra Papa'. I found this sweet and thoughtful. These days I'm proud to consider her one of my daughters.

I moved in with Marly on 5th May 2002. This is an important date in the Netherlands, they call it Bevrijdingsdag – Liberation Day – and it marks the date when the British and their allies freed the Dutch people from Nazi rule. The day after I moved in, Pim Fortuyn, the flamboyant, right-wing leader of the Lijst Pim Fortuyn party, was assassinated by an environmental and animal rights activist called Volkert van der Graaf. When the news broke early that evening, Marly was visibly shaken. She told me that it was the first time she had seen such real life violence, especially in broad daylight in her country, and it made her feel unsafe.

Marly had lived as a single mum with Madelief for two years in a newly built house, near the fields on the edge of town. I was madly in love with her, but nervous about moving in. We both had a history of things that hadn't worked out and we'd both had our hearts broken. We told each other that we still believed in love. I wanted a family and I know Marly felt the same way. The space I moved into was very feminine and bright. She had two white couches, the walls were white, the floor was light timber and around the glass-topped dining table were four white plastic chairs. I'd been used to living in a cluttered, one-room apartment with thick-brown velvet curtains that were almost always drawn and walls that were painted chocolate brown. I craved the dark.

Marly lived a structured life with a 9-to-5 job. She was used to everything being organised. I had been pleasing myself for years, living the life of a travelling musician; I ate when I was hungry, slept when I was tired. She would come home and cook a meal every night. I hadn't given food a second thought for years. In fact I was a poor eater, not an unhealthy one, but with a limited diet. I'd sit all day writing songs and sending out emails, it never occurred to me to experiment with nice recipes or anything like that. Marly would come home at just after five and say, 'What do you fancy for dinner?' Invariably I'd say, 'I just had three sandwiches an hour ago so I'm not hungry.' Food was never part of my consciousness and I didn't realise it was such an important part of family life. This was frustrating for Marly and in the beginning of our relationship, the source of some tension. Eventually, I began to get the hang of it. I made a decision not to eat after lunch so that we could eat an evening meal together. Then when Marly came home and said 'Are you hungry?' I went from 'I just ate three sandwiches' to 'I could be' to 'I could manage something light'. These days, I find myself asking, 'What's for dinner?'

It's through Marly that I've finally learned to go on holiday. I realise it may sound strange but musicians traditionally don't take holidays. In a way, what we do is one long vacation as we don't punch a clock. It's a mindset. We think we don't need holidays when in fact we really do. The problem is that's it's seldom a physical weariness and therefore difficult to spot. It sounds so mind-numbingly simple but I had to learn to do it. I now find it unbelievably refreshing to travel to some distant, sun-soaked location, taking along a great book and occasionally a guitar to simply relax and read and play. Maybe drink a little too much. I still have moments of anxiety when I'm on holiday and remember an important chore I should have taken care of before I left, but all things considered I now find that I like going away with my family on holiday.

There were some cultural things for Marly and I to overcome at first. I don't speak Dutch, so whenever we were in a social situation, Marly found herself having to repeat everything. This became a source of frustration, especially when I started to question her accuracy of translation. Many times she said to me, 'Okay, next time let's do it in Dutch and see how you like it!' I try, but I still haven't got the hang of the language. As in music, I'm a lazy learner.

We had our ups and downs like any other couple moving in and sharing a life together. Ours was complicated by cultural differences, the age difference, the language barrier and the baggage that we both brought from our past lives. We also found in the beginning that we didn't have too much in common, but we worked on it and found things. We did however care deeply for each other and felt a very strong psychological connection. So strong was that connection that each time we argued and told each other 'It's over' we knew it never was. It was Marly's house of course and she did tell me to go a few times. Each time I'd say, 'I'm not leaving, I live here,' and we'd make up.

Marly and I have a great fondness for Café Cambrinus, after all it's where we met. We like to stroll up there from our house for a drink and a chat at least a couple of times a week. Cambrinus is a classic neighbourhood bar that welcomes the world and its wife for good times and music. It proudly displays a chalkboard that features over a hundred beers, mainly from the Belgian brewing art, but from all over Europe too. For a while, Jan even brewed his own beers.

One night, Jan came and sat with us and asked if I might consider performing the *If You Saw Thro' My Eyes* album in its entirety, at his café. He told me that he had his original album from 1971 and it was still his favourite record of mine. He offered me two nights. I thought about it, but had to say no on the grounds that it was far too much work for such a short run. These were mostly songs that I had never performed live and the potential workload of figuring out arrangements, hiring a band and rehearsing was enormous. Not to mention paying them for their efforts.

However, Jan had planted a seed and in subsequent months I mulled it over. I was working steadily with Ad at the time and I broached the idea with him. He embraced the concept, but like me realised that something on that scale would need to have a longer shelf life than two nights in a local café, and that it would take more than two people to pull it off, with a lot of concentrated rehearsal.

The previous year, again at Cambrinus and at Jan's suggestion, I'd been to see a Limburg band called Blowbeat and had met their fretless bass player, a man called Eric Coenen. He lived an hour down the road from me in a village called Panningen. Eric and I became friends and ended up doing a short club tour together. I was in awe of his musical skills. I recognised an element of Fotheringay's Pat Donaldson in his playing. Pat had been the bass player on my album *If You Saw Thro' My Eyes* and I could envision Eric playing Pat's parts. The idea was now percolating.

One night Marly and I were talking about the original album. She asked me when it first came out. We totted up the years and realised it was coming up to 33 years ago, to be precise 33⅓ years ago. Marly said, 'Why is that important?' As I explained to her that is the speed the old LPs run at on a turntable, it occurred to me that I could do a celebratory tour entitled '33⅓' and perform the album live in its entirety, with anecdotes and stories about the making of it. The train was running. Eric, Ad and I began rehearsals.

One Sunday morning Jan called me and said, 'This afternoon at 4pm we have a jazz combo here that you simply must come and see.' This was Searing Quartet, a classic piano-based foursome with saxophone, drums and upright bass. The piano player, Egbert Derix, and the saxophonist, Peter Hermesdorf, wrote most of the material and they used these compositions as a springboard for improvisation. The quartet were stellar, one of the best I'd seen, but I was particularly taken by Egbert's otherworldly piano artistry. I realised that this was the kind of person I needed to work with. After the concert we spoke. He knew of my work. I told him about the 33⅓ tour plans and asked if he might consider being a part of it. He liked the idea and even more so when I told him that Keith Tippett had played most of the piano parts on the original album.

I contacted Ruud de Graaf, my Dutch theatre booker. It was perfect timing. He was at the beginning of his booking season and embraced the concept with great enthusiasm. He put us into 200-to 300-seat theatres and art centres across the Netherlands, eighteen venues in total. It became apparent after just a couple of shows that the choice of Egbert was an inspired one. Not only did he accompany Ad, Eric and I with great sensitivity, he took on the task of transcribing the orchestrated parts of that album, which was a feat in itself. Egbert had trained at the Conservatorium Maastricht. He used his considerable knowledge, particularly on a piece called 'Hinge' which originally linked the two sides of the LP. The strings on 'Hinge' had been two separate recordings and I had cross-faded them halfway through to form one continuous piece. With seemingly little effort, Egbert charted them as one piece and programmed the string sounds directly into his Roland keyboard and played it live.

Much to the delight of Jan, two of the nights on that tour were at Café Cambrinus and it was there, in that intimate candlelit space, that we decided to record the entire show. Up to that point we had been a drummerless quartet, but realised that for the purpose of the recording we were going to need a drummer. It would be a task to learn the parts in such a short time, as we only came up with the idea the night before. Eric suggested his colleague from Blowbeat, Arthur Lijten. Arthur was up for the challenge and we overnighted the original album to him in Amsterdam. He miraculously learned his parts on the two-and-a-half hour drive to Horst and fine-tuned them during soundcheck.

My friend Léon Bartels set up a portable control room in the café's kitchen. I was as nervous as a cat in a thunderstorm about the whole affair, particularly because of Arthur's last-minute participation. I needn't have been, he pulled it off with great panache. They all did, inspiring me to one of my better live vocal performances. The recording was briefly available as *Thro' My Eyes Live* on my own record label, MK2 (Matthews Kleeven Squared) where the musicianship is plain to hear.

For Jan, the live recording of *If You Saw Thro' My Eyes* was the culmination of a dream. Jan is a great character and his enthusiasm for bringing the outside world to a café bar in his local town is second to none. He had the vision to see that even on a small scale you can present quality. Over the years he has programmed music that would be the envy of the many far bigger venues across the country and he does it with good grace from a small country town called Horst. I feel blessed to have moved to a town with such an asset. And of course it's where I met my soulmate Marly, and Bart-Jan Baartmans and Egbert Derix, who were to become my musical mainstays.

Marly and I were married on 5th February 2004. The proposal had come eighteen months earlier. I was about to fly to Austria for a charity concert. Marly decided to accompany me. We arrived at the airport to be confronted by what the Americans call a 'Puddle Hopper' – a very small, propeller-driven eighteen-seater. Flying is not Marly's favourite thing in the world at the best of times. As we walked to the gate, Marly grabbed my arm.

'Please don't tell me that little aeroplane is ours.'

'I don't think so.'

Of course it was. We boarded the plane, strapped ourselves in and Marly turned to me and said, 'Will you marry me?' I didn't hesitate. I just said, 'Hell yeah!'

When we returned from Austria, Marly went to see her mom to give her the good news. Her mother was delighted because she had not long since seen her daughter pregnant and heartbroken. Marly mentioned that I was quite a bit older. Mom just smiled and said, 'You're just like me then.'

We were married in the old town hall. It occurred to me that I wasn't just marrying Marly, but her daughter Madelief too, so we bought Madelief a ring. The service was conducted in two languages. Andy Roberts flew over to be my best man. Marly had her best friend Lidia as maid of honour and Yvonne Elenbaas came down from Amsterdam to be witness for the both of us. We had a grand wedding party at Cambrinus. Ad Vanderveen, Julian Dawson, BJ, Andy and I played impromptu music on a makeshift stage. The most moving moment of the evening for me came when Marly's mom came and took my hand. She whispered into my ear in her strong Limburgian accent, 'Wal good veur eur zorge weh,' which means, 'Take good care of her.' I said, 'Of course I will.'

JOY MINING

Joy mining, don't look back
Get off that straight and narrow track
Joy mining, don't despair
Just dig in deep it's waiting there

You shudder at the sound of distant thunder
You say how everything is so divine
If all these weary blues don't suck you under
You'll be fine

You say you've heard about a door
But you just can't find it
You want to feel the joy but the joy won't come
You'd love to stick around but you've decided
You'll just run

Joy mining, don't look back
Get off that straight and narrow track
Joy mining, fill your soul
Just tap into that vein of gold

You take a walk in the morning glory
And you feel the heat of a brand-new sun
You're at the feet of a whole new story
This one's done

You used to spend your days in a state of wonder
You could not keep your feet on solid ground
Now you don't hang around there any longer
Since you found

Joy mining, don't look back
 Get off that straight and narrow track
Joy mining, don't despair
Just dig in deep it's waiting there
Joy mining, fill your soul
Just tap into that vein of gold
Joy mining

20. JAZZ IS AN ACCIDENT WAITING TO HAPPEN

Throughout my career I've made it a habit to revisit past projects. I wasn't sure that I would ever revisit Matthews Southern Comfort though until I did an interview in 2005 with a journalist who was constantly asking me in-depth questions about the band. To be fair, they were sensible questions and they set me thinking.

I was just a year shy of being sixty and had been a professional musician for forty years. My musical tastes had developed and jazz was something I was dying to dip a toe into. I wasn't thinking hardcore jazz, just something that had an edge and left room for improvisation. I pondered on reforming Matthews Southern Comfort based on these thoughts, but without the restrictions of the pedal steel that had so dominated the sound of the original band.

A year or so before I had recorded a solo album called *Zumbach's Coat*. It's an album based around the idea of shedding the cloak of expectation and embracing experimentation. When we took the record on the road I put together a trio of Mike Roelofs, a Dutch jazz pianist, and Richard Kennedy, a left-handed acoustic guitar player from New Zealand who, like Hendrix, plays a right-handed guitar strung upside down. The sound we made together was different from anything I'd done before and very much a departure for me. It picked me up and hurled me in a completely new direction. I liked it, and began to think that these two players might be the beginnings of a new Matthews Southern Comfort.

With that thought in mind, I went to see my good friend BJ Baartmans, a Dutch multi-instrumentalist who at that time was on tour with an American singer-songwriter by the name of Terri Binion. Terri lives in Orlando, Florida. They were playing an in-store at Sounds in Venlo. BJ had called me and said, 'You need to come down here and see this woman because I think she is really special.' I've worked with BJ on and off since I first saw him play in Cambrinus not long after I moved to Horst and I always trust his judgement on these matters. If he thinks I need to be there, then I need to be there.

I hustled on down to Sounds and I was blown away both by Terri's songwriting and her voice. There was something else too, the combination of Terri and BJ felt right. Together they created a comfortable, but edgy sound. I bought her album and drove home humming one of her songs. A good sign. When I got home it dawned on me that if I added Terri and BJ, I had all the pieces in place for re-launching Matthews Southern Comfort. All I had to do was convince BJ that for this band he would be the bass player, not the guitar player. I already had Richard to play guitar, but I needed to explain this without sounding as though I lacked confidence in Bart-Jan's guitar playing. Fortunately for me he saw my point and being a producer, he could visualise the sound I was imagining.

I got everyone together, inviting Mike Roelofs, Richard, BJ and Terri for ten days of experimentation at Léon's Farm Studio, a funky little recording studio owned by Léon Bartels, virtually down the road in Boekend. During that ten-day period we laid down about fifteen tracks, a combination of mine and Terri's songs and some old reimagined Matthews Southern Comfort tunes. Everyone had the complete freedom to be who they were. The four of them were excited by the end result and I thought there was enough potential to move forward with the idea, so much so that I got in touch with my English booking agent to ask him to put a tour together for us, which he agreed to do. However, towards the end of our experiments, I began to have the odd doubt. Something didn't seem quite right to me. I expressed my doubts to Marly.

'What is it you're feeling?' she asked. I didn't know. It was just a sense that things were somehow not working. 'If you are not feeling it, don't do it. I know you, you'll regret it,' she told me.

I understood what she was saying, but I didn't want to let these people down after all of their initial excitement. The more I dwelled on it, the more I realised I wasn't in the right frame of mind. I couldn't put my finger on the reason why, but I felt flat and uninspired and the music we were making seemed dull. The English promoter came back and told me he'd had a great reaction and had booked some nice shows, including a two-day showcase at Peter Gabriel's Real World Studios at Box near Bath. I was unsure what to do.

I sat down again with Marly and told her that everything I was hearing sounded nothing like I wanted it to. I played some tracks for her. She thought it sounded good. Now I was becoming confused. Was I imagining it? Through the simple exercise of talking about it, I came to realise that it was only me feeling uncomfortable, while the others were doing great work. I just couldn't get myself revved up at the sessions. I had no concrete ideas, I couldn't feel anything new and finally, in my fretful state, going to the studio became a chore.

Throughout my entire life, the role of bandleader or musical director hasn't come naturally. The creativity and vision comes instinctively, but assuming the role of leader is something I have struggled to come to grips with. Okay, I've had a fair amount of success and sustained a long career. Many musicians seem drawn to me because of my history, but often what they don't realise is that I am also attracted to working with them because they are far more musically knowledgeable and adept than I am. There's the rub. I'm not sure this will ever change. I think it is rooted somewhere deep in my childhood psyche, from my mother urging me to stay small. I guess all human beings have their moments of self-doubt, none of us are immune, it's part of the condition. We each have our ways of resolving it too. My way of dealing with the new Matthews Southern Comfort situation was not unlike the first incarnation – I threw all of the recordings into a drawer, cancelled the tour and walked away. I came home to contemplate, but also to support a heavily pregnant wife. Marly was expecting our first child, Luca Mae, in June of that year.

We wanted Luca to experience music, even while she was still in the womb. We played seminal Stevie Wonder albums throughout Marly's pregnancy; *Songs in the Key of Life*, *Innervisions*, *Talking Book* and *Fulfillingness' First Finale*. We played those records over and over again. We planned a home birth. It's not unusual in the Netherlands, in fact it's accepted as the norm. You make regular visits to the midwife's practice, which in our case was just a ten-minute walk from the house.

Very early in the morning of 9th June, Marly woke me and said, 'I think this is it.' She called the midwife and took a shower while I set up the room so that it was calm and harmonious. I lit candles and incense and put on a CD of ambient music.

Through my eyes the birth appeared to go very smoothly. I was in awe of the entire process from the moment Luca's little pink head appeared. I sat at Marly's right shoulder, holding tightly onto her hand, breathing with her, feeling her grip tighten with every contraction. As Luca lay in the midwife's hands, Marly turned her head to me and smiled. 'I'm done,' she said. I was asked if I would like to cut the umbilical cord. I wasn't surprised by the offer, Marly had already prepped me that they would give me the chance to do it, but when the moment came I baulked. It didn't feel right to be given the responsibility of separating my child from her mother. The midwife then explained to me that the cord was of no further use, it had served its purpose and therefore it was safe to cut it. With Marly's encouragement, I went ahead and made the cut. I was entranced by the whole magical experience.

When Luca was still a toddler, I put on Stevie Wonder's *Innervisions* album. The opening bars of 'Living for the City' came through the speakers. Luca was playing on the floor with a toy. She stopped what she was doing and cocked her head as if to say, 'I know that music!' Or did I imagine it?

In 2008 with – let's face it – a more than considerable career under my belt, I reimagined the concept I'd flimsily introduced at a coffee shop in Austin several years previous, Common Grounds, a series of events based around performing and explaining the art of songwriting. In Austin I hadn't thought it through properly and it proved muddled and ill-conceived, stumbling over its own enthusiasm. It was truly based around giving back, with free entrance. We would field questions between songs, which proved to be a bad idea when people soon began shouting out 'shut up and play'. They either completely missed the point, or simply didn't give a damn. That initial series lasted three performances before imploding.

I was prepared to try again and approached a generous benefactor in Leiden, a city close to Den Haag in the province of South Holland. Leiden is a university 'stadt' known for its centuries-old architecture and boasts the country's oldest university, dating from 1575. The city has an old weigh house – the Waag – which at the time was being used as a performance venue. I'd already played there twice. It's a stone building with marble floors; a very ambient room with a pleasant reverberation that felt perfect for my concept. My benefactor was the programme director for the city who quickly agreed to grant me a year of monthly concerts.

Each concert evening would feature two acts, one established and the other a newcomer. I would open the proceedings with a couple of songs and talk a little about the evening's guests. The newcomer would play for thirty minutes, followed by a short interval, after which the headliner played for an hour. There would then be a ten-minute break before all the performers came back on stage to field questions related to music from the audience. No holds barred. I was excited about it and arranged a dozen concerts with twenty-four interesting and diverse acts, ranging from the Godfather of English folk, Martin Carthy, to the man who wrote 'Eve of Destruction', P.F. Sloan, plus a brilliant up-and-coming New England songwriter, Jeffrey Foucault, and my friends Searing Quartet. In principle it was a wonderful idea. I spoke about it in newspaper articles and promoted it heavily at my own shows. I even persuaded a second room, The Beauforthuis near the town of Austerlitz, to agree to host Common Grounds on a Sunday, the night after Leiden. It all fell together nicely.

The series however did not take off. It seemed that people once again did not want to be educated about music, they just wanted to hear and experience it. Most would stay for the music but leave before the Q&A portion of the evening, possibly too shy to voice a question. I've been told that aspect is true of the Dutch. Or they were simply disinterested in the whys and wherefores. I take responsibility for its failure and feel that my expectations were perhaps a little too lofty. I had believed that audiences might have been curious enough about the inner workings of being a songwriter and a performer and all that entails, but they were not and they either did not stick around to find out, or stayed away altogether. Musically it was a raging success. I became friends with some of the artists and worked together with them later on other stages. But financially it was just short of a disaster for both rooms. The Beauforthuis cancelled their commitment to the series halfway through and I was crestfallen. I still believe the series has merit and may try it again in the future, but for now, audiences in general want to be entertained not put to the test, and venues are there to make money not lose it.

After our good experience on the *Thro' My Eyes* tour, Egbert and I had the notion to write together. I had written a lyric for a song about my father called 'God's Eye View' and gave it to Egbert to set to music. This set a precedent we have yet to veer from. Once given the words, Egbert wanted to be left to his own devices to create the music and then we'd get together to fine-tune the songs. I was astonished by how easily he captured the spirit of that lyric. I had handed him one of my most personal recollections, based on the ripped photograph from my parents' wedding day. I had often wondered why my Auntie Carrie had scissored my mother out of the picture and tried to interpret my feelings in 'God's Eye View'. When we listened to the completed song, I realised many things, but most of all that in Egbert I had found my perfect songwriting partner.

We pursued our songwriting at a great pace, rehearsed an evening's worth of music and soon began performing as a duo. In all ways it was the ideal scenario for the both of us. I was able for the first time to pursue my jazz leanings and Egbert found a way to access a different genre of music. Together we released what I consider to be two of my very best studio albums, *Joy Mining* in 2008 and *In the Now* in 2012. They contain some of my most mature lyric writing and Egbert's musical contributions easily mirror that. On *Joy Mining* there's a song called 'Fishing'. The first lines are:

> Have you ever gone fishing and tangled your line
> Never considering what you might find

The first draft of that lyric was:

> Marly went fishing and tangled her line

I don't know why I changed it. It was early in our relationship and I wasn't sure she would want to be subject matter so soon. Songs develop a life of their own once they're written down. Those two albums are packed with songs that have lived lives of their own.

Through Egbert's musical arrangements, I learned to stretch my vocal abilities. In my sixties I was hearing things in my own voice that I had never previously heard. With every composition, he would almost imperceptibly make it slightly more difficult and I relished the task before me. A critic, who shall remain nameless, caught wind of my jazz aspirations and let it be known in print that he was dubious. His exact words were, 'Iain Matthews! Jazz! Right. Pull the other one!' I found it hurtful at the time. I don't often respond to the ravings of critics but on this occasion I felt it necessary. Based on it, I wrote a song for *Joy Mining* called 'Shakespeare's Typewriter'. I had once seen two antiques experts on TV having a discussion. Their jocular term for a fake was 'Shakespeare's typewriter'. This gave me a foundation to build a song on.

> Next time you see me, you may not recognise
> The power of my conviction, or the twinkle in my eye
> In fact everything about me may just come as a surprise
> Next time you see me

Egbert was in on the joke. When he created the accompanying music, I thought, 'Yeah, that's jazz.' And it was.

Joy Mining was my first jazz album and I was more than ably supported by the Searing Quartet. We released the record on a label that Egbert and I set up – Matrix (Matthews/Derix) records – and then began to pursue a major label. One Sunday morning we were invited to perform on a prominent Dutch TV show called *Vrije Geluiden*. It's an eccentric show that presents styles of music you wouldn't normally see on mainstream television, particularly on a Sunday morning. On the show you get jazz, classical and global music as well as the occasional singer-songwriter performing their own material. We played two songs, 'God's Eye View' and 'Waves' from our self-released *Joy Mining*. The host for the show gave out information for anyone interested in buying the album. In this case it was Egbert's and my website addresses. I got home from the recording and sat down to check my email. I clicked on 'Mail' and for the next ten minutes orders for the album scrolled down the screen. I thought my laptop had gone mad and taken on a life of its own. I called Egbert to tell him.

'I can't talk now,' he said, 'I've got hundreds of orders coming in on my website. I think my computer's gone mad.'

That week, between us we sold almost a thousand CDs of *Joy Mining*. But that wasn't the end of it. The following week we received a message from Willem Hubers, a manager in Arnhem, telling us that he's worked with some of the jazz greats including Dave Brubeck. He'd seen the show and had been taken by our performance. He said he wanted to manage us. Egbert and I drove to Arnhem to meet with Willem. He was a likeable character and talked a good game, it was clear that he had a lot of experience. Egbert and I were impressed enough to agree to work with him.

Willem presented our self-released album to several labels. He then called us to say that he had a very positive response from Blue Note, the label of John Coltrane, Art Blakey, Jimmy Smith and any number of jazz greats from the hard bop period, and more recently John Scofield and Cassandra Wilson, two of my current favourites. He said he was pursuing an offer from them with great enthusiasm. This excited Egbert and I enough to share the good news with the band at rehearsal one day.

'We're going to be on Blue Note boys, we have finally made it,' I announced.

Pete Hermesdorf, our saxophonist, shook his finger at me to add a note of caution.

'Maybe,' he said.

'No Peter, it's a done deal,' I responded, 'we're gonna be on Blue Note, trust me.'

It was a silly thing to say. I should have known better. Neither I nor Egbert knew it at that time, but Willem Hubers was a Dutch version of Walter Mitty. He lived in a fantasy world of his own creation, built on limited past glories and imaginings. I distinctly remember Willem saying to me and Egbert, 'Put the champagne on ice boys, we're going to be on Blue Note.' That champagne has yet to be drunk. There never was a Blue Note deal. As far as we now know, Blue Note had simply been in touch with Willem to acknowledge receipt of the CD he sent to them.

Egbert and I were crushed by the whole affair and it caused him irreparable tension within the band. They splintered shortly afterwards. We severed our relationship with Willem. A short time later, we received news that he had died. Egbert and I both thought it proper that we should go to his funeral. I don't know why, but I guess we still had a grudging affection for the old boy. From the eulogies we heard at that funeral, which were mainly humorous ones, we came away realising that we weren't the only ones who had been taken in by Willem Hubers.

I was up in my attic searching through my archives for a piece of music I couldn't find. I opened and shut drawers, becoming more and more frustrated. In one drawer I found something I wasn't looking for. It was a disc with BJ's handwriting on it that said 'New Matthews Southern Comfort – Roughs'. I took it out of its plastic sleeve, turned it over in my hand and read the list of songs. It was four years now since the recordings and I had the urge to know if I had the same negative feelings about that music. I thought, 'What the fuck!' and put the disc into the player. It was an extraordinary experience. I pulled my chair round and sat directly in front of the speakers, eyes closed, until I had listened to all fifteen songs. By the end I was confused. It sounded completely different to the music I thought I remembered. In the years that this music had lain in the drawer it appeared that the ugly duckling had turned into a beautiful swan. Before the feeling faded, I emailed BJ, Terri, Richard and Mike. I was still emotionally choked as I wrote apologies to them all, vowing to them that I would finish the album and that it would see the light of day. Everyone gave their blessing, but with a certain amount of nodding and winking. Though it went unsaid, there was a degree of 'We told you so!'

Almost five years after those initial sessions I went back to Léon's Farm Studios, told Léon what I had just experienced and made a deal with him to finish the record. We hired in a drummer friend of his to overdub his kit on every track. Mike came by and laid down some gorgeous acoustic piano. BJ fixed some bass parts that didn't really need fixing. He was convinced he could do them better so I let him and he did. Finally, I recorded my vocal parts. We had all of Terri's lead vocals, but none of mine. I spent a week on vocals alone. The backgrounds were a challenge, imagining them all by myself, using Léon as a sounding board. Some I'd keep, others we would erase and begin again, double-tracking for effect as we went. On the re-invented 'Woodstock' there are thirty tracks of vocals.

The album was released in Europe with the title *Kind of New*, a nod towards my musical hero Miles Davis and because it was. By the time the CD came out, some of the band had moved on to other projects, so we didn't tour to promote it until almost a year later when Bart-Jan and I put yet another new version of Matthews Southern Comfort together and hit the road.

Kind of New remains an album I'm immensely proud of, a record I point people towards as an example of some of my finest work and an important lesson for me as an artist. Always trust your instincts, but at the same time, listen to those you trust.

Egbert and I were bloodied but unbowed by the Willem Hubers swindle. Undaunted, we hit our songwriting stride again on *In the Now*. The lyrics were flowing out of me and Egbert was interpreting them with great verve. I felt I surpassed myself with the range of subject matter. There were songs on there about Buddha, my hometown, my musical journey in the sixties, Thelonious Monk and personal growth. The album is like my autobiography before I had written it.

I found a list online in the hand of the jazz saxophonist Steve Lacy. He had played in Thelonious Monk's band and it was a fun compilation of the sayings of the great Monk. It struck me that I ought to incorporate some of these sayings into a song, by way of paying tribute to one of my jazz heroes. Egbert's writing caused me to rise to one of my most challenging vocals to date. The Steinway piano we rented for the sessions had at one time been the house piano at the original Blue Note Club in New York. Jan Huijbers, the man who rented us the piano, stated that he believed Thelonious himself had played that piano many times. Egbert recorded the song about Monk on the very keyboard that Monk himself had allegedly performed on all those years ago.

We decided to pursue a major label for a second time. I have a dear friend called Roy Teysse, a fellow Gene Clark fan. He is quite influential at Universal Records in the Netherlands so I played him the album. He told me he loved it. I was cheeky enough to ask him, 'Do you think Verve might be interested?' Alongside Blue Note, Verve is one of the pre-eminent jazz labels: Ella, Ben Webster, Nina Simone, Stan Getz and Billie Holiday all recorded for Verve. Roy played our recording for Paul Popma, Verve's A&R chief in Hilversum. Paul also loved the album and offered us a deal. This time it was no fantasy, we really did end up on a bespoke jazz label. The downside was, having licensed the album, the parent company Universal did very little to promote it and the album sales reflected that. Egbert and I sold roughly four times as many copies of our self-released *Joy Mining* as Verve did with *In the Now*. C'est la vie. You can't win em all.

It was a great shame, because *In the Now* was a suite of songs to compare with anything I'd ever done. 'Pebbles in the Road' in all respects is my musical autobiography. It begins in the now in the Netherlands:

> There's a hot wind blowing off the Maas tonight
> It's shaking the trailers in the caravan site

It then retraces footsteps to other periods of my life:

> Now I'm thinking about my old man
> And how his life was nothing more
> Than pushing hard against the undertow

Then we shift to a minor key for:

> It's autumn 1974
> There's a full house at the Troubadour

'When the Floyd Were on the Prowl' is a story on the album about the 1960s music scene in London. Nick Mason, Pink Floyd's drummer, wrote a book that I read and liked about the band's dalliance with Timothy Leary. He mentioned the mantra 'Turn On, Tune In, Drop Out', or as The Floyd would have it, 'Turn Up, Shell Out, Get Lost'. It was a wry, sideways glance at the success they were having back then. 'Buddha Dials Your Number' is about things written in the sand, about destiny. One line was originally 'Even Buddy Holly had to stop and toe the line'. I later changed the name to Eckhart Tolle. The song also nods towards my own flirtation with spiritualism and Buddhism in particular. I'm not a religious man. I have used the word God in a number of songs over the years, but God is quite a flexible word. When people ask me, 'Are you religious?' my answer remains the same, 'I don't believe in organised religion, but I do consider myself to be a spiritual person.'

The last song on the record is 'Gone is Gone', inspired by something Marly said. She went to a farewell party for a business colleague and casually asked him, 'Rudi, will you stay in touch with everyone?' He simply replied, 'No Marly, gone is gone.' This is the only song from the two studio recordings Egbert and I made together with any vocal harmony on it. It plays out the album and the harmony sneaks in quite subliminally as the song begins to fade. Rain, rain, rain. Rain, rain, rain.

PEBBLES IN THE ROAD

There's a hot wind blowing off the Maas tonight
It's shaking the trailers in the caravan site
Some Johnny come lately's whining on the radio
He's nervous as a homeless cat
Wishing this, regretting that
He just can't seem to understand the flow
Complaining about his record deal
But he's got no idea how it feels
When there's only a handful of people at the show
Then I see my borderline career's
a whole lot more than his appears to be
Another pebble in the road

Now I'm thinking about my old man
And how his life was nothing more
than pushing hard against the undertow
And I see this gift that keeps on giving
This precious gift that I'm still living
And I think he'd understand, in fact I know
It's a fast train running down a one-way track
No jumping off, no turning back
No stepping on the brakes and no control
My disappointments reconciled
I realise it's been worthwhile
To be another pebble in the road

Oh, turn me over
I'm just another pebble in the road
Oh, turn me over
Know that I will never break the code
History will not repeat
Apollo Nine or Merseybeat
They're all pebbles in the road

It's autumn 1974
There's a full house at the Troubadour
They're dimming down the lights all set to go
Expectations on the street are optimistically upbeat
The Hollywood Reporter's at the show
But it's only music after all
And here beneath the waterfall
We're praying that the muse will start to flow
I'm not a complicated man
I simply do the best I can
To be another pebble in the road

There's a hot wind blowing off the Maas tonight
Swirling around at the traffic light
Some disco's pumping sixteen to the bar
I try to sleep, but who am I fooling
So I crack the seal on the Lagavulin
And think about just how I came so far
Some will do it for the cash
While others shake their heads and laugh
They laugh about those crazy episodes
Me, I do it for the song
I go in hard, I come out strong
But still, I'm just a pebble in the road

Oh, turn me over
I'm just another pebble in the road
Oh, turn me over
You and I will never crack the code
History will not repeat
Apollo Nine or Merseybeat
It's just another pebble in the road
History cannot repeat
The glory days of Bleecker Street
We're all just pebbles in the road
Pebbles in the road

21. ALL THAT IS

During my early days with Fairport, I was introduced to the music of Gene Clark. I was already familiar with The Byrds, but only as a band. I was somewhat unfamiliar with the parts that had come together to form the whole. One of Gene's songs, 'Tried So Hard', was already a solid fixture in the live set when I joined and I enjoyed performing the song so much that it went into my little black book, to be considered later.

One morning in mid-December of 2013 I awoke to find an email from a sender whose name I didn't recognise. A man called Alex Scally. In his message Alex explained that he was the male half of an American duo called Beach House along with his partner Victoria Legrand and they were taking a break from playing their own original music to pay tribute to an artist and an album they both had long and deeply admired. The album was *No Other* by Gene Clark. Alex said the wheels were already in motion to present the album live and he asked if I was interested in being involved as a lead vocalist. I was both humbled and honoured to have been considered and, much to their apparent delight, I instantly accepted the invitation, no questions asked.

Victoria and Alex live in Baltimore, Maryland and had put together a fifteen-piece band with some of the finest players and singers on the Eastern Seaboard. The album was lovingly recreated, note for note and, apart from an absent pedal steel guitar, instrument for instrument. It involved splitting the eight songs on *No Other* between four lead vocalists. Already on board were Robin Pecknold of Fleet Foxes, Grizzly Bear's Daniel Rossen and a very tall character with the exotic moniker of Hamilton Leithauser. Hamilton was part of a band called The Walkmen. I hurriedly checked on their credentials through various mediums and discovered they were all terrifically talented and expressive front men. The individual song selection scenario was only just underway and I virtually had the pick of the bunch. After careful consideration I chose 'Silver Raven' and 'The True One'. I then knuckled down to try and do them justice.

I own most, if not all of Gene's recordings and this particular album, apart from being a work of genius, holds fond memories for me. Gene and I were on the same label in 1974, Elektra/Asylum. His album and my own *Some Days You Eat the Bear* we're both set free that same year. My album had an interpretation of 'Tried So Hard' on it and while we were mastering the album at Elektra Studios in Hollywood, Gene happened to be walking down the hallway, heard his song and popped his head around the door to investigate. He didn't say much but grinned quite a lot. Which I suppose is as good an endorsement as any.

I flew to Baltimore and after two long days of rehearsal we played four sold-out shows in Philadelphia, Washington, Baltimore and New York. With each show we improved in leaps and bounds. For a travelling unit of that size it was surprisingly harmonious and ego free, with every one of us working for the common good. It was all about the songs and the sheer joy of sharing them. By the time we hit New York, the set was practically flawless. What we thought would be the final show was filmed for posterity by a streaming company called Pitchfork. The group then unexpectedly reconvened several months later for a final fling when we headlined at the End of the Road Festival just outside Bristol in the UK. The tour was a brief but highly-successful affair and will live long in my memory as one of the most enjoyable collaborations of my career.

I'm told that during that short period of time between the announcement and conclusion of the American tour, Amazon sales of Gene Clark's *No Other* album increased some 4,000% and the album's chart position rose more than 1,200 spots. Now that news alone made all the hard work worthwhile.

In 2014 I made what I vowed and declared to be my last solo album. *The Art of Obscurity* is for me about looking back to find a peace with the here and now. I actually went back to Texas to record it with my old friend Bradley Kopp. We spent three weeks in his home studio in Buda, just south of Austin. I arrived with fifteen songs in my backpack. The process of writing these songs had not been easy. I had trouble finishing a lot of them because after years of co-writing I was trying too hard to be clever with the music. Just before I left for Texas I had a short run of dates in the UK with Egbert. I told him about my struggle and asked him if he would help me to finish my songs. He said that as soon as we could find some downtime he would take a look at them.

Halfway through the tour we found ourselves with cancellations and a three-day gap. We holed up with some old friends of mine, John and Beverly Walsh in Halifax, West Yorkshire. I first met John and Bev when I was touring with Al Stewart. They were big followers of Al and soon became fans of my music too. John has a business renting fruit machines and pool tables to pubs and working men's clubs. He is now into his fourth year of hosting a small, but blossoming songwriter festival in the area. Bev owns an antiques shop just around the corner from their home. They were wedding guests when Marly and I married and have become part of our extended family. They appeared more than happy to have me and Egbert around for a few days as we turned their living room into a music workshop. Egbert set up his keyboards in front of the fireplace and I sat opposite on the couch. John made dinner for us all every night and due to the relaxed atmosphere, in that short space of time we completed eight songs.

There's one cover song on the album, written by a relatively unknown songwriter by the name of Nemo Jones. Nemo has toured and recorded with Urban Species, Galliano and Faithless. His mother is Eve Libertine, who was once in the anarcho-punk band Crass. Nemo is also married to my daughter Darcy and is the father of my three grandchildren: Obe, Kiska and Jupiter. The song in question is simply called 'Music'. I first heard it when I brought Nemo over to play my Common Ground series with Boo Hewerdine. I heard him play it and instantly fell in love with the song and its sentiment. It's about being truly thankful for the healing power of music. Right up my street. After I recorded my interpretation, I sent the mix to Darcy. She called me to say that she had sat and listened to it together with Nemo and that it had moved them both to tears.

I hadn't played solo for a number of years. I wanted to get back on the horse that threw me. I had an offer to play a one-off solo concert in Trondheim, Norway. I accepted it to see if I still had it in me. I played to a sold-out crowd in a small club in the city centre. I will always remember that show because my voice made it to Trondheim but my guitar got stuck in Copenhagen and I had to borrow one from a local music shop. Regardless, I had a wonderful time and realised that my mojo was still intact.

Back in the winter of 2002, Andy and I decided to give Plainsong one more run. Together with Griff we invited Julian Dawson back into the band. Julian had recently gone through a traumatic period in his life where he discovered that he had breast cancer and needed surgery. He considered it a life-changing experience and emerged from it, as he said, 'a different man'. He was again ready to be part of a band. We made plans to record and convened at his cottage in Somerset to make an album we called *Pangolins* – yet another anagram. Without attaching blame, for me it's an album that lacks inspiration and verve. There was an element of friction over song choice that we never resolved and I have to say, between us, there was no great enthusiasm to go back on the road. I'm still not quite sure why we made that record. It felt to me at the time that it was just another means to work and the simple joy of playing together had deserted us.

We did take to the road and toured quite extensively, and in very good rooms. Towards the end of that tour I found myself playing yet again in Café Cambrinus in Horst. The day following the show we went into Léon's Farm Studio and recorded nineteen songs live, sequenced in order, before an invited audience who we then edited out of the recording but were listed as guests in the album booklet. We were thrilled with the results and presented the recording to Edgar Heckmann at Blue Rose. His response was positive but surprising.

'It sounds great,' he said, 'but it's too good to put out as a live album. There's no audience on it and to me it doesn't sound live.'

He declined to release it. It was to be a further nine years before we would reconvene.

At the beginning of 2012, Julian called us all again and said, 'I've been thinking, we need to put Plainsong to bed properly, why don't we do a farewell tour?' We all agreed it sounded like a good idea and had our various bookers set up a big European tour, with two nights in a Tokyo venue at the conclusion. An independent promoter in Japan had heard that it was to be our final fling and desperately wanted to be a part of it. I'd played in Japan several times over the years and had always enjoyed the experience, but by 2012 the halcyon days of Plainsong and indeed Iain Matthews were long over. When the much anticipated night arrived, we played to a miniscule audience in a modest out of the way club in an area of Tokyo I have no desire to ever visit again. It was basically a five-day holiday, with lots of good ramen and sushi.

Before the tour started we contacted Edgar at Blue Rose to see if he'd like to release the Léon's Farm live album to coincide with the tour. His opinion of it had loosened somewhat over the years and he thought it was a great idea. We threw titles around for both album and tour and it was Julian who eventually came up with *Fat Lady Singing*. And that was that. Except whenever Plainsong are involved, that was very much not that.

In 2014 I did a short solo tour on the west coast of America. A good friend of mine, Pat Thomas, an author and musicologist, travelled with me. Pat is well known for *Listen, Whitey!*, a book about the Black Panther movement and racial tensions in the late sixties. I like Pat a lot and had invited him mainly for the company and banter, but also because he's an accomplished percussionist. I asked him if he might consider bringing a pair of bongos along and maybe join me on some songs. Pat was delighted to be asked.

It's a five-hour trip from Los Angeles to the Bay Area and during our drive we talked about records we both liked and somehow found ourselves discussing tribute albums. We talked about who'd had one, who hadn't and who perhaps deserved one.

'No one's ever done a Richard Fariña tribute album,' said Pat. 'That's a fantastic idea.'

'Well you're the Fariña man, why don't you do it?'

I'd hugely admired Fariña's writing since being introduced to it in my Fairport days. In fact 'Reno Nevada' is the first Richard Fariña song I ever heard, the first I ever sang and the first I ever recorded. It became a Fairport staple in the early years, leading me to all of his recordings with his wife Mimi (Baez) Fariña. I've maintained that love for his work throughout my life, though getting through his infamous book *Been Down So Long It Looks Like Up To Me* was far more difficult than listening to his songs. I once talked to Tom Paxton about him. He said, 'Ahhhh! Fariña. Now there's an operator!'

When I came home from the California tour, I talked to Marly about the idea. She knew that Andy Roberts was as much a fan of Richard's work as I was and it was she who suggested that I should invite him to participate. Andy was instantly smitten by the offer for us to work together again. I made several trips to Brighton, each one for just a few days. He and I sat in his basement studio and listened through every song that Richard Fariña had ever written. We talked about how we might reinterpret the material.

'How about we call the album *Reinventing Richard*?' I suggested.

'Perhaps it should be *Reinventing Richard Fariña*,' countered Andy.

'No, just Richard.'

'People might think it's Richard Thompson.'

'Let them figure it out.'

We recorded all of the basic tracks in Andy's little basement studio, sitting opposite one another with acoustic guitars. We had two rules. First rule: no dulcimers. We made this rule because if you have a dulcimer on a Fariña tune it will automatically be recognisable as a Richard Fariña song and the point was to pay tribute not to emulate. The second rule was that we wouldn't record any Fariña songs that either of us had done before. This ruled out the likes of 'Reno Nevada' and 'House un-American Blues Activity Dream'. When we decided to record 'The Quiet Joys of Brotherhood' we both agreed that no vocal version could ever surpass the one that Sandy Denny had so brilliantly done, so we presented it as two short instrumentals, a prelude and a conclusion. Andy played the prelude on his bouzouki, complete with noisy Brighton seagulls circling overhead. This decision meant that while paying tribute to Fariña, we also paid secret homage to Sandy Denny.

Once we had recorded all of the basic tracks with a guide vocal we sat back and listened to them. A couple of the songs seemed a little loose and flighty, so we decided to call Griff and ask if he would add a little fretless bass to anchor them, adding, 'If you think they need anything else, just go for it, knock yourself out.' While Andy and I busied ourselves with some of the other songs, a few days later the two tracks came back from Griff for us to hear. We loaded the data back into Andy's system, hit play and sat back to listen. What flowed from the speakers was completely unexpected, an audible delight of what can only described as sonic heaven. Not only had Griff added his fretless bass, he'd also expertly programmed a drum track that I would swear was a real human playing. There was a smudge of mandolin, plus some wonderful ambient clouds of electric guitar and a little background splash of electronic keyboards. He'd taken a simple little acoustic folk idea and made it into something far bigger and far better. Andy and I were gobsmacked at the result and decided there and then to invite Mark into the project. From that moment on, once Andy and I were finished with our parts, we jetted the tracks off through the ether to Mark, who proceeded to shake his fairy dust all over them.

When all the recording was done, we loved what we had, but there was one slight hitch. We were ecstatic with the interpretations and the recorded sound but neither Andy, Griff nor I were accomplished sound mixers. We tried our best, but because of Andy's outdated digital program, the mixes sounded muddy and unrefined. But we hadn't done all of this great work only to fall at the final fence. I had an idea. I called Brad Kopp in Texas. Brad is one of, if not the best sound mixer I have ever worked with.

'Send me one track, aahll open it up and see what aah can do,' he said.

We decided to send him what we considered to be one of the more difficult mixes, 'Children of Darkness'. When it came back it had been given the full Kopp treatment and sounded glorious. At that point, despite having very little budget left, I decided to foot the remixing bill myself and we committed the entire album into Bradley's hands.

When we got round to designing the artwork, I emailed a good friend of mine, John Sellards. John is a fine graphic designer living near Boston, Massachusetts. He is one of those invisible people, conjuring up artwork for reissue labels around the globe, labels like Ace, Cherry Red and Sanctuary in the UK. I told him what we envisioned, that we pictured it with a contemporary, cutting-edge feel, yet with a nod towards the sixties. Within days he came back with a simple silhouette of Fariña on the front, and silhouettes of Andy, Griff and myself on the back. The one reservation we had was that with all three of our names on the cover, plus the long title, there was so much text that the eye was being drawn away from Fariña's image. It looked muddled.

The record was being partly funded by David Suff, our friend and owner of Fledg'ling Records. We showed him the artwork and he immediately said, 'Guys, why don't you just call it Plainsong?' It had crossed our minds and we'd been fighting it, but as soon as David said it, it made perfect sense and Plainsong it was.

After an album is finished, I'm saturated with the music and for several months I try to create as much distance from it as I can. This record was no exception. But in retrospect it may just be the best one I've ever made. It didn't sell in any great numbers, though – and I don't mean this as a gripe – as is typical in my later career, it was a critical success whilst being a commercial flop.

We did have a couple of brief moments in the sun with it. Andy and I (it was too expensive for all three of us to go) showcased at the International Folk Alliance Conference in Kansas City in February 2017. Folk legend Tom Paxton was in the audience. Afterwards he spied us in the restaurant. I watched as he got up from where he was sitting, walked over to our table, a wide, lumbering bear of a man. I stood up to greet him and he gave me the biggest hug I can remember getting from anyone. I virtually disappeared into him. Andy and I gifted him a copy of the CD. Sometime after our encounter in Kansas City, Tom mailed us his endorsement, 'What a beautiful tribute to a major artist of the early sixties, gone far before his time. The choice of tunes, the arrangements and the sheer musicianship is first rate. Somewhere, Dick Fariña is smiling and telling us to stay the hell away from motorcycles.'

At the Cropredy festival later that same year, Fairport Convention celebrated their fiftieth anniversary to sold-out crowds. All surviving members were invited to perform – and perform we did. Back in the day, Judy and I were almost like hired underlings, but at the anniversary we both felt acceptance; after fifty years of grafting at our trade, we were all on an equal footing.

The warm-up show for the festival was for me the zenith of the entire weekend. We played at the Banbury Trades and Labour Club with the 1967 line-up, plus the great Dave Mattacks on drums. It felt as though our fifty years of practise had paid off that night and we received a standing ovation from the sold-out crowd. More was yet to come for Plainsong at the festival itself. We got the chance to spend forty minutes sharing our versions of Richard Fariña songs to twenty thousand people, most of whom had been there at the beginning when Fairport had introduced his song 'Reno Nevada'. The effect we'd had was obvious at the signing tent afterwards. People queued for two-and-a-half hours to get their CDs signed. The question most asked by the folk in the queue that day was, 'Is Plainsong really over?' I hadn't thought to prepare an answer for that one. I guess only time will tell.

I'm 72 years old now. From The Rebels, a Scunthorpe rock'n'roll band in 1963, through Pyramid and Fairport Convention, to Matthews Southern Comfort, Plainsong and more than twenty-five solo albums and just as many collaborations, I've been fortunate to have a life in music. Music is in my blood, it motivates me. Music is my mistress.

In spring 2017, I called Bart-Jan Baartmans with a thought.

'Hi BJ it's Iain, what do you think about giving Matthews Southern Comfort another try?'

'I think that's a great idea.'

Fast forward to March 2018 and *Like a Radio*, the new Matthews Southern Comfort album, is in the shops. Back on the road are a quartet comprising BJ on electric guitar, mandolin and vocals; Eric Devries, acoustic guitar and vocals; Bart de Win, keyboards and vocals; and me.

On a chilly March lunchtime in 2018, I pack my guitar into the boot of my car, turn on Google Maps and head north east from my home. Tonight I play a concert at the Cobblestone Club, a place that operates from a beautiful seventeenth-century town house in Oldenzaal. The club is dedicated to roots, blues and world music. Oldenzaal is an old Dutch merchants' town in the north, just a stone's throw from the German border. In the Middle Ages it was part of the powerful Hanseatic League. It's a traditional town where they like to drink their local brew, a famous beer called Grolsch.

First stop is an afternoon visit to RTV Oost, a regional TV and radio station. They are having a seventies week on the radio and have invited Matthews Southern Comfort to play a couple of songs live in the studio. Even though it's already sold out, it's an opportunity to mention tonight's show and a festival appearance in Hengelo coming up in May. I meet the rest of the band in the reception area and we're given coffee. The DJ comes out and greets us warmly, asking which one of us is Iain Matthews.

'You have time to play two songs. What will you play?' he asks.

We start to discuss amongst ourselves what we might like to play when the DJ interjects.

'Can I suggest "Woodstock" should be one of the songs to fit in with our seventies theme.'

He then dashes off to be back in the studio in time for the weather slot. We set up our gear in the little control room which happens to have an in-tune upright piano in one corner. We soundcheck 'To Love', the old Carole King song, and 'Woodstock'. The DJ puts on his best seventies radio voice and says, 'Wow! Cool.' Then he tells us that we will wait now until the 2.30 news bulletin finishes. The news tells of cars crashing into lampposts in the wintry weather and stolen bicycles being recovered after tip-offs to the local police. As soon as the news is over, the DJ picks up where he left off.

'Okay music lovers, we continue our seventies week with a live treat from the studio. It's Matthew and his Southern Comfort ... take it away boys.'

We play 'To Love' and as we finish the DJ says 'Wow! Cool' again. He decides he has time for an impromptu interview and asks me if I can come to the desk microphone. I have no idea what he is going to ask me. It transpires that neither does he. He seems to be the squarest guy on Planet Radio and it's obvious that he hasn't done the slightest bit of research. He asks me his first question in Dutch. I ask him if we can talk in English.

'You have lived in the Netherlands for eighteen years and you didn't speak Dutch, why is that?' he asks.

'I prefer to speak in English.'

Now he suddenly seems to realise that he has no idea what he wants to talk about.

'You will play "Woodstock" next yes?'

I say 'Yes'.

'It was a big hit back in the day no?'

'Yes.'

'It was a hit in the 1970s wasn't it?'

'Yes, 1970 to be precise.'

'Well that's great because this week we are dedicated to the 1970s and if it had been a hit in the 1960s we wouldn't have been able to include it.'

'Right, I get it.'

'It was written by Joni Mitchell.'

'Yes.'

'She also wrote "Big Yellow Taxi" didn't she?'

I have no idea now where this is going so I just say 'Yes' again.

I think the DJ has even less of a clue where he's going, so he smiles at me before launching his introduction.

'Okay, it's time for a live in the studio sounds of the seventies special from wonderful Radio Oost and Matthews Southern Comfort doing "Woodstock".'

At least he gets the name of the band right this time. We play

'Woodstock'. As we finish, our host says 'Yeah! Super cool' then begins to read the results of a competition they have been having. We pack up our equipment and head for tonight's venue.

When we arrive at the Cobblestone Club, the place is packed to its seventeenth-century rafters. There's a buzz of expectation. We work our way through a mixture of the 1969 incarnation of the band, the more recent *Kind of New* era and some brand-new material. It's a crowd mainly made up of the baby boomer generation. I make a joke about today's new songs being tomorrow's classics. We launch into 'The Age of Isolation' a song that Eric and I wrote for the new album as a counterpoint to the hippy idealism of the late sixties.

> As far as I can gather
> Nothing seems to matter
> But that telephone's vibration
> Welcome to the age of isolation

As usual the audience is waiting to hear the hit. And we keep them waiting until the very end. I step up to the microphone and clear my throat.

'Without this next song, I probably wouldn't be standing on your stage tonight. It's a song with a strong, clear message. The sentiment might be a little dated, but when Joni Mitchell wrote it, she meant every word of it. It's a song that has helped prolong my career beyond my wildest dreams and I feel it my duty to honour it whenever I can.'

We play a rousing ten-minute version of 'Woodstock' then leave them wanting more.

RAINS OF '62

I grew up with a borrowed name
A little heart of porcelain
Here a hustle, there a shove
A kid to take advantage of
I guess it was a big surprise
When I appeared before your very eyes

Brothers yeah, I had a few
I know they thought the world of you
In your eyes they could do no wrong
Me, that was a different song
My life was a compromise
As I grew up before your very eyes
I know your life was misery
So deep and wide
Now my life's a memory ten storeys high

When I left for London in the rains of '62
When I left home it didn't mean that much to you
Now I look back on all the changes I went through
Growing up in the rains of '62

I still remember coming home
And running to the telephone
In time to hear somebody say
You'd better get here right away
Your daddy left us in the night
He's disappeared before our very eyes

Man I know your life was misery
So deep and wide
Now my life's a memory ten storeys high

When I left for London in the rains of '62
When I left home it didn't mean that much to you
Now I look back on all the changes I went through
Growing up in the rains of '62
Growing up in the rains of '62

ACKNOWLEDGEMENTS

For my girls Darcy, Madelief and Luca Mae. The real music in my life.

Without the guidance and encouragement from my dear friend and glowing example, Ian Clayton, this book may never have seen the light of day.

Here's to you Lewis Shiner for convincing me, against my constant barrage of protestations, that I always had it in me

A mighty hurrah for Ian Daley and Isabel Galan at Route who took this on, sight unseen, to crack open the marble and chisel out my David. Gracias.

Steve Hiett and Al Jackson of Pyramid. My ground zero.

To all the members of Fairport Convention, past and present. My starting gate. Particularly to Richard Thompson, the benchmark against whose creations all of my endeavours have been measured.

To Matthews Southern Comfort, then and now. The rubber band around my career that has stretched but never broken. In particular, Mark Griffiths and Bart-Jan Baartmans.

My fellow Gemini, Andy Roberts, there for me at the beginning and with me still. You're an inspiration.

Egbert Derix, who pushed me beyond my self-imposed boundaries and helped me become the singer I never knew I could be.

All of my dear friends around this big round ball who have taken me into their hearts, lives and homes without a second thought. Sherwin Strull and Lois Listopad. Yvonne Elenbaas and Jack. Kim and Greg Boone. Lindsay Gilmour. Joe and Gail Patrick. Sally Kennedy. Jan and Henny Brinus. Beverly and John Walsh. Chris and Liz Maxwell. Bruce and Sheri Barrow. Lorrie Singer. Wiel Janssen and Jolanda Arts.

I thank my galaxy of managers and producers. You all had your own vision of who I might have been. Sandy Roberton, Bradley Kopp and Mark Hallman, and Frank van der Meijden came close.

To the legion of writers and players I've ever had the honour to interpret and the great fortune to share a stage or even be in a room with. Ad Vanderveen, Jim Fogarty, Jay Lacy, Al Stewart, Michael Fracasso, Julian Dawson, Richard Fariña, Nanci Griffith and David Surkamp spring to mind.

My bulging catalogue of recordings would not exist were it not for the army of record companies willing to take a chance on me. Here's to you Roy Teysse. RIP Heinz Geissler.

A huge thanks to my solid core of fans and believers. I may not have always given what you wanted and yet you always embraced what you were given. I love and respect you all for your non-judgemental and unconditional support.

To the music, all the way from Alma Cogan to Snarky Puppy.

To Yorkshire Tea and McVitie's digestive biscuits for getting me out of bed in the morning. I couldn't have made it without you.

INDEX OF SONGS

Thro' My Eyes *If You Saw Thro' My Eyes*	7
When I Was a Boy *The Art of Obscurity*	17
This Train *God Looked Down*	29
In London *The Dark Ride*	47
Even the Guiding Light *Fat Lady Singing*	63
Knowing the Game *Journeys from Gospel Oak*	81
Road to Ronderlin *Kind of New*	97
In Spite of Myself *Joy Mining*	111
Jive Pyjamas *Like a Radio*	129
Rhythm of the West *Go for Broke*	145
You Don't See Me *Siamese Friends*	163
Money *Kind of New*	185
God's Eye View *Joy Mining*	201

Ghost Changes   213
The Art of Obscurity

Sight Unseen   225
Excerpts from Swine Lake

God Looked Down   235
A Baker's Dozen

Tigers Will Survive. Part II (Darcy's Song)   247
The Dark Ride

Back of the Bus   259
Live Unissued

Meaning to Life   279
More Than a Song

One Door Opens   291
Zumbach's Coat

Joy Mining   305
Demo Unissued

Pebbles in the Road   319
The Art of Obscurity

Rains of '62   333
Pure and Crooked

★ Source albums for songs on the complementary *Thro' My Eyes* double CD distributed with Deluxe Hardback Edition of this book.

DISCOGRAPHY

Iain's first commercially available recording was a 45rpm single with the group Pyramid. 'Summer of Last Year'/'Summer Evening' on Deram 1967.

Solo Artist

Original and Live Recordings on LP and CD
1971 *If You Saw Thro' My Eyes*. UK and US Vertigo.
1972 *Tigers Will Survive*. UK and US Vertigo.
1973 *Valley Hi*. Elektra.
1974 *Some Days You Eat the Bear*. Elektra.
1974 *Journeys from Gospel Oak*. UK Mooncrest.
1976 *Go for Broke*. UK CBS. US Columbia.
1977 *Hit and Run*. UK CBS. US Columbia.
1978 *Stealin' Home*. UK Rockburgh. US Mushroom.
1979 *Siamese Friends*. UK Rockburgh. US Mushroom.
1980 *Spot of Interference*. UK Rockburgh. US RSO.
1984 *Shook*. Polydor.
1988 *Walking a Changing Line*. Windham Hill.
1990 *Pure and Crooked*. Gold Castle.
1991 *Nights in Manhattan*. (Live at The Bottom Line). Taxim.
1991 *Live Alone. Notebook Series No.2*. Perfect Pitch.
1991 *Orphans and Outcasts Vol. One. (1969-79)*. Dirty Linen.
1992 *Skeleton Keys*. Line/Mesa.
1993 *Intimate Wash. The Notebook Series No.3*. Perfect Pitch.
1993 *Orphans and Outcasts Vol. Two. (1981-89)*. Dirty Linen.
1994 *The Dark Ride*. Watermelon.
1995 *Camouflage. Notebook Series No. 4*. Perfect Pitch.
1996 *God Looked Down*. Watermelon.
1998 *Excerpts from Swine Lake*. Blue Rose (Germany). UK Demon.
1999 *Orphans and Outcasts Vol. Three*. Perfect Pitch.
2000 *A Tiniest Wham/A Live Wham*. Perfect Pitch/Blue Rose.
2004 *Zumbach's Coat*. MK2 (The Netherlands).
2006 *If You Saw Thro' My Eyes Live*. Vinyl Japan. Also *Sparkler* bonus disc.
2006 *Brosella Live*. It's About Music (US).
2007 *Contact Live* (With bonus DVD). Blue Rose.
2009 *Amen. Slimline Series One*. Perfect Pitch.

2009 *Woodshedding. Slimline Series Two*. Perfect Pitch.
2013 *The Art of Obscurity*. MK2. UK Fledg'ling. US Omnivore.
2017 *A Baker's Dozen*. MK2.
2020 *Fake Tan* (With The Salmon Smokers). New Noise (LP). Talking Elephant (CD).

Reissues with Bonus Material
1994 *Pure and Crooked*. (4 bonus tracks). Watermelon.
1997 *Nights in Manhattan and Points West*. (4 live bonus tracks). DCC.
1998 *Excerpts from Swine Lake*. (4 bonus demos). Tangible (US).
2003 *If You Saw Thro' My Eyes*. Remastered. MK2.
2004 *Zumbach's Coat*. (6 live songs with Ad Vanderveen on DVD). Blue Rose.
2006 *Journeys from Gospel Oak*. (5 songs rerecorded in 2005). Castle.
2007 *Go for Broke*. (6 live songs from Denver 1976). Vinyl Japan.
2007 *Hit and Run*. (7 live concert rehearsal tracks from LA). Vinyl Japan.
2012 *If You Saw Thro' My Eyes*. Remastered. Esoteric.
2012 *Tigers Will Survive*. Remastered. (1 bonus track). Esoteric.
2014 *Stealin' Home*. (9 live bonus tracks rec. Texas 1978). Omnivore.
2017 *Walking a Changing Line*. (Second CD of outtakes). MIG

Compilations and Box Sets
1980 *Discreet Repeat*. Rockburgh.
1993 *The Soul of Many Places. Elektra Years 1972-74*. Elektra.
1996 *The Seattle Years. 1978-84*. Varèse Sarabande.
2002 *The Complete Notebook Series*. (Ltd. ed. 5 CD box). Coast to Coast.
2005 *Sparkler. Best of the Texas Recordings 1989-2004*. Blue Rose.
2011 *Collected*. (3 CD box). Universal.
2018 *Thro' My Eyes*. (Ltd. ed 2 CD). Route.
2019 *Orphans and Outcasts Volumes I-IV*. Cherry Red.

Remastered Reissues
2005 *Stealin' Home/Siamese Friends*. BGO.
2005 *Spot of Interference/Shook*. BGO.
2006 *Go for Broke/Hit and Run*. BGO.
2006 *The Dark Ride/God Looked Down*. BGO.
2009 *Pure and Crooked/Skeleton Keys*. BGO.
2017 *Valley Hi/ Some Days You Eat the Bear*. BGO.

Video/DVD
1984 *London Revisited*. Video. Castle Hendring.
1997 *Compass and Chart*. Video. Perfect Pitch.
1998 with Nanci Griffith. *Other Voices, Too*. Video. Elektra.
2003 with More Than a Song. *Witness*. Inbetweens Records.

2005 *Osolomeo (A Night in Colorado)*. (Includes a bonus CD of *Live at Brosella*, Belgium 1992 with Andy Roberts). Inbetweens Records.
2006 *I Can't Fade Away*. London Concert 1984. Cherry Red.
2007 *Contact*. (Bonus disc with CD of same name). Blue Rose.
2010 *Afterwords*. (Bonus DVD with CD, live in Den Haag 2009). Matrix.
2012 with Egbert Derix. *That is to Say*. Matrix.
2014 with Egbert Derix. *The Making of In the Now*. Matrix.
2017 *Live at Rockpalast*. (With 2 bonus CDs of live and studio versions). MIG

Fairport Convention

Original, Live, Retrospectives and Box Sets
1968 *Fairport Convention*. UK Polydor. US Cotillion.
1969 *What We Did on Our Holidays*. UK Island. US A&M.
1969 *Unhalfbricking*. UK Island. US A&M.
1986 *Heyday. The BBC Sessions*. UK Island. US Hannibal.
1987 *The Other Boot*. Woodworm.
1999 *Meet on the Ledge. The Classic Years 1967-75*. Island.
2002 *Heyday*. Expanded edition. (8 bonus tracks). Island.
2002 *Cropredy 2002, Another Gig: Another Palindrome*. Woodworm.
2004 *Cropredy Capers*. Free Reed.
2004 *The Quiet Joys of Brotherhood (Live At The Cropredy Festivals 1986 and 1987)*. Shakedown.
2007 *Live At The BBC*. Island.
2008 *The Fairport Companion*. Sanctuary.
2017 *Fairport Convention Come All Ye – The First 10 Years (1968-78)*. Universal.
2018 *What We Did on Our Saturday*. Matty Grooves.
2018 *A Tree With Roots – Fairport Convention And The Songs Of Bob Dylan*. Universal.

DVD
2007. *Tony Palmer Film of Fairport Convention and Matthews Southern Comfort*. Live in Maidstone in 1970. Voiceprint.

Matthews Southern Comfort

Original and Live Material and Issues with Bonus Material
1969 *Matthews Southern Comfort*. UK Uni. US Decca.
1969 *Second Spring*. UK Uni. US Decca.
1970 *Later That Same Year*. UK Uni. US Decca.
1994 *Scion*. (BBC recordings and outtakes). Band of Joy.
2008 *Later That Same Year*. (With 4 bonus tracks). BGO.

2010 *Kind of New*. Brilliant/Genepool.
2011 *Kind of Live*. MK2.
2012 *Kind of New/Kind of Live*. Esoteric.
2017 *A Simple History Vol.1*. MK2.
2018 *Like a Radio*. MIG.
2018 *Bits and Pieces*. (10 inch EP). MIG.
2020 *The New Mine*. MIG.

Compilations
1970 *One, Two, Three... Too Good*. Teldec (Germany).
1974 *Best of...* (Reissued on CD in 1989). MCA.
1997 *The Essential Collection*. Half Moon.

Plainsong

Original and Live albums. Reissues with Extra Material
1972 *In Search of Amelia Earhart*. Elektra.
1992 *Dark Side of the Room*. Line.
1992 *On Air, BBC Recordings*. Band of Joy.
1992 *And That's That*. Demos. Taxim.
1994 *Voices Electric*. Line.
1996 *Sister Flute*. Line.
1997 *On Air, BBC Recordings*. (With 2 bonus tracks). Strange Fruit.
1998 *New Place Now*. Spin Along/Blue Rose.
1999 *Live in Austria*. Self-released.
2001 *Plainsong A to B*. (With Andy Roberts). Spin Along.
2003 *Pangolins*. Blue Rose.
2005 *Plainsong*. (Contains *In Search of Amelia Earhart* and the previously unissued second Plainsong album *Now We Are 3* and bonus live material). Water.
2012 *Fat Lady Singing*. Blue Rose.
2015 *Reinventing Richard*. UK Fledg'ling. US Omnivore.

Hi-Fi

1981 *Demonstration Record*. SP&S Records.
1983 *Moods for Mallards*. First American.
2002 *Complete Works*. Blue Rose.
2012 *The Complete Collection*. (With DVD footage). Rockville.

Collaborations with Other Artists

1995 *Hamilton Pool*. Watermelon.
2000 *No Grey Faith. Secrets All Told (Songs of Sandy Denny)*. Perfect Pitch.

2000 with Ad Vanderveen. *Iain Ad Venture*. Perfect Pitch/Blue Rose.
2001 with Elliott Murphy. *La Terre Commune*. Last Call (France)/Blue Rose.
2001 with Elliott Murphy. *Official Bootleg* (Live). Blue Rose.
2001 with Elliott Murphy and Olivier Durand. *CD-Ticket*. (A rare live recording from a German concert in May 2001). Blue Rose.
2001 *More Than a Song*. Perfect Pitch/Unique Gravity.
2002 More Than a Song. *Witness*. (Live). Turtle.
2002 with Julian Dawson. *Songs from the Red Couch*. Iglhauser.
2002 with Julian Dawson. *Flood Damage*. Live in Austria. Key-Wi.
2008 with Searing Quartet. *Joy Mining*. UK Matrix/Fledg'ling. US Omnivore.
2010 with Egbert Derix. *Afterwords*. Matrix.
2010 with Ad Vanderveen. *Ride the Times*. Turtle.
2012 with Egbert Derix. *In the Now*. Europe Verve. UK Fledg'ling. US Omnivore.

As a Featured Artist
1998 *Other Voices, Too*. Nanci Griffith. Elektra.
2007 with various artists. *Blue Rose Christmas Party*. Blue Rose.
2009 with Nick Vernier Band. 'Woodstock'. (Download). Brinker.
2010 with Nick Vernier Band. 'Time Will Show the Wiser'. (Download). Brinker.

As a Guest Artist
1969 Marc Ellington. *Marc Ellington*. Philips.
1971 Marc Ellington. *Rains/Reins of Changes*. B&C.
1971 Andy Roberts. *Nina and The Dream Tree*. Pegasus.
1972 Longdancer. *It Was So Simple*. Rocket.
1972 Allan Taylor. *The Lady*. United Artists.
1973 Marc Ellington. *Restoration*. Philips.
1973 Andy Roberts. *Urban Cowboy*. Elektra.
1974 Bob Neuwirth. *Bob Neuwirth*. Asylum.
1975 Steve Gillette. *Back on the Street Again*. Outpost.
1976 Jackie Lomax. *Livin' for the Lovin'*. Capitol.
1976 Richard Thompson. *(guitar, vocal)*. Island.
1978 Julie Covington. *Julie Covington*. Virgin.
1978 Richard and Linda Thompson. *First Light*. Chrysalis.
1983 Any Trouble. *Any Trouble*. EMI America.
1986 Bourgeois Tagg. *Bourgeois Tagg*. Island USA.
1988 Fred Simon. *Usually/Always*. Windham Hill.
1990 Christine Albert. *You Are Gold*. Gambini Global Recordings.
1995 Eric Taylor. *Eric Taylor*. Watermelon.
1997 Denice Franke. *You Don't Know Me*. de nICE gIRL.
1999 Mike Rosenthal. *Mike Rosenthal*. Red Truck.

1999 Rainravens. *Rose Of Jericho*. Blue Rose.
2000 Jeff Talmadge. *Spinning Of The World*. Bozart.
2000 Ad Vanderveen. *Here Now*. Hunter Music.
2001 Henning Kvitnes. *Scandicana*. Bonnier Music.
2003 Ad Vanderveen. *The Moment That Matters*. Blue Rose.
2003 Willy Russell. *Hoovering The Moon*. WR Ltd.
2004 Ad Vanderveen & The O'Neils. *"Bürgerhaus" Heilbronn (Germany) 7.6.2004* (Live). Blue Rose.
2004 BJ Baartmans. *Where Lovers Go*. Inbetweens.
2008 Jelle Paulusma. *iRECORD*. Munich.
2010 BJ Baartmans. *Voor en Achter*. Continental Europe.
2011 Lorrie Singer/Bradley Kopp. *A Deep Oasis*. Redboot.
2012 Egbert Derix. *Paintings in Minor Lila*. Eggy D.
2012 Bart de Win. *Easy To See*. Shine A Light.
2017 Pete Mancini. *Foothill Freeway*. Paradiddle.

Unique Compilation Albums
Compilations containing material not available elsewhere:

1993 Various. *2 Meter Sessies, Volume 4*. 'A Cross To Bear', recorded 8th September 1992, NOB radio session. Radio Records.
1994 Various. *Broadcasts Vol. 2*. 'Evening Sun', recorded live for 107.1 KGSR/Radio Austin. KGSR.
1994 Various. *Liner New Tracks 2*. 'Meet On The Ledge', Iain Matthews & Ian Cussick, recorded live at the Knust Club, Hamburg. Line Records.
1995 Various. *SXSW Live Vol.3*. 'God Looked Down', recorded Austin, Texas 17th/19th March 1994. SXSW Recording.
1995 Various. *Three Two One… It's Alive! From Studio A WCBE Vol. 3*. 'Jumping Off The Roof', WCBE radio session. WCBE.
1998 Various. *What's That I Hear? The Songs Of Phil Ochs*. 'Flower Lady'. Sliced Bread Records.
2000 Various. *Live På Halkær Kro (International Folkemusik)*. 'I Drove', Danish radio recording. Halkær Kro.
2003 Various. *30 Jaar Hubert On The Air*. 'Ballad Of Gruene Hall', 'Heart Of A Man', 'Bare Necessities', Iain Matthews / Eliza Gilkyson / Ad VanderVeen . 1Limburg Dutch radio session. L1records.
2016 Various. *Ever After: Tree Of Life*. 'Alone Again Blues' (Live). Fyify! Records & Publishing.

For more on this book, please visit:

www.iainmatthewsmemoir.wordpress.com
www.iainmatthews.nl
www.route-online.com